Buridan lecturing on logic. From the copy of Buridan's *Sophismata* (Paris: Denys Roce) in the Bodleian Library.

REFERENCE *and* GENERALITY

An Examination of
Some Medieval and Modern Theories

BY PETER THOMAS GEACH

Professor of Logic, University of Leeds

Third Edition

Cornell University Press

ITHACA AND LONDON

First edition published 1962 by Cornell University Press.
Emended edition published 1968.
Third edition published 1980.
Published in the United Kingdom by Cornell University Press Ltd.,
2–4 Brook Street, London W1Y 1AA.

Library of Congress Cataloging in Publication Data

Geach, Peter Thomas.
    Reference and generality.

    (Contemporary philosophy)
    Bibliography: p.
    Includes Index.
    1. Logic. 2. Languages—Philosophy. 3. Reference (Philosophy)
I. Title. II. Series.
BC71.G34 1980   160   80-10977
ISBN 0-8014-1315-X

Printed in the United States of America

DEDICATED,

WITH MANY GRATEFUL AND HAPPY MEMORIES,

TO TELLURIDE HOUSE, CORNELL UNIVERSITY;

LYDDON HALL, UNIVERSITY OF LEEDS;

AND VAN PELT HOUSE, UNIVERSITY OF PENNSYLVANIA

Preface, 1962

My title is going to arouse immediate objections from various classes of readers. Historicists will protest that every age has its own philosophical problems—how vain to look for any answer to modern problems, right or wrong, on the part of medieval writers! Yet my title is a claim to have found theories about the same problems of reference and generality in both medieval and modern logicians.

Again, it is a popular view that modern formal logic has application only to rigorous disciplines like algebra, geometry, and mechanics; not to arguments in a vernacular about more homely concerns (like the amusing examples about policemen, politicians, and crooks in Quine's *Methods of Logic*). The reason offered would be the complex and irregular logical syntax of vernacular languages. This view is held, not only by the philosophers of ordinary language, but also by some formal logicians whose main interest is mathematical. Now medieval logic is an attempt to state formal rules for inferences performed in medieval Latin—a language just as complex and irregular as everyday English. To the critics I am now discussing, this medieval enterprise must appear misconceived, and my own doubly misconceived.

Again, somebody might object on Carnapian lines that one cannot philosophize just about 'language'—that philosophical theses must be made to relate to the logical syntax of a particular language, e.g. medieval Latin. It is fairly easy to answer this objection. In spite of what some eccentric linguists and some people ignorant of the history of languages may have said, the general syntactical resemblances between English and medieval Latin are far more important than the differences that impress a superficial observer (e.g. the greater number of inflections in Latin). The cause of these resemblances is, of course, that English and Latin both belong to the Indo-European family; but they have much more than an historical interest. For what is important about a sign is not its outward guise but the use that is made of it; an English word is the same word whether it be written or spoken or transmitted in Morse code. And the uses of an English word often run so far parallel to those of a Latin word that as signs the two words are to all intents identical.

Just this is what is philosophically interesting—the employment of a word in a given sign-function, which may occur in many languages. It does not matter whether the word that does the job is "omnis" or "every"; what matters is the job done. Inquiry into etymology and sense-history and fine points of idiom is not the business of philosophy, even if amateur linguistics has recently been practiced by philosophers. In point of fact, none of the medieval discussions I shall cite will lose any of their force through being made to relate to English translations of Latin sentences and arguments rather than to the Latin originals; and I shall not assume even a schoolboy knowledge of Latin grammar. I shall, however, often be obliged just to take over some medieval technical term, because no current term would be an adequate substitute; whenever I do this I shall try to explain, or at least illustrate, how the term was used.

The only difference between English and Latin syntax that will have any importance for us is that Latin has no article, definite or indefinite. A medieval logician could not puzzle himself over the role of "a" in "I met a man", since the Latin sentence has no word for "a". (The Latin numeral word for "one" is indeed sometimes used by medieval writers to mean not "one" but merely "a", as happens with the corresponding words in German and the Romance languages; this is common in William of Ockham and in Buridan. But so far as I know they were never self-conscious about this use; it is not noticed in their discussions of logical examples.) Nevertheless, as we shall see, the lack of an indefinite article in Latin did not prevent the development of a theory remarkably similar to the theory expounded in Russell's *Principles of Mathematics* about 'denoting' phrases of the form "an A". The lack of a definite article, on the other hand, means that no 'theory of definite descriptions' may be looked for in medieval writers.

In view, however, of the syntactical similarities between English and medieval Latin, the historicist objection to my undertaking breaks down over other concrete examples. Consider this problem: If "every man" has reference to every man, and if a reflexive pronoun has the same reference as the subject of the verb, how can "Every man sees every man" be a different statement from "Every man sees himself"? The actual sentences just given are English ones, but they stand in strict syntactical correspondence, word for word, with the Latin ones discussed by medieval logicians, and the problem is just the same. If a modern logician were debarred from discussing this problem for lack of a medieval *Weltanschauung*, then modern algebraists ought equally to feel debarred from discussing the problems of Diophantus.

I shall not here argue against the people who wish to deny formal logic any application to arguments in everyday language, for the whole book will refute them by being such an application. I have no quarrel with logicians whose interests are predominantly mathematical, so long as they do not positively oppose other applications of formal logic, so long as they do not perversely attempt to cut logic off from roots that long have nourished it and still do. At its very origins formal logic was used by Aristotle and the Stoics to appraise ordinary arguments; it has been so used whenever it has flourished; it still is so used by distinguished modern logicians like Prior and Quine.

The 'ordinary language' philosophers, who want to keep the estate they claim strictly preserved against the poaching of formal logicians, are, I think, people with a vested interest in confusion.

Preface

One of them, I remember, compared formal logicians to map makers who should try to map everything in constructible geometrical figures; no doubt he forgot that countries actually are mapped by triangulation. It is no accident that the argument devised in Oxford against the Frege-Russell analysis of existence statements has been eagerly seized upon by theologians wedded to nonsensical doctrines about Being—little as such an application would please the authors of the argument.

The extension I am giving to the term "medieval logic" is practically the same as that which Moody gives it in his *Truth and Consequence in Mediaeval Logic*; namely, the logic taught in the Arts faculties at Oxford and Paris, which flourished particularly in the thirteenth and fourteenth centuries. I shall also cite the writings of Aquinas, both as evidence for the doctrine of the contemporary formal logicians (*sophistae*) and also because, though Aquinas was not a logician *ex professo* and never wrote a *Summa logicae*, his views on the philosophy of logic are often of the highest value.

A principle that I have repeatedly used to eliminate false theories of reference is the principle that the reference of an expression *E* must be specifiable in some way that does not involve first determining whether the proposition in which *E* occurs is true. The first explicit statement of this principle that I have found is in Buridan's *Sophismata* (c.vi, *sophisma* v); the principle might suitably be called Buridan's Law.

The substance of this book was first delivered as a course of lectures in Blackfriars, Oxford, while I was acting as deputy for the University Reader in Medieval Philosophy in Trinity term 1957; I am most grateful to the University of Oxford for inviting me, and to the Prior and Community of Blackfriars for the use of their aula. I have since discussed the topics of the book extensively in a seminar at Cornell University during the fall term 1959–1960 and cannot adequately say how much the book owes to the suggestions and criticisms of those who took part in the discussions. I wish also to express my gratitude to the staff of the Cornell University Library for procuring me photographic copies of rare medieval logic books. Chapters One and Two appeared in a rather different form in *Mind* of January 1956 and October

Preface

1950 respectively; the Editor has kindly allowed me to reprint this material.

University of Birmingham

Preface, 1980

Reference and Generality has now been in print since 1962. In previous reprintings only minor changes could be made; even though the reprint in 1968 was called an emended edition, it contained only minor emendations except in sections 20 and 31. I am grateful for the opportunity afforded me by Cornell University Press to effect more radical repairs.

In Chapter One I had strangely omitted to state and criticize the two rules against fallacy that were supposed to be the main use of the "distributed/undistributed" contrast: the 'illicit process' rule and the 'undistributed middle' rule. A new section 13 is now devoted to these rules. Other changes that deserve mention here were motivated by my wish to do justice to the memory of Neville Keynes; his *Formal Logic* was the first logic book I read, with that excellent teacher my father, Professor George Hender Geach, before we moved on to *Principia Mathematica*; I count it extreme good fortune to have begun with such a teacher and such a textbook. It distressed me very much that from my criticizing the doctrine of distribution as it occurs in Keynes, reviewers concluded that I had a low opinion of Keynes, and that he was one of the 'fools' referred to elsewhere in this book. In fact I was acting on a principle I learned from Wittgenstein: to criticize a position effectively, attack it in its strongest form. I could have quoted statements of the doctrine of distribution from any one of a dozen current bad logic texts; I chose Keynes's statement because he was likely to make out the best possible case for the doctrine.

Many attempted defenses of the doctrine have come to my notice since 1962; but I think they are one and all either invalid or irrelevant. I call irrelevant those defenses which construct a theory quite alien to the tradition but labeled with the old name. This is like a patent medicine manufacturer with an old family remedy whose one active ingredient has turned out to be noxious: he removes the active ingredient, replaces it by one at least harmless, and then announces, "This fine old remedy is now prepared on a new formula, in accordance with current medical trends." So I have commented on none of the defenses, and withdrawn none of my strictures in response; indeed, I have added a few more.

In Chapter Two I have tried to clarify the role played in sentences by such phrases as "this man" and the contribution made by criteria of identity to the sense of proper and common names. There is also a new emphasis on the important distinction between a name *for* an A and a name *of* an A; the verbal expression I have used for this is my own choice, but the need to bring out the distinction was impressed on me by the many discussions I have had with Dr. Harold Noonan of Trinity Hall, Cambridge. The sections most affected by these changes are sections 32, 34, and 35. I rearranged the matter of sections 30 and 31.

The only major change in Chapter Three is in section 36. I there explain 'referring' phrases as a species of what I now call "applicatival phrases"; and I now supply a differentia for this species that makes "most" or "almost every" phrases belong to the species along with "some" and "every" phrases. The similarity of the quantifier "most" to the classical quantifiers is thus further stressed; and some awkward passages later on, in which "most" phrases had to be treated like 'referring' phrases although my explanation excluded them from that class, could now be streamlined.

In Chapter Four I have completely rewritten section 56, on the *dictum de omni*. When I first wrote it, and for long afterward, I shared a prevalent confusion between two kinds of logical rules: schematic rules, which directly give us valid schemata or patterns of inference, and thematic rules, which show us how to start with valid argument(s) and derive from thence a new valid argument. This led to a muddled exposition of the *dictum*; I have now removed the muddle and made all the consequential changes required by the new exposition; these particularly affected sections 57, 58, and 59.

In Chapter Five I have revised my account of how, and in what sense, substantival general terms may be defined, and have therefore rewritten sections 74 and 75. Section 82 came in for revision because of the new account of the *dictum de omni*.

In Chapter Six I have eliminated the notorious example of Heraclitus' dip in the river. This had the disadvantage that in the phrases "the same river" and "the same water" one noun is a count noun, the other a mass term. I do not think anyone as yet has a satisfactory theory of mass terms; certainly I have not. By changing to an example with two count nouns I make it possible to concentrate on what is essential for my purpose. This change affects sections 91, 95, and 98. I have also reworked section 92, with an improved criticism of Frege's theory concerning *Zahlangaben* and one-one correspondence. I feel too uncertain on problems of intentionality to have made more than small alterations in what I have said on this topic; I could not be confident that my second thoughts would be better than my first.

As regards lists, the subject matter of Chapter Seven, I ought to remark that lists do not form a special category of expressions: it is simply that sometimes a predicable can admit into an argument-place either a single name, or several names at a time all on a level. This idea of a logical procedure's being applicable to more or fewer arguments is familiar in propositional logic; this is a feature of "and" and of "or" and of "neither . . . nor . . ." in the vernacular, and of Wittgenstein's operator "N" in the *Tractatus*.

Actual changes in the text of Chapter Seven were made for two main reasons. The less important reason was that I found it convenient to discuss two sorts of exclusive proposition, which I have called *unrestricted* and *restricted*; examples of the two sorts would respectively be: "Only a man can laugh" and "Among men, only Adam and Eve had no father". The recognition of restricted exclusive propositions enabled me to improve some of the analyses given in section 108 and to clear up some unfinished business from Chapter Five about introducing names via "A that is P" phrases. The last paragraph of section 108, being concerned with the pronouns "the same" and "(an)other" rather than with "only", is now the beginning of section 109, which continues discussion of those pronouns; section 109 has been expanded slightly at the end—also, I hope, clarified.

The major change is that I have canceled the inconclusive final paragraph of the book and replaced it by a new section 110, in which I discuss how a proper name for an A relates to the predicable "—— is the same A as ——". Slow as I have been to take the point, it seems clear that on my general view of numbers and identity it is quite useless, indeed nonsensical, to characterize a proper name as a name whose sense restricts it to naming only one *thing*; instead, what has to be explained is a name's being a proper name *for an* A; and such a name may be a shared name of several *B*s, so long as each such *B* is the same A as any other. I thus came to accept the view of Leśniewski and other Polish logicians that there is no distinct syntactical category of *proper* names. Whether a name is a proper name depends on the kind of thing it is a name *for*, and this is a matter of its sense, not of its syntactical category; in syntax there is only the category of *names*. (I must not therefore be taken to agree with the followers of Leśniewski on other matters; they advocate a sophisticated version of the two-name doctrine of predication, which I firmly reject.)

A consequential change is that I can no longer hold, as I did in earlier editions of the book, to the line that empty proper names are inadmissible, but empty names that are not proper names are admissible. This has required some rewriting of section 106 and cancellation of a paragraph in section 108. I now hold the Fregean view that in logic empty names are always inadmissible.

Apart from these structural repairs and alterations I have tried to do a thorough spring-cleaning of the whole fabric. Part of this tidying-up has been an improved system of bibliographical references, including (as many readers have requested) more references to such medieval source books as are readily accessible in modern printed editions.

Of all those who have helped me during these years, I owe special mention to Prior and Quine for constant friendship, interest, and support.

The book has been much criticized; in revising it I have done little to please most of its critics, nor have I wished to do so. Wrong views of reference are prevalent in the world of philosophy, and I could not conciliate committed partisans of these. I have been gratified, however, to notice over the years that some of my ideas and my terms of art have been favorably noticed by linguists, professionally concerned as they are with patiently unraveling the tangled skein of language.

P. T. GEACH

University of Leeds

Analytical Table of Contents

ONE   *The Doctrine of Distribution*   27

1 The traditional doctrine of distribution is commonly accepted without examination.   27
2 Keynes's formulation needs to be amended, because he confusedly uses schematic letters like "S" to represent both general terms and singular designations of classes.   28
3 What difference is supposed to exist between the relations of denoting and of referring to?   29
4 We cannot coherently take "some man" to refer to some man.   30
5 A person who uses the words "some man" may be referring to some particular man, but what he actually says does not convey this reference.   31
6 An argument of Miss Anscombe's shows that at any rate there could not be just one way that "some man" referred to some man. This robs the doctrine of its intuitive simplicity.   32
7 The idea that speaking of some men leaves us 'in ignorance with regard to the remainder' has been refuted by Keynes himself, and cannot serve to explain the nondistribution of the term "man" or "men".   34
8 "No men" assuredly does not refer to no men or to a

Analytical Table of Contents

class consisting of o men. We should equally doubt the view that "all men" refers to all men and "some men" to some men. 34

9 In a thoroughgoing class reading of categoricals there is no place for distribution. 35

10 The question whether a predicate term is distributed or undistributed does not really make sense. 36

11 This is specially manifest for the predicate terms of singular propositions. 36

12 The traditional 'proofs' that particular negative propositions have distributed predicate terms contain gross fallacies. 37

13 The rules against 'illicit process' and 'undistributed middle' are unsound. 38

14 A medieval example shows that these rules do not in general supply a workable test for validity. 43

15 Hamilton's quantification of the predicate (apart from his incidental mistakes) would be a natural extension of the doctrine of distribution. But a difficulty about simple conversion exposes a radical defect in the doctrine. 45

16 The doctrine of distribution is thus quite indefensible. 48

TWO *Subject and Predicate* 49

17 "Subject" and "predicate" in this work are always linguistic terms. Provisional explanation of these terms. 49

18 It is convenient to say that an expression is a *predicable* when it can be attached to a subject, a *predicate* only when it actually is so attached. 50

19 In predicating we are not necessarily making an assertion or statement. Advantages and disadvantages of the term "proposition". 51

20 Names can be recognized from their use in acts of naming. 52

21 Proper names are parts of the language in which they are embedded. 53

22 The role of demonstrative pronouns in simple assertoric sentences. 53

23 A subject may be picked out of a proposition as an expression that could be linked up with an act of naming. 54

24 A proposition may admit of more than one subject-predicate analysis. 54

Analytical Table of Contents

25 The name refers to its bearer regardless of time. 55

26 We got a predicate by removing a proper name from a proposition. 56

27 Names and predicables, *referring to* and *being true of*, are irreducibly different. 57

28 The 'Aristotelian' doctrine is confused as regards the notion of 'term', and as to the role of the copula. The two-name theory of predication is demonstrably wrong. 59

29 The modern theory of varieties of copula is equally erroneous. 61

30 Substantival and adjectival terms. 63

31 The problem whether there can be negative terms. 64

32 When can substantial general terms occur as logical subjects? 65

33 A proper name can never be used predicatively. 67

34 The use of proper names as logical subjects seems to involve a subject-use of substantival general terms. 67

35 How does such a term refer to the several objects it can be used to name? 71

THREE   *Referring Phrases* 73

36 Explanation of the term "referring phrase". The relation of referring phrases to lists of proper names. 73

37 Russellian and medieval theories of referring phrases and their various modes of reference. 79

38 These theories were unnecessarily complicated by bringing in concepts 'meant' by referring phrases and (in Russell's case) nonrelational 'combinations' of objects. 81

39 The multiply ambiguous term "denoting" is best avoided. *Suppositio.* 83

40 A referring phrase is only a quasi subject, not a subject. 84

41 Frege's analysis of propositions containing referring phrases. 85

42 The 'scope' of referring phrases. 86

43 The canceling-out fallacy. 88

44 The modes of reference of "some" and "any" phrases. 88

45 Confused *suppositio*—the mode of reference of "a" phrases. 90

46 Referring phrases do not require namely-riders if their *suppositio* is confused. 91

47 Confused *suppositio* and disjunctions of proper names. 91

Analytical Table of Contents

48 A paralogism of Berkeley's explained in terms of confused *suppositio*.   95

49 The mode of reference of "every" phrases: conjunctive *suppositio*.   96

50 This kind of *suppositio*, as distinct from the distributive *suppositio* of "any" phrases, was not noticed by most medieval logicians, but was so by Russell.   98

51 My explanation fits almost all Russell's examples of referring phrases.   98

52 Russell's attempted explanation of the distinction between "any" and "every" is different, but is anyhow inconsistent with his own examples.   102

53 The distinction between "every" and "any" enables us to avoid fallacies.   104

54 It will, however, be shown that this no more justifies us in accepting the doctrine of *suppositio* than the fallaciousness of syllogisms with 'undistributed middle' justified our accepting the doctrine of distribution.   104

FOUR   *The Shipwreck of a Theory*   105

55 Truth-conditions for propositions that contain referring phrases formed with the applicative "some", "any", "most", "every", or "a".   105

56 Exposition of the *dictum de omni* principle.   107

57 By applying the *dictum de omni* to "most" phrases, we clear up an old puzzle.   116

58 Apparent exceptions to the *dictum de omni*, where we are dealing with portmanteau propositions.   118

59 A proposition may be an apparent exception because it is not genuinely formed, as it appears to be, by attaching a predicable to a referring phrase as quasi subject. Illustrations with "most", "a", and "every" phrases.   120

60 At first sight the medieval or Russellian type of theory seems to give a very good account of propositions got by filling the blanks of a two-place predicable with referring phrases.   123

61 If, however, we fill up the two blanks with a "some" phrase and an "any" phrase, the rules land us in difficulty.   125

62 Russell and the medievals could dodge this difficulty with supplementary rules.   126

Analytical Table of Contents

63 These rules are awkward and artificial, and no such device would remove a similar difficulty over a pair of "most" phrases.   127

64 The key to our problem is that the order of insertion of the two phrases into the proposition makes a difference.   128

65 William of Sherwood unwittingly attained this conception.   131

66 The fallacies that the referring-phrase theory sought to avoid, and the apparent exceptions to the *dictum de omni* that it generates, can all be dealt with in terms of the two notions: order of filling up, and scope. We may therefore reject the alleged distinction between "any" and "every", and between "some" and "a".   132

67 Our results help us to understand the modern symbolism of quantifiers and bound variables.   134

FIVE   *Pronominal Reference: Relative Pronouns*   136

68 Further remarks on the relation of bound variables to pronouns in the vernacular.   136

69 Logically and grammatically relative pronouns.   139

70 Defining and qualifying relative clauses. A provisional account of the difference.   141

71 Are complex terms of the form "A that is P" genuine logical units?   142

72 Reasons for denying this: in such phrases we have to split up "that" into a connective (not always the same one) and a logically relative pronoun, and with this the whole appearance of a complex term vanishes like a mirage.   143

73 "Such that" is an all-purpose connective whose ambiguity is resolved contextually.   145

74 Cannot definitions of terms be given in the form "A that is P"? Solution of this difficulty. All names, and all substantival terms, are syntactically simple.   147

75 Proper names and definite descriptions.   149

76 Do relative pronouns ever pick up a reference made by a term used elsewhere? 'Pronouns of laziness' may, but others do not.   151

77 A sort of example given by Strawson is no exception.   153

78 We must be cautious over classifying a pronoun as one of laziness.   155

79 Sometimes the work of pronouns answering to bound

Analytical Table of Contents

variables is work that could be done by the logical constants of the calculus of relations—which shows how superficial the jargon of "variable" and "constant" really is.   156

80   A reflexive pronoun does not have the same reference as its antecedent.   158

81   Walter Burleigh on the *suppositio* of reflexive pronouns.   159

82   A reflexive pronoun cannot be taken as filling up one blank in a two- or many-place predicable.   161

83   Rather, a reflexive pronoun fills up both places in a two-place predicable, but its own requirement for an antecedent reintroduces an empty place. This account is easily extended to many-place predicables. The matter illustrated by diagrams.   162

84   There are connected puzzles about those uses of bound variables which correspond to the use of reflexive pronouns.   165

SIX   *Pronominal Reference: Indefinite Pronouns*   169

85   List of the pronouns to be discussed—a miscellaneous lot.   169

86   "Anything, everything, something" and the noun "thing".   169

87   We might try splitting up "something that is *F*" into "some" and "thing-that is *F*"; here "thing-that" would be a logically simple sign with the role of transforming a predicable "is *F*" into something that can occur in subject position.   170

88   This might be used to explain the systematic ambiguity whereby a substantival general term can shift about between subject and predicate position.   171

89   But to take "thing that is *F*" as a sort of complex name is open to some of the objections raised in section 72 to a similar view of "A that is *F*".   172

90   Analyzing away this sort of phrase leaves us once more with unanalyzed occurrences of "anything", "something", and the like.   173

91   Are phrases like "any A" and "some A" analyzable in terms of the corresponding "-thing" pronouns and merely predicative occurrences of "A"? Reasons to deny this.   173

Analytical Table of Contents

92 Frege's views on identity and countability.   176

93 An alternative view of unrestricted quantifiers.   177

94 Application of this view to quantifiers that reach into an *oratio obliqua* clause.   179

95 Quantifiers with proper-name variables and with general-term variables. These two sorts of quantifier relate to the same entities. Proper-name variables can occur in a language that includes no proper names.   183

96 The error of Quine's slogan "To be is to be the value of a variable". Only predicable expressions can fill the blank in "There is ——"; and empty proper names, unlike empty predicables, have no place in language used to convey information.   185

97 Empty proper names in *oratio obliqua* clauses constitute only an apparent exception.   186

98 The forms "For some *x*, *x* is *F*", "There is something that is *F*", "Something or other is *F*", "There exists something that is *F*", are in very many cases equivalent.   188

SEVEN *The Logic of Lists*   191

99 Lists of proper names; their mode of significance. A proper name is a one-item list.   191

100 The modification of a predicable by an applicative (of a certain class) yields a predicable that can be attached to an arbitrarily long list as subject; the truth-condition of this predication is that a certain disjunction of conjunctions of singular propositions should be true.   192

101 The interpretation of predicates that take lists as subjects, for the degenerate case of one-item lists.   195

102 It is only an incidental effect of applicatives to remove ambiguities in truth-conditions.   195

103 Solution of an old puzzle about *suppositio*. There is no need to ascribe to a list various modes of reference; one must 'separate the concept *all* from the truth-function'.   196

104 Generalization of our results to many-place predicables and to lists of arbitrary finite length.   198

105 A substantival general term can take the place of a list as a logical subject; it is by itself a logical subject and does not go with an applicative to form a quasi subject.   200

106 Truth-conditions for categoricals with empty general terms as logical subjects.   202

23

Analytical Table of Contents

107 What are we to say when the things covered by a general term cannot be listed? 205

108 The applicative "only": restricted and unrestricted exclusive propositions. 207

109 The pronouns "the same" and "(an)other". 211

110 Proper and common names. 215

Appendix 219

Bibliography 221

Index 223

REFERENCE AND GENERALITY

An Examination of
Some Medieval and Modern Theories

One

The Doctrine of Distribution

1.   Before modern quantification theory, logic books would signify a term's logical quantity by prefixing "all" or "any" or "every", or on the other hand "some". It was held that when a
general term, say "man", is used in making a statement, the
statement is not fully understood unless we know how much of
the extension of the term the statement covers—the whole extension, any and every man, or just part of the extension, some man
or men. This question "how much?" is answered by noticing the
signs "all", "any", "every", or again "some", prefixed to the term;
so these are *quantifiers* or signs of logical quantity, universal or
particular as the case may be. The use of the verb "quantify" and
the noun "quantification" in this connection appears to derive
from Sir William Hamilton.

This doctrine of the quantifiers is a part of the traditional
doctrine of distribution. Now the concept of distribution has a
very peculiar position in logic. Although this concept is used by
people who think Aristotelian logic is the only logic a philosopher
ought to recognize, it was wholly unknown to Aristotle; there is
no Greek word for "distributed" or "distribution", and the appearance of such terminology in the Oxford translation of the
Organon is just a mistake. Aristotle never tests the validity of

syllogisms and inferences by rules of distribution; he has entirely different tests. Łukasiewicz's work on Aristotle's syllogistic rightly makes no mention of distribution.

Logicians have indeed been remarkably incurious as to the origin and validity of the distribution doctrine; one textbook writer will simply copy the stuff about distribution from another. This practice is not confined to traditional 'Aristotelian' textbooks; such elementary textbooks of modern symbolic logic as include a treatment of syllogistic (rightly regarded as a valid, though restricted, formal theory) commonly include the doctrine of distribution as something unquestionably correct, even if other details of the 'Aristotelian' tradition (e.g. the validity of *Darapti*) are called in question.

2.   Now we need only look at the doctrine of distribution with a little care to see how incoherent it is. I shall use as a source book Keynes's *Formal Logic*. Keynes was a good logician; his merits were great, his logical perceptions unusually keen; if he could not make good sense out of the doctrine of distribution, I think nobody could. In fact, later expositions are certainly no better than his.

A term is said to be distributed when reference is made to *all* the individuals denoted by it; . . . undistributed when they are referred to only *partially*, that is, when information is given with regard to a portion of the class denoted by the term, but we are left in ignorance with regard to the remainder of the class.[1]

It is worth notice that in this account, and quite standardly, "undistributed" does not simply mean "not distributed"; the term "distributed" is associated in the explanation with the particle "all", and "undistributed" with the adverb "partially", a literary variant for "some". Moreover, we must unsnarl a small tangle that arises from a conflation of a more recent class logic with an older logic of terms. The whole talk about classes as such in this passage is inessential. We might in fact imagine Keynes's text emended so as to read: ". . . information is given with regard to

[1]Keynes, p. 95.

28

some individual(s) among those denoted by the term, but we are left in ignorance about the rest of them." This rewording would not introduce any concept or doctrine that Keynes would object to; it would simply make the position clearer by not raising irrelevant puzzles about classes.

Keynes, like many writers, plays fast and loose in his use of schematic letters like "S" and "P"; you find, for example, in one and the same context the phrase "every S", which requires that "S" be read as a general term like "man", and the phrase "the whole of S", which requires that "S" be a singular designation of a class taken collectively, like "the class of men"; obviously "man" and "the class of men" are wholly different sorts of expression. The term "class name", which may be applied to either sort of expression, serves only to perpetuate confusion, and I shall avoid it. I shall also avoid the phrase "all S", as in "All S is P"; for here also "S" may be taken as a general term (as in "All gold is malleable") or as a singular designation of a class ("all the class of men"). "All Ss" on the other hand is unexceptionable, since here "S" must be taken as a general term that has a plural.

3. Taking Keynes's text as amended, we find mention of two distinct semantic relations in which a term may stand to an individual, say "man" to an individual man: denoting and referring. "Man" regularly denotes each and every man; it refers, however, now to some men only, now to all men, according to context, and is accordingly undistributed in the one sort of context, distributed in the other. For example, Keynes goes on, it 'follows immediately' that "man" is distributed in a statement about every man, "Every man is P", and undistributed in a statement about some man, "Some man is P".

What then is 'referring', and how does it differ from denoting? The whole doctrine hinges on this distinction, but neither Keynes's nor any later exposition tells us what the distinction is. The term "denoting", as here used, is itself none too clear; I think it covers up a fundamental confusion, between the relations of a name to the thing named and of a predicate to what it is true of.

Indeed, the doctrine of distribution gets all its plausibility from assimilating nouns and noun-phrases generally to proper names as regards their manner of signification. "Churchill" stands for Churchill; so "man" stands for man—for any man; and "every man" stands for every man; and "some man" just stands for some man. Only we said just now that "man" regularly stands for any man! No matter; we can set things straight by using a pair of distinctive terms, instead of the one term "stands for". "Churchill" denotes, and also refers to, Churchill; "man" always denotes every man, but refers to every man when preceded by "every" and not when preceded by "some". We can then define a distributed term as a term that refers to whatever it denotes; thus "Churchill", and "man" in the context "Every man is *P*", will both be distributed terms. Making sense of this depends on the distinction between denoting and referring; but who is going to ask what that distinction is, so long as there are the two words to use?

4. Even if we knew what 'referring' was, how could we say that "some man" refers just to some man? The question at once arises: Who can be the man or men referred to? When I say "Some men are *P*", does the subject-term refer to just such men as the predicate is true of? But then which men will the subject-term refer to if a predication of this sort is false? No way suggests itself for specifying which men from among all men would then be referred to; so are we to say that, when "Some men are *P*" is false, all men without exception are referred to—and "men" is thus distributed?

One might try saying that, when "Some men are *P*" is false, "some men" is an expression intended to refer to some men, but in fact fails so to refer. But if in the sentence represented by "Some men are *P*" the subject-term is meant to refer to some men, but fails to do so, then the sentence as a whole is intended to convey a statement about some men, but fails to do so—and therefore does not convey a false statement about some men, which contradicts our hypothesis. Nor could one say that what the subject-term is referring to is just some man or men, not a definite man or a definite number of men; for, *pace* Meinong, nothing in this world or any possible world can be just some man or men without being any definite man or any definite number of men.

5.   The view that in an assertion of the form "Some man is *P*" "some man" refers to some man seems to make sense because as regards any assertion of this form the question "Which man?" is in order, and if the assertion is true the question can be answered by naming a man who is *P*. But we get into difficulties even if we ignore false assertions of this form. Suppose Smith says, as it happens truly: "Some man has been on top of Mount Everest." If we now ask Smith "Which man?" we may mean "Which man has been on top of Mount Everest?" or "Which man were you, Smith, referring to?". Either question is in order; and if what Smith says is true the first must have an answer, whether or not Smith knows the answer. But though it is in order to ask whom Smith was referring to, this question need not have an answer; Smith may have learned only that some man has been on top of Mount Everest without learning who has, and then he will not have had any definite man in mind.

I here mention personal reference—i.e. reference in a sense corresponding to the verb "refer" as predicated of persons rather than of expressions—only in order to get it out of the way. Let me take an example: Smith says indignantly to his wife, "The fat old humbug we saw yesterday has just been made a full professor!". His wife may know whom he refers to, and will consider herself misinformed if and only if that person has not been made a full professor. But the actual expression "the fat old humbug we saw yesterday" will refer to somebody only if Mr. and Mrs. Smith did meet someone rightly describable as a fat old humbug on the day before Smith's indignant remark; if this is not so, then Smith's actual words will not have conveyed true information, even if what Mrs. Smith gathered from them was true.

In any case, as Keynes is using the verb "refer", what matters is not which individual the utterer of a proposition had in mind, but what reference was conveyed by the actual expressions used. If Smith did not have any definite man in mind, then obviously Smith's use of the phrase "some man" did not convey a reference to any definite man. If Smith did have a definite man in mind, there is, as we just saw, a common use of "refer" in which we can say Smith referred to that man; but it does not follow that the actual phrase "some man" referred then and there to the man in question. Suppose that when Smith made his statement he had in mind Sir Vivian Fuchs, whom he falsely believes to have been on top of Mount Everest: then Smith may be said to have been referring to Sir Vivian Fuchs, but what he actually said conveyed no such reference. For what Smith actually said was true; but if it conveyed a reference to Sir Vivian Fuchs, it would have to be taken as a predication about him, and then it would be false. So even if the person who uses the phrase "some man" may be said to have referred to some definite man, that is no reason for saying that the phrase "some man" actually conveys a reference to some man.

6. An argument devised by Miss Elizabeth Anscombe shows that at least we cannot suppose "some man" to refer to some man in one single way; we should have to distinguish several types of reference—it is not easy to see how many. Let us suppose that we can say "some man" refers to some man in a statement like this:

(1) Joan admires some man

that is, a statement in regard to which the question "Which man?" would be in order. Let us call this type of reference type A. Then in a statement like the following one:

(2) Every girl admires some man

"some man" must refer to some man in a different way, since the question "Which man?" is plainly silly. If, however, we take a case coming under the general statement (2), such as (1), the question "Which man?" will be in order. Thus we might distinguish a second sort of reference: "some man" has type-B reference to some man in general statements like (2), under which there come particular cases, like (1), that exemplify type-A reference.

But now consider this very statement:

(3) In general statements of the type just described, "some man" has type-B reference to some man.

Plainly "some man" occurring at the end of (3) has not a type-A reference to some man, since the question "To which man?" would be silly. We might suppose that since (3) is a general statement there would here again be a type-B reference as in (2). If that were so, in any particular case under (3) "some man" would have type-A reference. This, however, is false; for if we take the following case under (3):

(4) At the end of (2), "some man" has type-B reference to some man

then here again, as with (2) itself, the question "Which man?" is silly; so (4) is not an instance of type-A reference; so (3) cannot be an instance of type-B reference. Thus (3) exemplifies a third type of reference that "some man" has to some man.

Thus far I have given Miss Anscombe's argument. As I have said, it is hard to see how many types of reference we should have to distinguish on these lines. For instance, we might go on to ask what sort of reference "some man" has at the end of (4). The fact that (4) is about the occurrence of "some man" at the end of (2) certainly does not prove that "some man" at the end of (4) has the same sort of reference as "some man" at the end of (2); and one might argue on the other side that (4), unlike both (2) and (3), is a singular statement from which we cannot descend to particular cases, and therefore presumably exemplifies a different sort of reference from both (2) and (3). We have already seen that "some man" at the end of (4) has not type-A reference; if it has not type-B reference either, it will have its own type of reference, say type C; and then (3) would have yet another type of reference, type D, related to type C as type B is to type A—that is, if we take a general statement in which type-D reference of "some man" occurs, then in particular cases under that general statement we shall have "some man" occurring with a type-C reference to some man.

To these complexities it is hard to see an end. Of course they do not show that it is wrong to take "some man" as referring to some man; but they do rob this view of the simplicity and straightforwardness that made it intuitively acceptable.

7. We have not made much of the idea that an undistributed term refers to some of the things it denotes; can we make anything of Keynes's other statement about an undistributed term—that we get information only about some of the individuals denoted by the term, and 'are left in ignorance with regard to the remainder' of them? Many writers have used this sort of language about undistributed terms quite unsuspectingly; Keynes seems to have had an obscure idea that something was wrong, since he adds in a footnote that, if by "some" we understand "some but not all", then the information that some *S*s are *P*s does not really leave us in ignorance as to the remainder of the *S*s. Yet Keynes does not go on to deny that the subject-term in "Some *S*s are *P*s" is undistributed when "some" is taken to mean "some but not all". Thus a clear and reliable criterion for a term's being undistributed is not supplied by the two distinguishing marks that Keynes gives us; we cannot get a coherent idea either of a term's referring to 'some' of the individuals it denotes, or of the way its use 'leaves us in ignorance' about 'the remainder' of these individuals.

8. Many logicians have taken for granted that "all men" refers to all men and "some men" just to some men; and I have even sometimes come across the view that "no men" refers to *no* men, or to a class consisting of o men. Do not suppose that this is too absurd a view to have been put forward by a logician; for Boole and Schroeder introduced the null class into logic with a forged passport identifying it as the class signified by the word "nothing"—a procedure that has been followed by some more recent logicians in order to jolly their young readers into accepting the null class. The actual idea of a class consisting of o cats seems to be involved in the following sophism, traditional among schoolboys:

> Some cat has one more tail than no cats have;
> Three tails is one more tail than two tails;
> No cats have two tails;
> *Ergo*, some cat has three tails.

The first premise suggests that, since n (normal) cats have n tails between them, o cats have o tails between them, and that accordingly there is some cat that, having one tail, has one more tail than o cats have between them.

We can see, however, that this is nonsense. If a class were taken as consisting of its members, there could be no place for a null class in logic; when "nothing" or "no man" stands as a grammatical subject, it is ridiculous to ask what it refers to. The phrases "no men" and "men alone" are grammatically formed like "wise men", by attaching an adjective to "men"; but whereas "wise men" might be said to 'denote' certain men, who form a definite part of the class of men, this is clearly not true of "no men" or of "men alone". Although it might seem sensible to ask which portion of the class of men is constituted by the men referred to as "all men" or "some men", we may be led to doubt the legitimacy of this question; if we once think of comparing the adjectival uses of "all", "some", "no", and "alone"—"all men laugh, some men laugh, no men laugh, men alone laugh"—we see that none of these has the role of marking out part of a class.

9.   As I said earlier, modern writers on the doctrine of distribution fall into needless obscurities because they halfheartedly use a class terminology which came into fashion long after the doctrine had become stereotyped and does not really fit in with it. Indeed, on a thoroughgoing class interpretation of categoricals there is just no place for distribution. If the terms "S" and "P" are consistently understood to stand for two classes taken collectively, then they cannot be taken to refer to 'portions' of these classes, nor yet to individual members; so there can now be no question when a term is distributed—no question when it means 'the whole' of a class and when just 'a portion' of it, or when it means all the members and when just some of them. Phrases like "all men" and "some men" will not on this interpretation have any reference at all; "all" and "some" will be significant, not as prefixes to single terms, but as parts of logical frameworks with places for two terms, "All —— are ——", "Some —— are ——", "Some —— are not ——"; similarly, "no" and "alone" will be significant as parts of the frameworks "No —— are ——", "—— alone are

———"; each such framework will express a definite relation between two classes taken as wholes. I am not here advocating such a class interpretation of categoricals, but only pointing out that it cannot be combined with a doctrine of distribution.

10.   I have argued that the doctrine of distribution, though it looks intuitively acceptable when applied to subject-terms, will not really work even there; and its application to predicate-terms is even more open to exception. On the face of it, if I use the term "man" in the context ". . . is a man" or ". . . isn't a man", it is mere nonsense to ask which man or men would be referred to, or whether every man or just some man would be meant. If I said "Tibbles isn't a dog" and some nonphilosopher asked me with apparent seriousness "Which dog?", I should be quite bewildered—I might conjecture that he was a foreigner who took "isn't" to be the past tense of a transitive verb.

There are ways, however, of making this sort of question look like sense. If "man" occurs as a predicate in some true proposition with the general term "S" as subject, then "S" is truly predicable of some man, but not necessarily of every man; this is supposed to show that "man" is undistributed in "Every (*or* Some) S is a man". Likewise, if "No S is a man" is true, then we can truly say of every man that he is not an S; this is supposed to show that "man" is distributed in "No S is a man". In some such way, students are led to accept the traditional laws: In a universal or particular affirmative, the predicate-term is undistributed; in a universal negative, the predicate-term is distributed.

11.   As we saw, singular terms are counted as distributed, because they refer to whatever they denote; so singular propositions are traditionally assimilated to universal ones as regards the distribution of their terms. The subject-terms being distributed alike in both sorts of proposition, it is presumed that the predicate-term will be distributed or not in a singular proposition according as it is distributed or not in a corresponding universal proposition— i.e. "man" would be undistributed in "John is a man", as in "Every S is a man", and distributed in "John is not a man", as in "No S is a man".

Doctrine of Distribution

Here the doctrine limps at every step. Even if we waive objections to treating as 'distributed terms' both singular terms and general terms prefaced with "every" or "no", it would not follow that the predicate-terms in singular propositions must correspond in their distribution or nondistribution to those of universal propositions. For now we can no longer test for the distribution of "man" in "John is (isn't) a man" by asking whether, if this proposition were true, the subject-term would be truly predicable of every man or some man or no man; a proper name cannot stand as a predicate-term at all—it stands for an individual, not for something that does or does not hold good of individuals. Perhaps the best that can be done is to use the predicable term "identical with John" as proxy for "John" in predicate position, and convert "John is (isn't) a man" into "Some (No) man is identical with John". But bad is the best.

12. Difficulties arise also for the predicate-terms of particular negatives; for from "Some S is not P" it is not possible within the traditional system to infer any categorical beginning either "Every P is . . ." or "Some P is . . .". The traditional doctrine that "P" is here a distributed term, referring to every P, is upheld by mere fallacies; writers hurry over the topic, as over a thin patch of ice. Keynes gives us a typical 'proof' that "P" is distributed:

Again, if I say *Some S is not P*, although I make an assertion with regard to a part only of S, I exclude this part from the whole of P, and therefore the whole of P from it.[2]

As before, Keynes's class terminology obscures the matter: let us amend "with regard to a part only . . . the whole of P from it" to "about only some of the Ss, I exclude these from among all the Ps, and therefore exclude all the Ps from among them". We may now ask: From among which Ss are all the Ps being excluded? Clearly no definite answer is possible; so Keynes has simply failed to exhibit "Some S is not P" as an assertion about all the Ps, in which the term "P" is distributed.

[2]Keynes, p. 95.

Of course, if "Some S is not a man" is true, then of every man we can truly say: "Not he alone is an S". But obviously such a form of predication as "Not —— alone is an S" falls right outside the traditional scheme; and the admission of such forms would wreck the doctrine of distribution anyhow. If we say that in "Some S is not a man" "man" is distributed, on the score that this sort of statement about every man is inferable, then we must also allow that "dog" in "Some dog is white" is distributed, on the score that it entails that we can say as regards every dog "Either he is white, or not he alone is a dog".

13.   The doctrine of distribution has been supposed to be useful as supplying a test for the validity of inferences. The two rules by which invalid forms of reasoning are supposed to be eliminated are the rule against 'illicit process' and the rule against 'undistributed middle'.

The 'illicit process' rule is not restricted to arguments of syllogistic structure: it is e.g. traditionally applied to 'immediate', single-premise, arguments. It forbids our inferring a conclusion in which a term occurs distributed from a premise or premises in which the term's only occurrence is undistributed. Otherwise, it is argued, we shall be trying to get information about *every* S when in the premise(s) we are informed only about *some* S; and how can that possibly be legitimate?

I answer that it may very well be legitimate. Certainly this is an invalid schema:

(A) Some S is P; *ergo* every S is P.

But an invalid schema may have valid arguments as instances, and this one in particular has. We need not develop this objection, however, for the argument-forms traditionally stigmatized as involving 'illicit process' neither are overtly of form (A) nor can be shown to involve an argumentative step of that form. Rather, they conform e.g. to one of these patterns:

(B) Some S is P; *ergo* every (no) S is Q,

(C) *p*; some S is P; *ergo* every (no) S is Q

where "p" stands in for a premise in which "S" does not occur. But the invalidity of (A) gives us no shadow of reason for stamping a schema as invalid because it can be assimilated to (B) or to (C). It may be that all the schemata picked out by this test from some restricted class are in fact invalid; that does not mean the test is sound. People who uphold the 'illicit process' rule on the grounds usually given may be suspected of first considering form (A) and then reasoning thus:

> (D) Some arguments from *some* to *all* are invalid; *ergo*, all arguments from *some* to *all* are invalid.

And (D) of course must itself be invalid, just because its premise is true; for if (D) is valid, its conclusion is true; and in that case, being itself an argument from *some* to *all*, (D) will be invalid. The conclusion of (D) is in fact easily shown to be false: the following schema is assimilable to pattern (B), but is valid:

> (E) Some S is P; *ergo* every S (is such that) either (it) is P or not (it) alone is S.

We have already found how hard it is to make sense of the traditional view that "S" in "Some Q is not S" is distributed; but if we waive these difficulties, we find that on that view the 'illicit process' doctrine breaks down altogether, even within traditional logic. For it has long been known that by a series of steps each counted as valid in traditional logic finally "Some Q is not S" may be inferred although the only occurrence of "S" in the original premise(s) is undistributed.[3] Keynes honestly states, but does not satisfactorily resolve, this difficulty.

As we have so far considered it, violation of the 'illicit process' rule involves that a term shall occur *undistributed* in a premise although distributed in the conclusion, and we have construed "undistributed", in traditional style, as meaning implicit or explicit quantification of a term with "some". A variant form of the rule, also to be found in traditionalist logicians, would make an argument invalid if the term T occurring distributed in the

---

[3]See Keynes, pp. 139f., 297f., and Geach, pp. 62–64.

conclusion were merely *not distributed* at its sole occurrence in a premise. This imposes a stronger requirement, for of course *T* need not occur quantified either with "every" or with "some", whether explicitly or implicitly. In this form, the rule is more vulnerable by counterexamples, like this one:

(F) Most *S*s are *M*; most *Q*s that are *S* are not *M*; *ergo*, some *S* is not *Q*.

"*Q*" is not distributed nor undistributed at its sole occurrence in the premises; neither "all *Q*s" nor "some *Q*s" could replace "most *Q*s" without altering the premise essentially; on the other hand, "*Q*" would count as distributed in the conclusion. But (F) is formally valid, and this can be shown by a purely logical consideration, not by reasoning about the numbers of elements in classes: if the conclusion were false, then the *S*s would be the same as the *Q*s that are *S*, and then both premises could not be true.

The logic of the quantifier "most" has been strangely neglected since Sir William Hamilton urged that "most" ought to be recognized on a level with "some" and "all". Consideration of this quantifier is however useful to logicians, if only because it may rid them of prejudices got by concentrating on "some" and "all" (which are indeed far more important). I have just been using an example with "most" in it to refute one form of the rule against 'illicit process'. Friends of the traditional logic may protest that the rule was never intended to apply to such examples. But if the expositors of the rule were appealing to genuine logical insights, as they purport to be doing, then the rule could be extended to cover my example too; the way the rule breaks down here shows on the contrary that it embodies nothing but inherited superstition.

One objectionable feature of traditional doctrine is the statement, copied from one textbook into another, that for syllogistic purposes "Most *S*s are *P*" has to be 'put into logical form' as "Some *S*s are *P*". For example, Luce tells us that "most" is one way of introducing a particular proposition, along with "some";[4]

[4]Luce, p. 54.

Copi similarly tells us we have to ignore the difference between "most students" and "some students."[5] Obviously "Most *S*s are *P*" is stronger than "Some *S*s are *P*"; but the idea seems to be that this added logical strength is unusable (it is, so to say, energy that the engine cannot convert into mechanical work but must reject as waste heat). It comes as no surprise that Keynes had long since explicitly rejected this falsehood.[6] The example of a valid argument with two "most" premises that I have just given would turn into an invalid argument if in either premise "most" were replaced by "some".

The rule against 'illicit process' appeals, though in an unsound way, to general considerations about what can be derived from what, and is not restricted to arguments of one special form. The rule against 'undistributed middle' on the other hand is restricted to arguments of syllogistic form: in the two premises, a 'middle term' is predicatively linked to another term, and this term disappears in the conclusion, where the two other terms are linked together. The rule requires that the middle term shall occur distributed in at least one of the two premises. (In spite of the traditional meaning of "undistributed", the rule is *prescribing* such *distributed* occurrence; not *forbidding* the occurrence in the premises of a middle term *undistributed*, i.e. explicitly or implicitly quantified with "some".)

The attempts to show that this rule has an intuitive basis are pitifully feeble. The best that Keynes can do is to produce a certain pair of premises from which no conclusion can be drawn combining "*S*" and "*P*", this pair being, as it happens, one in which the middle term "*M*" is not distributed: as if this showed that *all* arguments lacking a distributed middle term are invalid.[7] Keynes was indeed aware, as we shall see (section 57), that there are cases in which this rule breaks down: no wonder he was not able to say much in its support.

Let us then take a typical exposition of the rule from a contemporary textbook of traditional logic: A. A. Luce tells us that if the middle term is not distributed at least once "it might be taken in

[5]Copi, p. 232.
[6]Keynes, pp. 104, 377.
[7]Keynes, p. 288.

one part of its extension in one premise, and in a different part of its extension in the other: and then the premises would fall asunder."[8] The idea no doubt is that one premise might be true in virtue of what held good of one lot of things covered by the middle term and the other premise in virtue of what held good of another such lot, and then these two bits of information might not be combinable to yield a categorical conclusion that linked the two remaining terms. The sort of case that makes this plausible is the premise-pair "Some *S* is *P*; some *S* is *Q*", from which we certainly cannot infer anything about *Ps'* being *Q* or *Qs'* being *P*.

Let us however take another example. From the premise-pair:

Every *A* is *M*; most *Ms* are *B*

we of course cannot infer "Some *A* is *B*"; and the supporters of the 'undistributed middle' rule would no doubt explain this by saying that on an interpretation of the terms that makes both the premises true, the *As* might all fall among the minority of *Ms* that were not *B*. Similarly we cannot infer "Some *A* is *B*" from the premise-pair:

Most *Ns* are *A*; every *B* is *N*.

But now let us combine the two premise-pairs. Obviously "*M*" cannot become distributed in the premises in which it occurs because we add two more premises in which it does not occur; and the same goes for "*N*". And indeed by the doctrine of distribution we can no more infer a conclusion from two premise-pairs with 'undistributed middle' in each pair than from one such pair. But these four premises *do* yield the conclusion "Some *A* is *B*".

Nor is this conclusion obtainable only by algebraic considerations about the supposed numbers of individuals in each of the classes involved. It is possible to derive a contradiction from the conjunction of our two premise-pairs with the negation of the conclusion, "No *A* is *B*", by a series of steps each of which would count as purely logical by the canons of traditional logic, if only the quantifier were "some" or "all" instead of "most".

[8]Luce, p. 88.

(G) (1) Every A is M. (2) Every B is N.
(3) Most Ms are B. (4) Most Ns are A.

From (1) we get: (5) Every A is MA; and from (2), similarly: (6) Every B is NB.

From (4) and (5) we get: (7) Most Ns are MA.

From (3) and (6) similarly we get: (8) Most Ms are NB.

From (7) we get: (9) Most MNs are A.

From (8) similarly we get: (10) Most MNs are B.

Notice that each of these last four steps would remain valid if we replaced the quantifier "most" in the premise and the conclusion by "all" both times or by "some" both times. So also would the following step remain valid under such substitutions:

From (9) and "No A is B" we get: (11) Most MNs are not B. But (10) and (11) are inconsistent. So (1), (2), (3), (4), and "No A is B" are an inconsistent set. So from (1), (2), (3), and (4) this follows: "Some A is B". Q.E.D.

Although the moves of inference I have here performed with "most" propositions may fairly count as purely logical, traditionalist logicians may be expected to object to the use of such premises at all. But it does not lie in their mouths to do so if they are prepared to appeal to their intuitive grounds for the 'undistributed middle' rule as explaining why in the deduction (G) the conclusion does not follow from (1) and (3) alone, nor from (2) and (4) alone. And they have still less of a case if they put out the preposterous untruth that by purely logical manipulations a "most" premise cannot yield a stronger conclusion than the corresponding "some" proposition. Argument (G) is a further refutation of this untruth, for "Some A is B" could not be deduced if either (3) or (4) were replaced with a "some" proposition.

14.   Difficulties about the rule against 'illicit process' have in fact long been known. In one old statement of the rule, there is mentioned as a difficult case an argument essentially like the following one:

> Every donkey that belongs to a villager is running in the
>   race;
> Brownie is not running in the race;
> *Ergo*, Brownie is not a donkey that belongs to a villager.

The difficulty was that "villager" seemed to be distributed in the conclusion but undistributed in the premise.[9]

What suggested this difficulty to my old author? I suppose he was puzzled by the fact that in the premise "a villager" is replaceable by "some villager", and not replaceable by "every villager", without changing the force of the premise; whereas in the conclusion "a villager" is replaceable by "any villager" without changing the force of the conclusion. This reasoning is not decisive; for in the premise too "a villager" is replaceable by "any villager", though not by "every villager". But then, the doctrine of distribution has no room for a distinction between "any" and "every"—either word is just a sign of distribution.

My old author has no such distinction; his solution is that what counts as distributed or undistributed for the purpose of syllogistic theory is not "villager" but "donkey that belongs to a villager". This term is distributed in the premise as in the conclusion; he argues that validity of the syllogism requires only that "donkey that belongs to a villager" be unambiguously used in premise and conclusion—the internal structure of this complex term is irrelevant. But this does not answer, nor can it stop us from asking, the question whether "villager" is undistributed in the premise and distributed in the conclusion.

If we tried saying that "villager" is distributed in the premise, the traditional theory still could not stand. First, we should need to distinguish "every" and "any", in a quite untraditional way. Secondly, we should have to say that in this equivalent form of the premise:

> Every donkey that belongs to some villager is running in the race

"villager" is distributed, and refers to any villager. On the other hand, in this proposition:

> Every donkey that belongs to every villager is running in the race

[9]This example comes from an appendix at the end of the *Modernorum summulae Logicales* (Mainz: Peter Drach, 1489). I owe this reference to Professor Kneale.

we must say that "villager" is not distributed and does not refer to
every villager. For we could not go on to syllogize thus:

> Hobson is a villager;
> *Ergo,* every donkey that belongs to Hobson is running in
> the race

since a donkey could very well be one of Hobson's donkeys without being a communal donkey that belongs to every villager. Nor
could we say that in the proposition:

> Every donkey that belongs to every villager is running in
> the race

"villager" refers to some villager. At least, it is not clear what we
could mean by doing this; and certainly this proposition does not
require that the formula:

> Every donkey that belongs to X is running in the race

should be true for even one interpretation of "X" as a proper
name of a villager. (We see this clearly if we suppose that every
villager has at least one private donkey, whereas only the communal donkeys are racing.) Thus in the context:

> Every donkey that belongs to —— is running in the race

"villager" is distributed when preceded by "some", since in this
case it seems to refer to any villager; in the same context, we
could hardly take "villager" preceded by "every" as referring
either to every villager or to some villager, and thus on the traditional account it would be neither distributed nor undistributed.
(Remember that in traditional explanations "undistributed" does
not mean "not distributed" but rather "having reference just to
some of the things denoted".) Once we leave the hackneyed
examples, the doctrine of distribution is no guide at all.

15.   If a predicate-term "P" can indeed be understood to refer
now to any and every P, and now only to some P, then it seems
natural to mark this fact by attaching quantifiers to the predicate
as well as the subject—"Any S is some P"; "No S is any P";
"Some S is (isn't) some P". Explicit quantification of the predi-

cate is, however, actually rejected by upholders of the doctrine of distribution. Admittedly, the work of Sir William Hamilton, who first advocated a systematic quantification of the predicate, is full of mistakes, confusions, and inconsistencies; but to fasten on these in discussing the subject is a matter of "No case; abuse plaintiff's attorney"; one might as well denounce Boolean algebra by fastening on Boole's mistakes and confusions. If the predicate is understood as distributed or undistributed, then it is understood as quantified; and then what is wrong with Hamilton's demand that we be allowed to state in language all that is implicitly contained in thought?

Like the statements of the traditional doctrine itself, the criticisms of Hamilton's theory have been copied from one textbook to another. Writers keep on denouncing him for taking "some" to mean "some but not all", although he himself did not consistently adhere to this reading and although one could perfectly well quantify the predicate without adopting this reading; their triumph over him is thus merely forensic. The actual cause for opposition to Hamilton is mere conservatism, which comes out amusingly in Keynes; if an explicit quantification renders the quantity of the predicate independent of the quality (affirmative or negative) of the proposition, then we have to admit new forms of categorical falling outside the traditional fourfold scheme, like "No *S* is some *P*" and "Some *S* is not some *P*"; and Keynes is unwilling that such an enlarged schedule should 'supersede the fourfold schedule in the main body of logical doctrine'.[10]

The form "Some *S* is not some *P*" has come in for specially fierce criticism. Keynes raises the difficulty that in a schedule of propositions with quantified predicates any affirmative form is compatible with this verbally negative form, which thus 'is of absolutely no logical importance'.[11] But just as "Some knife is no sharper than some spoon" is contradicted by "Any knife is sharper than any spoon", we might well take the contradictory of "Some *S* is not some *P*" to be "Any *S* is any *P*".

In Hamilton's own schedule this last form does not appear: the

[10]Keynes, p. 207, n. 4.
[11]Keynes, pp. 206f.

affirmative form with both subject and predicate universally quantified is "All S is all P". Indeed, if we study Hamilton's schedule, [12] we find him oscillating between two ways of reading the letters "S" and "P". In "All S is all P", "All S is some P", "Some S is all P", and possibly in "Some S is (not) some P", "S" and "P" go proxy for singular designations of classes, like "the class *men*", and "all" and "some" respectively mean "the whole of" and "a part of". On the other hand, in "No S is any P", "Any S is not some P", "Some S is not any P", "S" and "P" must go proxy for general terms like "man" and "animal", and this reading is also possible for "Some S is (not) some P". Keynes did not observe this flaw in Hamilton's schedule, since he himself, as I remarked, habitually fell into the same confusion.

An amended schedule would read as follows:

1. Any (*or* Every) S is any (*or* every) P.
2. Any (*or* Every) S is some P.
3. Some S is any (*or* every) P.
4. Some S is some P.
5. Some S is not some P.
6. Some S is not any P.
7. Any S is not some P.
8. No S is any P.

The forms 1 and 5, 2 and 6, 3 and 7, 4 and 8, would be contradictories.

Hamilton claimed, and it would seem natural to think, that, with the predicate-term explicitly quantified, every categorical could be simply converted by interchanging its terms while retaining the quantification of each term. But in fact difficulties arise. In the schedule above, "Any (*or* Every) S is some P" would naturally be taken to mean that, for any S you take, there is some P that that S is; whereas "Some P is any (*or* every) S" is naturally taken to mean that there is some P that is any and every S, i.e., that is the one and only S. These are obviously not equivalent; yet there is no difference between them as regards the separate quantifications of the terms "S" and "P". Thus the import of a

---

[12]Keynes, p. 195.

categorical form is not completely determined by whether its 'quality' is affirmative or negative and whether the two terms in it are distributed or undistributed; something essential has been left out.

16.   The traditional doctrine of distribution combines the quantification of the predicate with an incoherent denial that the predicate is 'thought of' as quantified[13]—a denial which is irrelevant if meant psychologically, and inconsistent if meant logically; further, it includes what we have already shown to be an incoherent doctrine that "every man" refers to every man and "some man" to some man. Why has the doctrine survived so long? Well, it looks intelligible if you are not too curious; and it supplies easy mechanical rules for judging the validity of inferences.[14] And for the rest—England and the United States cling to their odd weights and measures, and all men measure angles the way the Babylonians did, because it would be too much trouble to change.

[13]Keynes, pp. 197f.
[14]These rules are in fact not foolproof: cf. Keynes, pp. 139f., 297f.

Two

Subject and Predicate

17.   We saw in the first chapter that the doctrine of distribution was clearly fallacious as regards predicate-terms but plausible as regards subject-terms; it seemed absurd to ask which dog or dogs the word "dog" referred to in "Jemima is (isn't) a dog", but not absurd to ask this when the word occurred as a grammatical subject, or again as part of the phrase "every dog" or "some dog". To see whether there is anything in this apparent difference, we must investigate the relation of subject and predicate.

As used in this work, the terms "subject" and "predicate" will always be linguistic terms. I shall never call a man a logical subject, but only the name of a man; the name "Peter", not the Apostle, is the subject of "Peter was an Apostle"; and not the property of being an Apostle but its verbal expression is a predicate. I shall say, however, that what the predicate in "Peter was an Apostle" is predicated of is Peter, not his name; for it is Peter, not his name, that is being said to have been an Apostle. In saying that something is predicated of Peter, I do not mean that this predicate is true of or applies to Peter, but only that in some significant sentence, true or false, it is predicated of Peter. I shall say that a predicate is *attached to* a subject, is *predicated of* what the subject stands for, and *applies to* or is *true of* this if the statement so formed is true.

The stipulations in the last paragraph are of course arbitrary; but it is convenient to make some such stipulations and adhere to them. For lack of this, logicians as distinguished as Aristotle and Russell have fallen into almost inextricable confusions, so that you just cannot tell whether a predicate is something within language or something represented by means of language.

Let us now try to get provisional explanations of the terms "subject" and "predicate". (These are *not* to be taken as proper definitions.) A *predicate* is an expression that gives us an assertion about something if we attach it to another expression that stands for what we are making the assertion about. A *subject* of a sentence S is an expression standing for something that S is about, S itself being formed by attaching a predicate to that expression.

18.   There is a divergence between these explanations: "subject" is defined as "subject of a sentence", but "predicate" is not defined as "predicate in a sentence". This divergence is deliberate. It would be very inconvenient not to recognize the same predicate in "Jim broke the bank at Monte Carlo" and in "The man who broke the bank at Monte Carlo died in misery"; but in the latter sentence the predicate in question is attached not to the name of somebody to whom the predicate allegedly applies, but to the relative pronoun "who", which is not anybody's name. What makes this predicate to be a predicate is that it can be attached to a person's name to make an assertion about him, not that it actually is so attached whenever it is used.

There are, however, also inconveniences about not having "subject" and "predicate" as correlatives. We can remove these by taking the explanation just given as an explanation not of "predicate" but of "predicable"; the older use of the noun "predicable" is too little current in recent philosophical literature to stop me from staking out my own claim to the term. Thus in "Jim broke the bank..." and "The man who broke the bank... died in misery", we have two occurrences of the same *predicable*, but only in the first sentence is it actually a *predicate* attached to the subject "Jim".

Subject and Predicate

19. A further difficulty arises over the expression "assertion about something". Round this and similar expressions there is piled a secular accumulation of logical error; we have here a suggestion that "*P*" is predicated of *S* only if it is actually asserted, affirmed, that *S* is *P*. A moment's consideration ought to have shown that this will not do: "*P*" may be predicated of *S* in an *if* or a *then* clause, or in a clause of a disjunction, without the speaker's being in the least committed to affirming that *S* is *P*. Yet it took the genius of the young Frege to dissolve the monstrous and unholy union that previous logicians had made between the import of a predicate and the assertoric force of a sentence. Even when a sentence has assertoric force, this attaches force to the sentence as a whole; not specially to the subject, or to the predicate, or to any part of the sentence.

Frege's lesson still has to be learned by many philosophers. A philosophical theory of certain predicables may win popularity, when it is not even plausible if we consider occurrences of them as predicates in hypothetical or disjunctive clauses. I have even read an author maintaining that "if... then..." itself means something different in an asserted hypothetical from what it means in a hypothetical that itself occurs as a subclause in a longer hypothetical. Would he say "and" meant something different in an asserted conjunctive proposition? Probably he would say in that case that the assertoric force attached not to "and" but to the clauses it joined. Such a position, however, is clearly arbitrary.

To avoid these absurdities, we had best reword our explanation of "predicable", using some term less objectionable than "assertion". "Statement" will hardly do; a statement is something we state, as an assertion is something we assert, and by both terms assertoric force is equally suggested. (How misleading is the fashionable talk about sentences being true or false only qua 'used to make statements'! Can we then not assign any truth-values to the clauses of a disjunction?) "Proposition" is much better; a proposition is something we propound or put forward—it may or may not be asserted. Unfortunately, though the traditional use of "proposition" makes a proposition something linguistic, there is a prevalent use of the term to mean a supposed kind of nonlinguistic entities, signified by what I call propositions. But we can avoid ambiguity very simply: in discussing the philosophers who intro-duce these nonlinguistic entities, I shall dignify "Proposition" with an initial capital. Thus our explanation of "predicable" and "predicate" will be: A *predicable* is an expression that gives us a proposition about something if we attach it to another expression that stands for what we are forming the proposition about; the predicable then becomes a *predicate*, and the other expression becomes its *subject*; I call such a proposition a *predication*.

20.   How are we to apply this definition of "subject"? How can we tell that an expression within a proposition is being used to stand for something that the proposition is about? If Frege and the young Wittgenstein were right, then a name stands for something only in the context of a proposition, and this question becomes formidably difficult: but I think they were clearly wrong. A name may be used outside the context of a sentence simply to call something by name—to acknowledge the presence of the thing. This act of naming is of course no proposition, and, while we may call it correct or incorrect, we cannot properly call it true or false. It does, however, as grammarians say concerning sen-tences, express a complete thought; it is not like the use of "Napo-leon" to answer the question "Who won the Battle of Hastings?", where we have to take the single word as short for the complete sentence "Napoleon won the Battle of Hastings".

I call this use of names "independent"; but I do not mean that it is independent of the language system to which the names belong or of the physical context that makes their use appropriate; I mean that names so used to not require any immediate context of words, uttered or understood—it is quite a different case when names are used to answer spoken or unspoken questions. Nouns in the vocative case used as greetings, and again ejaculations like "Wolf!" and "Fire!" illustrate this independent use of names; we get a very similar independent use of names when labels are stuck on things, e.g. "poison" on a bottle or the name labels sometimes worn at conferences.

It is noteworthy that common nouns and proper nouns equally admit of this use in acts of naming. I may greet the same animal with "Hullo, Jemima!" or "Hullo, cat!" The latter greeting refers to Jemima less determinately than the former; it would serve equally well to greet any other cat.

21. I have said by implication that the use of proper nouns is dependent on the language system to which they belong; perhaps, therefore, it will be as well to mention the odd view that proper names are not exactly words and do not quite belong to the language in which they are embedded, because you would hardly look for proper names in a dictionary. On the contrary: it is part of the job of a lexicographer to tell us that "Warsaw" is the English word for "Warszawa"; and a grammarian would say that "Warszawa" is a Polish word—a feminine noun declined like "mowa". And what is wrong with this way of speaking?

22. An assertoric sentence whose grammatical subject is a demonstrative pronoun often has the logical role not of an as- serted proposition but of a simple act of naming. The grammatical subject does not here name something concerning which an assertion is made; it simply points at an object, directs attention to it; it works like a pointer, not like a label. There is a well-known philosophical illusion that demonstratives are a sort of name, indeed the only genuine proper names. The source of the illusion must surely be a desire for an infallible method of naming or referring; when I say "this" or "that", what I mean by the word must for certain be there. But very often a demonstrative is no more of a term than "lo" or "ecce" or "voici", which might take its place.

We may get a clear view of the matter if we compare the respective roles of the pronoun and the noun in "That is gold" or "That is Sam" to those of the hands and the figures of a watch. The hands direct attention to the figures from which we are to read the time. In some watches the demonstrative role of the hands is not needed, because only the figures showing the current time are visible; similarly, in some environments "Gold!" or "Sam!" would be enough for an act of calling by name, without need for a demonstrative pronoun or gesture.

Demonstratives not only are not a superior sort of names, they just are not names at all, and regarding them as names is mere philosophical silliness. If a demonstrative were a name, it could function alone in an act of calling by name; but obviously it would be quite senseless to call out "That!" as one might call out "Gold!" or "Sam!" Of course in some alien language the word for "gold" might sound just like "that", but this is quite irrelevant to the use of the English word "that".

23. In many propositions we can pick out a part functioning as a name of something that the proposition is about; such an expression could always be used, outside the context of a sentence, for a simple act of naming, and it always makes sense to ask whether these two kinds of use fit together—whether an expression stands for the same object in a given use of a sentence as it does in a given act of naming, so that we have a proposition about the object then and there named. For example, if my friend points to a man and says "Smith!", I may ask him *sotto voce* "Is he the one you were telling me nearly went to prison?"; and if my friend assents, he is linking up his present use of "Smith" in an act of naming with his past use of it in "Smith nearly went to prison". Whenever an expression in a sentence could thus be linked up with an act of naming, the expression is a name, and the sentence will have the role of a proposition about the bearer of the name. The cases most easily recognized are certain uses of proper names (what Quine calls the 'purely referential' uses). Any proposition in which we can thus recognize the name of something the proposition is about may rightly be regarded as a predication, with that name as its logical subject.

24. We must beware of supposing that a proposition admits of only one subject-predicate analysis. "Peter struck Malchus" is at once a predication about Peter and a (different) predication about Malchus; either "Peter" or "Malchus" may be taken as a logical subject—as Aristotle observed long ago, a logical subject need not be in the nominative case.[1] A traditionalist might protest that only "Peter" can be treated as the subject, and some modern

[1] *Analytica priora*, I. 36.

logicians might say we have here a relational proposition, not admitting of subject-predicate analysis; both would be making the mistake of treating an analysis of a proposition as the only analysis. Logic would be hopelessly crippled if the same proposition could never be analyzed in several different ways. Some people hold that it is a matter of which name is emphasized, "Peter" being the subject of "*Peter* struck Malchus" and "Malchus" the subject of "Peter struck *Malchus*". I reply that for logic these are not different propositions; they have, on the contrary, just the same logical content—either implying and implied by just the same propositions as the other.

25. The object named by a name may be called its bearer. No reference to time is involved in the questions whether a proper name in a given use (e.g. "Peter" in the Gospels, "Cerberus" in Greek theology, "Vulcan" in astronomy) has a bearer, and whether such-and-such an object is that bearer. Thus, the proper noun "Augustus" as used in Roman history books has Octavian for its bearer; this is true without temporal qualifications, even though Octavian lived for years before being called by that name; it would be absurd to object to the question "When was Augustus born?" because the name was not conferred on him then. Again, after a woman has married, it may be a social solecism to call her by her maiden name; but this is not the sort of linguistic fault to make a sentence containing the name to be no longer a proposition with a sense and a truth-value.

Nor yet does it cease to be true that so-and-so is the bearer of a name because so-and-so is no more. Otherwise—if I may adopt the style of a Stoic logician—"Dion is dead" could not possibly be true, because if the person so called is not dead "Dion is dead" would be false and not true, and if the person so called is dead "Dion" would stand for nothing, and so "Dion is dead" would be no longer a proposition and again would not be true. There are, one would normally wish to say, things that can hold good of Dion even if Dion is no more—e.g. that Dion is loved and admired by Plato. Naturally, formal logic cannot sort out what can and what cannot be true of a man who is no more; that is no job for formal logic; it would be silly to cut the knot by saying that nothing at all is true of the dead. It suffices, for a name to have a bearer, that it could have been used to name that bearer in a simple act of naming; it does not matter if such use is not at present possible, because the bearer is too remote from the speaker, or has even ceased to be.

26. If we remove a proper name from a proposition, the whole of the rest of the proposition supplies what is being propounded concerning the bearer of the name, and is thus, by our explanation, the predicate attached to that name as subject. In "Peter struck Malchus" the predicate is "—— struck Malchus" if we take "Peter" as the subject and "Peter struck ——" if we take "Malchus". As I said in section 24, either choice of subject is legitimate. The proposition relates both to Peter and to Malchus; what is propounded concerning Peter is that he *struck Malchus*, and what is propounded concerning Malchus is that *Peter struck* him.

We may get the very same proposition by attaching different predicates to the same subject. The predicates "—— shaved Peter" and "Peter shaved ——" are quite different, and when attached to the subject "John" yield different propositions, but when attached to the subject "Peter" they yield the very same proposition "Peter shaved Peter". This simple example shows that the sense of a predicate cannot be determined, so to say, by subtracting the sense of the subject from that of the whole proposition. We need rather to consider a way of forming propositions; "—— shaved Peter" and "Peter shaved ——" represent two different ways of forming propositions, and this is what makes them two different predicates even in "Peter shaved Peter".

We may in some instances recognize a common predicate in two propositions even though this predicate is not an identifiable expression that can be picked out; for example, "John shaved John" propounds the very same thing concerning John as "Peter shaved Peter" does concerning Peter, and thus we may regard the two as containing a common predicate, but this is by no means identifiable with the mere word "shaved" occurring in both. This does not mean that the common predicate must here no longer be regarded as something linguistic; but on the linguistic level what we have is a shared pattern or way of formation of certain propositions, not a form of words extractable from all of them alike.

We could of course replace the second occurrences of the proper names in these propositions by the reflexive pronoun "himself", and then treat "—shaved himself" as a predicable which can occur even where it is not attached to a logical subject—as in "Nobody who shaved himself was shaved by the barber". But this is not what makes it legitimate to treat "John shaved John" and "Peter shaved Peter" as having a common predicate; it is the other way round—because these propositions have a common predicate, it is legitimate to rewrite them so that the common predicate takes the shape of an explicit predicable that can be extracted from each of them.

27.   Given my explanations of "subject" and "predicate", it follows that a name can occur in a proposition only as a logical subject; if the same expression appears to be used now predicatively, now as a name, that is a misleading feature of our language. Thus names and predicables are absolutely different. A name has a complete sense, and can stand by itself in a simple act of naming; a predicable, on the other hand, is a potential predicate, and a predicate never has a complete sense, since it does not show what the predication is about; it is what is left of a proposition when the subject is removed, and thus essentially contains an empty place to be filled by a subject. And though a predicable may occur in a proposition otherwise than as a predicate attached to a subject, it does not then lose its predicative, incomplete character; it has sense only as contributing toward the sense of a proposition, not all by itself.

A predicable applies to or is true of things; for example, "Peter struck ——" applies to Malchus (whether it is actually predicated of Malchus or not). This relation must be sharply distinguished from the relation of name to bearer, which is confounded with it in the 'Aristotelian' tradition under the term "denoting". A predicable never names what it is true of, and "Peter struck ——" does not even look like a name of Malchus.

Again, negation operating upon the whole of a subject-predicate proposition may be taken to go with the predicate in a way in which it cannot be taken to go with the subject. For predicables always occur in contradictory pairs, and by attaching the members of such a pair to a common subject we get a contradictory pair of propositions. But no name pairs off with another expression (whether we are to call this a name or not) so that by attaching the same predicable to both we always get a contradictory pair of propositions.

It is easy to prove this formally. Suppose that for a name "a" there were a complementary expression "Na" such that by attaching the same predicable to both we always got a contradictory pair of propositions. Consider now the predicables "$P(\ )$ & $Q(b)$" and "$P(\ )$ v $Q(b)$". By our hypothesis, these will be contradictory pairs:

"$P(a)$ & $Q(b)$" and "$P(Na)$ & $Q(b)$"
"$P(a)$ v $Q(b)$" and "$P(Na)$ v $Q(b)$"

But we can quickly show that this runs into inconsistency. Suppose "$Q(b)$" is true. Then "$P(a)$ v $Q(b)$" is true: so its contradictory "$P(Na)$ v $Q(b)$" is false. Then, however, "$Q(b)$" is false. —Suppose on the other hand that "$Q(b)$" is false. Then "$P(a)$ & $Q(b)$" is false; so its contradictory "$P(Na)$ & $Q(b)$" is true. But then "$Q(b)$" is true. —Either way we get inconsistency. So a name, unlike a predicable, cannot be replaced by a complementary expression with the result that the whole proposition is negated.

This reasoning of course depends on the possibility of analyzing "$P(Na)$ & $Q(b)$" or "$P(Na)$ v $Q(b)$" in two different ways: as the result of attacking a complex predicable to "Na" instead of "a", and as a conjunction or disjunction whose second limb is "$Q(b)$". Someone might protest that this merely shows an ambiguity of notation that could be removed by some sort of bracketing. But in the original propositions "$P(a)$ & $Q(b)$", "$P(a)$ v $Q(b)$", there was no such ambiguity: either of these admits of alternative analyses—as the result of attaching a complex predicable to "a", and as a conjunction or disjunction whose second limb is "$Q(b)$"—without thereby becoming two distinct propositions. And if a predicable is replaced in a proposition by its contradictory, again there is no resulting ambiguity. So if the replacement of a name by a complementary expression brought with it a need for some disambiguating device, this again only shows an irreducible difference between names and predicables.

If a name is used not as a subject of predication but in a simple act of naming, then we have a use of language which may be mistaken and thus may be contradicted or corrected: when a child says "Pussy" or "Jemima", I may say "Not pussy—dog" or "Not Jemima—another pussy". But "Not pussy" and "Not Jemima" are not themselves acts of naming. For as regards two uses of a single name in acts of naming we can always ask whether the same thing is named, and this is all right as regards "Jemima" or "pussy"; but it would be senseless to ask whether the same thing was named when on various occasions someone said "Not Jemima" or "Not pussy", since the reason for saying this could simply be that on none of the occasions was any cat present. So the negation of an act of naming is never the use of a negated name as a name.

Again, puzzling as tenses are, we can at least see that they attach to predicables; we may say not only of the proposition "Peter struck Malchus", but also of the predicables "Peter struck ——" and "—— struck Malchus", that they are in the past tense. But names are tenseless, as Aristotle observed;[2] the reference of a name to its bearer admits of no time-qualification. On the other hand, we may quite well say that since "—— struck Malchus" *does* apply to Peter, "—— is striking Malchus" *did* apply to Peter; and thus the relation of a predicable to what it applies to does admit of time-qualification.

We must thus make an absolute distinction between names and predicables; if a name and a predicable have the same external form, that is a defect of language, just as it is a defect in a language if it fails to distinguish the uses of "Peter" to talk about the man Peter and about the name "Peter".

28. A term, as conceived in Aristotelian logic, is supposed capable of being a subject in one proposition and a predicate in

[2] *De interpretatione*, c. 3.

another; since only names, not predicables, can be logical subjects, this notion of terms has no application whatsoever. This initial confusion has led to a multitude: *pessima in principiis corruptio*.

One center of confusion is the copula. Should a proposition be analyzed into subject and predicate, or into subject, predicate, and copula? Aristotle had little interest in the copula; he remarks casually at the beginning of the *Analytica priora* that a proposition is analyzable into a pair of terms, with or without the verb "to be". This was natural, because the Greek for "Socrates is a man" might be (literally rendered) either "Man the Socrates" or "Man is the Socrates". Frege repeatedly says that the bare copula has no special content; this is the view I shall defend.

If terms are thought of as (at least potential) names, then a natural idea is that the truth of a categorical consists in its putting together two names of the same thing. In fact, a categorical is true if its predicate is a predicable applying to that which its subject is a name of; the two-name theory of predication is derivable from this principle if one confounds the relation *being a predicable applying to* with the relation *being a name of*. Hobbes, who held the two-name theory of predication, held also that the copula was superfluous; but we might very well object that on the contrary it is necessary, because a pair of names is not a proposition but the beginning of a list, and a redundant list at that if the two names do name the same thing. (If I am listing the things in my room, I do not need to enter both a cat and Jemima.)

The two-name theory breaks down in any event—whether we have a copula or not. Of a name it always makes sense to ask what it names, but it is clearly nonsense to ask which cat "cat" stands for in "Jemima is a cat", or which dog "dog" stands for in "Jemima isn't a dog". I suppose somebody might try saying that in "Jemima is a cat" "cat" stands for Jemima, because the proposition is true. But what the names in a proposition stand for cannot be determined by whether the proposition is true or false: on the contrary, we can determine whether the proposition is true only when we know what it is about, and thus what the names contained in it do stand for.

Again, consider propositions like "Socrates became a

philosopher". "Philosopher" clearly has the same sort of predicative use as "cat" and "dog" did in the examples last discussed; in Polish, a language sensitive to the distinction of subject and predicate, all three nouns would take the predicative (instrumental) inflection. Now if Socrates did become a philosopher, he certainly did not become Socrates, nor did he become any other philosopher, say Plato; so "philosopher" does not stand for a philosopher—it does not serve to name a philosopher.

Even here a resolute champion of the two-name theory will not give up. Ockham for example regards propositions like "Socrates became a philosopher" as exponible, somehow like this: "First of all Socrates was not a philosopher and then Socrates was a philosopher"; the first half of this would be true in virtue of the predicate-term's referring to all the people (Anaxagoras, Parmenides, etc.) who were philosophers when Socrates was not one, and the second half would be true in virtue of the predicate-term's referring to the philosopher that Socrates eventually was—viz. Socrates.[3] But this ought not to satisfy us. It is clear that a two-name theory, though it starts off simple, is ultimately going to let us in for more and more futile subtleties: just as, if you insist on describing planetary motions in terms of uniform circular motions, you need an immense number of cycles and epicycles.

29. If this two-name theory is rejected but the terms are still thought of as names, people will naturally come to regard the copula as expressing a relation. As I said, two names by themselves cannot form a proposition; but this can be done if we join two names with a word for a relation, as in "Smith excels Robinson". It will then be a problem whether the relation expressed by the copula is always the same; logicians of our time commonly suppose that the copula may express either class membership or class inclusion, and some make even further distinctions. But it is quite wrong to say that "is" means different relations in "Socrates is an animal" and in "Every man is an animal"; there is the same unambiguous expression "is an animal" in both, and the propo-

[3]Ockham, c. 75.

sitions differ in just the same way as "Socrates can laugh" and "Every man can laugh", where there is no copula to be ambiguous.

Admittedly, if "animal" stood for the class of animals and "every man" stood for the class of man, then "is an" would have to mean different things in "Socrates is an animal" and "Every man is an animal"; but the supposition is plainly false, at least about "every man" (being in this case, I suppose, a hangover from the muddled fusion of the doctrine of distribution with class logic). Frege has sometimes been credited with distinguishing these two brands of copula; in criticism of Schroeder, Frege actually pointed out that if we turn "Every mammal is a vertebrate" into "The class of mammals is included in the class of vertebrates", the predicate is now not "vertebrate" but "included in the class of vertebrates", and "is included in" is not the copula but the copula plus a bit of the predicate.[4]

By my explanation of "predicable", there is a single predicable occurring in "Socrates is an animal" and in "Every man is an animal", viz. "is an animal"; the grammatical copula is thus part of this predicable. This does not settle the problem of the copula, but just determines how we state it. In a predicable like "is an animal", has the "is" any definite content? I can see no reason for saying so. Naturally, if a tensed proposition contains a copula, the tense will attach to the copula just because the copula is grammatically a verb; but a tensed proposition need not contain a copula, and anyhow tense is something utterly different from the copula's supposed role of linking two terms. The traditional logic drilled pupils in twisting propositions into a form where they had a predicable beginning "is" or "are", and preferably one consisting of that prefixed to a noun (-phrase); this was a pernicious training, which might well disable the pupils for recognizing predicables that had not this special form. Moreover, as we shall see, predicables consisting of "is" plus a noun (-phrase) have special logical difficulties about them, which ought not be gratuitously brought in by transforming other predicables into this shape.

[4]Frege (3), pp. 90–91.

30. We must here notice a restriction on the kind of general terms that can ever occur as names. When the same name is used in two acts of naming, we can always ask whether the same thing is named. It follows that a general term can occur as a name only if it makes sense to prefix the words "the same" to it; by no means all general terms satisfy this condition. And again, only in connection with some terms can the question be asked how many so-and-so's there are. For example, although we have the phrase "the seven seas", nobody could set out to determine how many seas there are; the term "sea" does not determine any division of the water area in the world into seas in the way that the term "letter" (in the typographical sense) does determine a division of the printed matter in the world into letters.

This second ground of distinction between terms was recognized by Frege and by Aquinas. Frege said that only such concepts as 'sharply delimited' what they applied to, so that it was not 'arbitrarily divisible,' could serve as units for counting; to link this up with what I have been saying, we need only observe that for Frege a concept was what language represented by a general term. Frege cagily remarked that in other cases, e.g. "red things", no finite number was determined.[5] But of course the trouble about counting the red things in a room is not that you cannot make an end of counting them, but that you cannot make a beginning; you never know whether you have counted one already, because "the same red thing" supplies no criterion of identity. Aquinas similarly mentions the grammatical fact that, in Latin, substantives have (singular or plural) number on their own account, whereas adjectives have a number determined by the nouns they qualify; I shall follow him in distinguishing general terms as *substantival* and *adjectival*.[6] Grammar is of course only a rough guide here: "sea", for example, could be an adjectival term, although grammatically a substantive.

I had here best interject a note on how I mean this term "criterion of identity". I maintain that it makes no sense to judge whether things are 'the same', or a thing remains 'the same',

---

[5]Frege (1), p. 66.
[6]Aquinas, Ia, q.39, art.3, c.; ad 1um; art.5, ad 5um.

unless we add or understand some general term—"the same *F*". That in accordance with which we judge whether identity holds I call a *criterion* of identity; this agrees with the etymology of "criterion". Frege sees clearly that "one" cannot significantly stand as a predicate of objects unless it is (at least understood as) attached to a general term; I am surprised he did not see that the like holds for the closely allied expression "the same". "The same *F*" does not express a possible way of judging as to identity for all interpretations of "*F*". I shall call "substantival" a general term for which "the same" does give a criterion of identity. Countability is a sufficient condition for considering a term as substantival; this is so because we (logically) cannot count As unless we know whether the A we are now counting is the same A as we counted before. But it is not necessary, in order that "the same A" shall make sense, for the question "How many As?" to make sense; we can speak of the same gold as being first a statue and then a great number of coins, but "How many golds?" does not make sense; thus "gold" is a substantival term, though we cannot use it for counting.

31.   Our distinction between names and predicables enables us to clear up the confusion, going right back to Aristotle, as to whether there are genuine negative terms: predicables come in contradictory pairs, but names do not, and if names and predicables are both called "terms" there will be a natural hesitation over the question "Are there negative terms?".

The negation of a substantival term is never itself a new substantival term. If "the same A" supplies an intelligible criterion of identity, "the same non-A" or "the same thing that is not an A" never of itself does so, though such a criterion may be smuggled in. ("The same non-A" may in context mean "the same B that is not A" where "*B*" is a substantival term; e.g., "the same nonsmoker" may mean "the same man—or, railway compartment—that is not a smoker".) So the fact that some general terms can both be predicated and be used as names in simple acts of naming does not threaten the distinction we drew—that predicables always, and names never, come in contradictory pairs; for a general term cannot be used as a name unless it is substantival, and if it is substantival its negation never is so, and therefore even in this sort of case we have only a pair of contradictory predicables, not a parallel pair of contradictory names.

32.   Common nouns can be used as names in simple acts of naming if they are substantival terms—and only then; for concerning this use of a name there may always arise the question whether the same so-and-so has been twice named (section 27); and for common nouns that are not substantival terms there can be no such question, as we have just remarked. Common nouns have, however, also a predicative use; so if in sentences, as well as in simple acts of naming, they can function as names, we need some way of recognizing when they do so.

There is one clear class of cases: a common name may often be clearly seen to be a logical subject when it occurs after a demonstrative pronoun. Suppose my friend whispers to me, meaning Smith who is in our presence: "That man nearly got sent to prison." It would be wrong to analyze this utterance as if it were a conjunctive proposition: "That is a man, and that nearly got sent to prison". As we saw, "That is a man" is not a predication with "that" as subject. The logical subject of my friend's proposition is "man", used on this occasion to name Smith. The demonstrative pronoun is not a name of Smith; in using it here, as in the simpler form "That is a man", we are acknowledging the presence of one of the objects sharing the name "man"; the use of the compound "that man" also shows that we are tying down the actual reference of the name "man" to just one of the objects that it has the general potentiality of naming.

I have argued that some assertive sentences beginning with demonstratives are not propositions but simply uses of the grammatical predicate as a name; but this account will not cover all such sentences. Moreover, in a sentence like "If that is gold, I'm a millionaire" "that is" could not be suppressed without yielding nonsense. The clause "that is gold" cannot be construed as a simple act of naming, for only a proposition can significantly be an *if* clause. I am inclined to say the demonstrative pronoun must here be understood as though it were a demonstrative adjective attached to some general term. E.g., in our example the sense might be "if that lump is gold"; and I have just tried to explain the logical role of phrases like "that lump".

What I have said here about demonstratives applies only when they 'demonstrate to the senses' as medieval writers say. When the use of "that man" relates not to a context in which the man is sensibly present, but to a context of discourse about a man, then "man" will not be used in an act of naming, and a radically different account must be given. [7]

Although it is part of the rationale of using an expression as a name in a proposition that the same expression could be used to name the same thing in a simple act of naming, it is also part of the rationale of names that they can be used to talk about what is named *in absentia*. (Unlike the wise men in *Gulliver's Travels*, a man need not carry around with him a peddler's pack filled with the objects he wishes to talk about.) As regards proper names, this raises no special difficulty; we recognize that a proper name used in a proposition could have been used in a simple act of naming the object to which the proposition was intended to relate.

We may be tempted to assimilate the following pairs of utterances:

(1) Jemima fought Towzer.—That's Towzer.
(2) Jemima fought a dog.—That's the dog.

In both cases we may look for a linkage between an act of naming and a predication, employing the same name, concerning the thing so named. But such an account of (2) would be quite wrong. For one thing, as we have seen, "a dog" in (2) should not be taken as referring to *a* dog, to some one dog; for another thing, "That's the dog" in (2) would not be a simple act of naming, rather it is a fragmentary utterance needing to be eked out with a linguistic context. "That's the dog" has to be understood as "That's the dog Jemima fought", or as "Jemima fought *that* dog", and thus not as a use of "dog" for a simple act of naming, like "Towzer" in the second member of (1). Thus far, then, only where common nouns are preceded by demonstratives have we

[7]Cf. Chapter Five infra.

any reason to recognize them as logical subjects; and even here their semantical relation to the things they name is more complicated than the one borne by proper names occurring in sentences. So it is simplest for the time being to concentrate on proper names as logical subjects: these are, so to say, the only pure samples we have thus far come across.

33. A proper name is never used predicatively—unless it ceases to be a proper name, as in "He is a Napoleon of finance" or (Frege's example) "Trieste is no Vienna"; in such cases the word alludes to certain attributes of the object customarily designated by the proper name. In statements of identity we may indeed say that the copula joining two proper names has a special role. I shall not here discuss the difficult question whether "Tully is Cicero" exemplifies the classical uses of "Tully" and "Cicero" as names, or whether we should rather regard it as a proposition about these names in this use; that is, whether its analysis is something like "Tully is the same man as Cicero", the names being used just as they might be in making historical statements, or rather something like "In history books the names 'Tully' and 'Cicero' are commonly used for the same man". But in any event the copula is no longer the trivial bit of grammatical form that it is in "Socrates is a man". On that very account, however, our absolute distinction of names and predicables is inviolate; for the predicable (say) "—— is the same man as Cicero" is totally different from the name "Cicero".

34. So far, as I said, we have not found any names other than proper names to be used as logical subjects of propositions *regardless of whether the things named are present or absent*; proper names are at any rate the only obvious examples. However, as I shall try to show, it is plausible to suggest that general terms (substantival ones, that is) also admit of such use as logical subjects. Indeed, although the use of proper names in that capacity is much more easily recognized, it is arguable that such use depends on the possibility of general terms' also being logical subjects.

People sometimes speak as if a proper name had meaning just

by having a bearer. This is absurd; we certainly do not give a man the meaning of a proper name by presenting him with the object named. In using a proper name we claim the ability (or at least acquaintance, direct or indirect, with somebody else who had the ability) to identify an object; and by giving somebody an object we do not tell him how to identify it. Different proper names of material objects convey different requirements as to identity; the name "Cleopatra's Needle" (which is logically a single word) conveys the requirement of material identity, but neither the name "Thames" nor any proper name of an animal conveys any such thing. For every proper name there is a corresponding use of a common noun preceded by "the same" to express what requirements as to identity the proper name conveys: "Cleopatra's Needle"—"the same (bit of) stone"; "Jemima"—"the same cat"; "Thames"—"the same river"; "Dr. Jekyll" or "Mr. Hyde"—"the same personality". In all these cases we may say that the proper name conveys a *nominal essence*; thus, "cat" expresses the nominal essence of the thing we call "Jemima", and Jemima's corpse will not be Jemima any more than it will be a cat. (It was for the same reason that I put forward the view that, in a case like "If that is gold I'm a millionaire", "that" must be understood as if it went with a noun like "lump"; otherwise reference would fail for lack of a way to identify *that*.)

I am here deliberately rejecting a well-known thesis of Locke's; but two points for which Locke would have contended must, I think, be granted: first, that the sense of the proper name "Jemima" *need* not include the sense of any predicables like "female" and "tabby" that apply to Jemima but not to all cats (and similarly for proper names of other kinds of things); secondly, that common nouns expressing the nominal essence need not be standing for a kind of substance. The first concession involves rejecting Russell's notorious disguised-description theory of proper names. Russell was obliged of course to admit that, for example, several men may converse intelligently about Bismarck even if the peculiar traits of Bismarck that each has in his mind should differ; this shows that the question which traits the name "Bismarck" recalls is purely psychological and has no bearing on the sense of the name.

Subject and Predicate

The reason for the second concession comes out from one of my examples: the nominal essence of the object called "Thames" is expressed by the common noun "river", and on any view "river" does not stand for a special kind of substance. In the traditional view of substance and accident, it is a mere accident of water that it should flow in a certain watercourse.

I might tell a story involving Jemima and the river Thames without using either of these proper names; I might refer to Jemima as "a cat" and the Thames as "a river" when I first mentioned them, and thereafter speak of "the cat" and "the river"—sc. "the same cat" and "the same river". A hearer unacquainted even by hearsay with Jemima and the Thames, and destined never to make such acquaintance, nor ever to discourse about them again, would lose absolutely nothing by this suppression of the proper names. So if "cat" in this storytelling did not retain the use of a logical subject, how could "Jemima" have such a use? How could we make out that "Jemima" has what it takes to be a logical subject, but "cat" has not?

Although repeated use of a proper name for acts of naming can express an identification, and repeated use of a common noun in this way cannot do so, nevertheless a common noun prefaced by "the same" *can* be used outside the context of a sentence to express an identification. Someone may be trained to say "Jemima" upon seeing Jemima, and "cat" upon seeing a cat; someone may also be trained so that he first says "cat" and then says "the same cat" when presented with the same cat as he saw on the first occasion. Now surely this use of "cat . . . the same cat . . . the same cat . . ."outside the context of a sentence is related to the use of "cat . . . the (same) cat . . . the (same) cat . . ."in telling a story in just the same way as the use of "Jemima" in a series of acts of naming is related to the use of the name in telling the story. And if so, then surely "cat" so used in telling the story is as much a logical subject as "Jemima" is.

If "cat" in such a story is a logical subject, then we need to say what it stands for. It does not stand for Jemima or some other definite cat; my story may have been in fact true (or substantially true) of Jemima, but as told it was not a story about Jemima or about any definite cat, and it need not have been even roughly true of any cat. We cannot say "cat" here stands for an indefinite cat: there is no such animal. In an act of naming, or again in a proposition where it is preceded by a demonstrative, "cat" potentially stands for any cat, and only the concrete application of the utterance to its context ties "cat" down to standing for a given cat then and there present; "cat" in the story is not thus tied down, so we must say that here it refers to any and every cat, equally and impartially. It may rouse our suspicions that though the story is just about *a* cat, the term "cat" used in it will on this view refer to *every* cat alike. But the suspicion can be dispelled: let us call to mind that, given some complete list of cats, a proposition making a predication "$F(\ \ )$", however complex, about *a* cat must have the same truth-value as would belong to a disjunction "F(Jemima) or F(Mehitabel) or F(Tibbles)..." (and so on for all the items of the list); and in this disjunction the names of each and every cat occur symmetrically.

A proper name carrying as part of its sense the criterion of identity expressed by "the same cat" may be called a name *for* a cat: even if "cat" is a name *of* any and every cat, it is not a name *for* any cat. Repeated use of a proper name for a cat requires an intention on the speaker's part to name the same cat each time; repeated use of the name "cat" does not. A proper name is a name *of* a cat if it is not an empty name but does actually name a cat. Each of the names in the list I have just imagined would be a name *of* and *for* a cat. When I speak of a name *of* and *for* an A in the sequel, I mean "A" to be read as going proxy for some substantial term, and a name *of* and *for* an A will be a nonempty proper name whose sense carries the criterion of identity expressed by "the same A". (The phrase in quotes, "the same A", in the last sentence is of course intended not as mention of that actual expression, but as schematically standing in for quotation of some English phrase in which the letter "A" is supplanted by a substantival term; such reading of expressions with schematic letters in them as schematic quotations rather than quoted schemata will often be needed in this work; I rely on the good will and intelligence of readers to see *where*.)

The outward guise of a proper name of course does not show

(usually at least) what criterion of identity the name's use carries with it. Many writers on the theory of meaning have been strangely misled by this fact; they have inferred that proper names lack 'connotation', an obscure expression but one that is certainly meant to exclude the proper name's having a sense that includes a criterion of identity. That out of a set of equiform names one may e.g. mean a man, one a dog, one a river or mountain, is another fact mentioned in this connection, and with equal irrelevance; equivocal terms are not confined to the class of proper names, and one might as well argue that "beetle" does not include being an insect as part of its sense because an equiform common noun means a large kind of hammer. (Some have even gone further and denied that proper nouns are words of the language in whose sentences they occur: see section 21.)

The right comment seems to be: What a sign conceals, its use reveals. In vernaculars misunderstanding of proper names is often avoided by adding a suitable common noun in apposition to the proper noun: "Mount Everest", "the river Arrow", "Lake Erie". This device is readily adoptable in formalized languages that contain both proper and common names: if "$a,b,c, \ldots$" are letters standing in for proper names and "$A,B,C, \ldots$" for common names, then "Ab" could be used to represent a name *for* an A, and "Bc", a name *for* a B. This would obviously be better than e.g. using a new fount of type when proper names for a new kind of object were required—a device that is sometimes employed. But the book contains no formalized proofs; so I shall simply stipulate what the names occurring in it are to be read as names *for*, from one occasion to another.

35.   The futility of the doctrine of distribution, that "some cat" refers to some cat, not to every cat, ought to convince us that, if a theory of common nouns' being logical subjects is to be taken seriously, it must make any (unambiguous) common noun refer in an impartial way to each of the objects that could be so named in a simple act of naming. But is this impartial reference the same kind in all propositions; or are there various species of reference? The latter alternative was chosen in medieval logical theories,

and was extensively worked upon; a similar, but historically independent, theory is sketched in Russell's *Principles of Mathematics*. [8] In the next chapter I shall expound these theories; and then I shall try to show why this whole way of thinking was, as Russell found, only a blind alley.

[8]Russell, secs. 56–62.

Three

Referring Phrases

36. The term 'referring phrase' as used in this book occurs in the exposition of theories which would make the term an appropriate one if they were themselves correct. By using it I am not prejudging the question of these theories' being correct, nor do I hold myself estopped from arguing later on that the term is a misnomer.

Referring phrases are a subspecies of what may be called applicatival phrases. Applicatival phrases are formed by combining substantival general terms with what W. E. Johnson[1] called *applicatives*: an applicative is an expression such as "a", "the", "some", "any", "every", "no", "most", "only", "just one", "more than one", "all but one". Any such expression may be combined with a substantival general term like "man" or "men" to form what intuitively appears to be a syntactical unity; in inflected languages applicatives are very often in grammatical concord of gender, number, and case with the nouns they are attached to. At this stage of our inquiry it will be convenient to count among applicatival phrases, not only ones formed simply from an applicative and a general term, but also complex phrases

[1]Johnson, p. 97.

like "some *white* man" or "more than one man *who broke the bank at Monte Carlo*", which we may call *restricted* applicatival phrases. There is no need to specify the class of applicatives otherwise than by such a list as I have given, for doubtful cases will be automatically cut out when I supply the added conditions that form the differentia of referring phrases.

If we substitute an applicatival phrase for a proper name, we never destroy the syntax of the proposition: e.g., starting from "Some boy loves Mary" we can form "Some boy loves every girl", "Some boy loves only pretty girls", "Some boy loves just one girl", and so on. Small changes may be needed to make the sentence fully grammatical if e.g. a phrase with "girl" in it replaces "Mary", but I think this happens only when we have a plural phrase like "most girls" instead of a proper name as a grammatical subject. This is wholly trivial; for this remnant of grammatical 'agreement' in English has no bearing on the informative content of propositions. A foreigner who decided not to bother about his concords in these cases would be in no danger of being misunderstood; indeed, the use of "they, them, their" with a singular applicatival phrase as antecedent has been established in English since the early 1500s. This usage avoids troubles about gender ("he/she") as well as number. (Grammarians have long condemned it; but Women's Liberation may beat them yet.) I shall henceforth ignore this complication. Occasionally I shall use "Almost every A is *P*" as a conventional substitute for "Most As are *P*", to avoid linguistic awkwardnesses.

I shall count an applicatival phrase as a referring phrase *only* when it stands where a proper name might have stood. When "a man", or "the man who broke the bank at Monte Carlo", occurs predicatively after "is", I shall not recognize it as a referring phrase; for if in such places a proper name is used referentially, this means there is a change in the force of "is", so that it amounts e.g. to "is the same man as". Certainly, the "is" or "was" in a proposition like "Louis XV was the King of France at that time", or "Smith is (was) the man who broke the bank at Monte Carlo", has been taken by many logicians to be a copula of identity, as in "Tully is (was) Cicero" or "The Thames is the Isis"; but I think this is quite wrong. The definite description is in such cases used predicatively or attributively, and in Polish would bear a predicative inflection, even if it came first in the sentence (as e.g. in "The King of France at that time was Louis XV"). Predicative uses of definite descriptions will be discussed in section 75.

It will be convenient for our purposes to introduce a little symbolism at this point. I shall use signs like "*" and "†" to go proxy for applicatives; the letters "A,B,C, . . .", for general terms; and the letters "a,b,c, . . .", for proper names. I shall use "$f(\ )$", "$g(\ )$", "$h(\ )$", and so forth to represent contexts into whose empty place we may insert either a proper name or an applicatival phrase. (The question will arise, for complex sentences, *how much* of the sentence is to be taken as the context "$f(\ )$"; this is the question of what logicians call *scope,* to which we shall return in section 42 below. For the present we shall assume that a schematic symbol like "$f(\ )$" represents the whole scope of the phrase "*A".)

Our next task is to state a condition which shall pick out from among applicatival phrases that subclass which I am going to count as referring phrases. Given an applicatival phrase "*A", we may have a list *L*, with items that are names *of* and *for* As, such that the following is true when "*A" is interpreted:

L is a list covering *A and covering only As.

(I include here the degenerate case where the list *L* contains only one name.) If, on this assumption about the list *L*, we are warranted in inferring "$f(^*A)$" when we have also a premise that is obtained from "$f(^*\ A)$" by inserting a suitably modified form of the list *L* instead of the applicatival phrase, then I call the phrase "*A" a *referring phrase;* otherwise not. The 'suitable modification' of *L*, if *L* has more than one item, is to be made by prefixing "each one of:"; if *L* consists of just one name, this name is to be inserted as it stands.

For example, imagine a small community of boys and girls, and suppose we have:

> "Mary, Jane, Kate" is a list covering all the girls/most girls/some girls/at least two girls, and covering only girls.

Then from the premise:

> Every boy admires each one of : Mary, Jane, Kate

we are warranted by this assumption about the list in passing to the conclusion:

> Every boy admires all the girls/most girls/some girls/at least two girls

where the applicatival phrase chosen corresponds to the one occurring in the assumption about the list. And similarly, since in this case we shall have:

> "Mary" is a (one-item) list covering a girl and covering only girls

from the premise:

> Every boy admires Mary

we are warranted in inferring

> Every boy admires a girl.

So "all the girls", "most girls", "some girls", "at least two girls", and "a girl" all pass the test for referring phrases. On the other hand, "just one girl" fails the test; for if we have:

> "Mary" is a list covering just one girl and covering only girls

then clearly from the premise "Every boy admires Mary" we are *not* hereby warranted in inferring the conclusion:

> Every boy admires just one girl.

For "no" phrases the test as stated simply cannot be applied; obviously, for no list L could the condition "L covers no A and covers only As" be fulfilled, if the items of L are names *of* and *for* As. By stipulation, we exclude "no" phrases from among referring phrases.

The applicative "any" is grammatically anomalous in English, but the conditions for it to be a means of forming a referring phrase are often clearly fulfilled. On the condition:

> The list "Mary, Jane, Kate" covers any girl and covers
> only girls

we may pass from the premise "Some boy will whistle at each one of: Mary, Jane, Kate" to the conclusion "Some boy will whistle at any girl". So here "any girl" passes the test. Some of the troubles about "any" are matters of scope: see section 42 below.

As we shall see, this way of bringing in lists is close to the thought of medieval logicians writing about *suppositio,* and to Russell's thought when he wrote about denoting phrases. A simple working criterion is all that we shall need; in the next chapter we shall see that this type of theory breaks down even for applicatival phrases that clearly pass the test for referring phrases, and even for simple finite models; so formulating a more refined criterion would be wasted labor in logic, as well as historically perverse.

It must be stressed that if we have a proposition *P* with a referring phrase in it, the truth of a proposition related to this one in the way our test stipulates is not in general more than a *sufficient* condition for the truth of *P*; the truth of *P* will not in general *require* the truth of some suitably related proposition with a list in it. For example, the truth of

> Every boy admires most girls

does *not* require the truth of some proposition like:

> Every boy admires each one of: Mary, Jane, Kate, . . .

For even if the objects of each boy's admiration form a majority of girls, it may be a different majority for each boy. But this in no way goes against the use of the test.

So far I have stated the condition for a referring phrase only as regards one class of applicatival phrases, namely those formed from an applicative and a logically simple general term; I must now consider also phrases of the form "*(A that is P)*", e.g. "some white man" ("some man that is white") or "the man who broke the bank at Monte Carlo". It is quite easy to make the required extension: we simply change the general form "$f(^* A)$" to "$f(^* A$ that is $P)$" throughout, and change the conditions imposed on the list *L* to the following:

L is a list covering *(A that is P) and covering only As, and whatever A there is that L covers is P.

For example, if in our small community we have:

"Minnie, Tibbles, Ahab, Jemima" is a list covering all the tabby cats/most tabby cats/some tabby cats, and covering only cats, and whatever cat this list covers is tabby

then from the premise:

Fido chases each one of: Minnie, Tibbles, Ahab, Jemima

we may pass to the conclusion:

Fido chases all/some/most (of the) tabby cats.

Similarly if we have:

"Jones" is a (one-item) list covering the man who broke the bank at Monte Carlo, and covering only men, and whatever man "Jones" covers broke the bank at Monte Carlo

(it is irrelevant that the parts of this following the first comma are in fact redundant), then from the premise "Smith met Jones" we may clearly infer:

Smith met the man who broke the bank at Monte Carlo.

Thus "all/some/most (of the) tabby cats" will pass the test for being a referring phrase, and so will "the man who broke the bank at Monte Carlo". But it is easy to see (I leave it to the reader to check this) that "just one man who broke the bank at Monte Carlo" will fail the test, and so will "at most two tabby cats".

Some reader may suspect a vicious circle because the very applicatival phrase whose semantics we are discussing occurs in one of the sentences employed in stating the test. Such a suspicion would be unfounded. We are supposed to know, at least in part, the logical powers of propositions containing a given applicatival phrase before we begin the test: the aim of the test is not to determine those logical powers, but to determine whether the applicatival phrase is to be classified as a referring phrase.

Again, doubts may be felt because I make use of the names of objects: is "all pebbles on Brighton beach" to be rejected as a referring phrase because every one of these pebbles may be nameless? or am I assuming, like advocates of 'substitutional' quantification, that our language ought to contain names for all the objects covered by the general terms that occur in our referring phrases? There is no need to accept either position. The criterion for an applicative's serving to form referring phrases can be employed when there *are* names of all the objects of the relevant sort; and according to the decision in that case, we shall count all similar applicatival phrases using that applicative as being or not being referring phrases. We shall however be mostly concerned with small finite models in which all the objects concerned *have* names; as I said, in the next chapter we shall see that theories of the medieval and Russellian type such as are expounded in this chapter already break down for these finite models, so any fuss about the semantics required for an applicatival phrase "*A" when nameless or infinitely numerous As are involved would be merely gratuitous.

37.   The essential feature both of Russell's theory of denoting in his *Principles of Mathematics*, and of many medieval theories is this: In a referring phrase "*A" such as I have been describing, the general term "A" refers impartially to each object so called; but there are various modes of reference that "A" may then have, and the use of one applicative in the phrase rather than another serves to specify which mode of reference there is to the thing(s) called "A". (Provisionally, I shall here assume, as the authors of the theories I am reconstructing would have, that a 'restricted' referring phrase like "some mouse in this house" may be put in the form "*A", with "A" read as a complex term "mouse in this house". We shall later see reason to deny this: see section 72 below.)

I must emphasize the difference between this sort of theory and the doctrine of distribution. On that doctrine, "some cat" will not just have a different mode of reference from "every cat"; it will also, in general, have a different reference—to some cat as apposed to every cat. What is worse, the reference of "some cat" would have to differ according as the proposition "Some cat is *P*" were true or false; in true propositions of this form "some cat" would refer to each cat of whom the predicable represented by "*P*" were true, whereas in false ones no such specification of 'some' among cats would be possible. This result is absurd; for, as Buridan pointed out long since, the reference of an expression can never depend on whether the proposition it occurs in is true or false.[2] The very same referring phrase as occurs in a true or false proposition will occur in a yes-or-no question to which that proposition is an answer; and if this expression does indeed give us something that the question is about, then this must be specifiable before the question is answered, and cannot depend on which answer is right.

On the sort of theory we are now considering, a phrase like "some cat" always stands in a certain relation of reference to each cat. I criticized Ockham for thinking that, in "Socrates was a philosopher", "a philosopher" refers to or names Socrates; but I was not imputing to Ockham the view that the phrase in this context refers only to Socrates; Ockham in fact held that "a philosopher" here refers after a fashion to every philosopher (at least every one among Socrates' contemporaries—I cannot here go into the difficulties about the so-called 'ampliation' of terms in tensed propositions). Of course it would only be the reference of the term "philosopher" to Socrates that made the proposition true; but the phrase "a philosopher" would refer, in some appropriate mode, to each philosopher (of that time at any rate), and this would not depend on the truth of the proposition "Socrates was a philosopher".

Are we to say that it is the term "cat" itself which has a different mode of reference in "some cat" and in "every cat", the signs "some" and "every" serving to show which mode occurs? or shall we rather say that what has reference is not the bare term "cat" but the whole phrase "some cat" or "every cat"? Plainly it makes little difference which we say. Russell in fact preferred the latter way of speaking, and medieval logicians the former. This was due to a syntactical difference between English and Latin; the Latin

---

[2] Buridan, *Sophismata*, c. vi, *sophisma* v.

expression answering to what I am calling a referring phrase would commonly be a noun or noun-phrase unaccompanied by an article or other applicative. The medieval theories of reference were devised so as to apply to such isolated common nouns, as well as to referring phrases formed with applicatives, and thus they naturally ascribed the various modes of reference to the common nouns themselves; which mode of reference a noun had in a given context would sometimes be shown by an applicative (*signum*), sometimes have to be gathered from the total sense of the proposition.

Ockham compares the applicative to the zero sign in the Hindu system of numerals, which had by his time reached Europe by way of the Arabs: it has no numerical value of its own, but alters the value of the numerals it follows.[3] Now it is plainly arbitrary whether we say that "20" means twenty, or that the "0" in "20" makes the "2" mean twenty. Russell, on the other hand, takes all his examples from English, in which language it is rather rare for a common noun in the singular number to stand as subject or object of a verb, or after a preposition, without having an article or other applicative prefixed to it. So it was natural for Russell to ascribe the mode of reference to the phrases as wholes, to "every man" and "some man" rather than to the plain "man". Since I too shall be using only English examples, I shall follow Russell; but this must be clearly understood to be only a terminological decision, of no deep significance.

38. Both Russell and the medieval logicians held that the relation of mere words to objects was only an indirect one: what primarily refers to a given dog, say Towser, is not the phrase "every dog" but the 'meaning' of the phrase; and similarly a whole verbal proposition containing the phrase "every dog" will have a 'meaning', of which the 'meaning' of "every dog" will be a part. The 'meaning' of a whole proposition would be built up out of the 'meanings' of its parts in a way roughly parallel to the syntax of the verbal proposition. For medieval logicians this 'meaning' was a content of an individual mind, an inner utter-

[3]Ockham, c. 4.

ance in an immaterial language; Ockham took this idea of mental language and its structure so seriously and so naïvely that he tries to determine which parts of speech, and which grammatical attributes like voice, case, and number, are to be found in the mental language. For Russell, on the other hand, the 'meaning' of a verbal proposition was objective, in Frege's sense; and sometimes at least the Proposition in Russell's sense—the meaning of the verbal proposition—would have as parts the actual entities, the individuals and universals, mentioned in the verbal proposition. It appears to me that, as regards the theory of referring phrases, both the medievals' mental proposition and Russell's objective Proposition were idle wheels, useless reduplications of the linguistic structures.

Russell held not only that a referring phrase was not what primarily did the referring, but also that what a referring phrase like "every dog" or "a dog" primarily referred to was not individual dogs like Tray and Towzer, but rather a certain 'combination' of dogs 'effected without the use of relations'. We can more or less make out what led him to use such language. The proposition "Jemima can lick every dog in town"would have the same truth-value as "Jemima can lick Tripod and Bonzo and Tray and Towzer . . ." (and so on for all the dogs in town); "Jemima can lick a dog in town" would have the same truth-value as "Jemima can lick Tripod or Bonzo or Tray or Towzer . . ." (and so on for all the dogs in town). If each of these lists of dogs' names, formed respectively with "and" and with "or", has to correspond to something *in rebus*, then there must be two distinct objects somehow formed out of the individual dogs, which may be called "combinations". Now the difference between these 'combinations', unlike that between two ordinary combinations of the same objects, is not to be regarded as due to different relations holding between the things; for Russell was not prepared to stomach *and* and *or* relations between concrete objects like men and dogs; this explains his expression "combinations effected without the use of relations".[4]

Such a combination, Russell thinks, is 'something absolutely

―――――――

[4]Russell, sec. 59.

peculiar... neither one nor many'. This odd language can be explained: Russell elsewhere[5] puzzles over the fact that though "every man" and "some man" are grammatically singular, the singular entity they would apparently refer to cannot be identified with Socrates or Plato or any other definite person. He concludes that *one* is denoted in every case, but in an impartial distributive manner. Yet how can reference be impartial or distributive as between *one* thing and itself? It is in this uneasy confusion—perhaps aggravated by a worry whether "Socrates or Plato or Aristotle" stands for *one* man or *three*—that Russell talks of something absolutely peculiar which is neither one nor many. This wild Realist metaphysics is, however, quite inessential to Russell's logical theory of referring phrases.

39.   I must now discuss the ambiguities of Russell's term "denoting". What I here call "referring phrases" Russell called "denoting phrases"; but he held that their denoting role was derivative—what primarily did the denoting were the 'meanings' of denoting phrases, objective parts of Propositions which he called "denoting concepts" or "denoting complexes". This ambiguity in the application of the adjective "denoting" was always, I think, rendered harmless by the context.

It was more troublesome when Russell abandoned the logic (along with the metaphysics) of *Principles of Mathematics*, but went on speaking of denoting phrases—particularly as he now counted "no men" as a denoting phrase. The really bad confusion, however, was caused by his statement that his own earlier use of the term "denote" corresponded to Frege's "*bedeuten*". This is a travesty of the truth: in fact, whereas Russell takes "every man" and "some man" as typical denoting phrases, Frege says it is merely absurd to ask what such expressions stand for (*bedeuten*).[6] (I shall discuss this view of Frege's presently.)

Russell's use of the term "denote" is thus most confusing; but then, the whole previous history of the term is a sad tale of confusion. Our contemporaries too have added their quota by

[5]Russell, secs. 75, 88.
[6]Frege (3), pp. 14, 48, 93.

using it in a number of different senses; thus, Church has used "denote" to render Frege's "*bedeuten*", and Quine has used it for that relation of predicables to objects which I express by "apply to" or "be true of". High time that so battered and defaced a coin were withdrawn from philosophical currency; I shall avoid it as much as possible, even when reporting Russell.

The medieval term for what I call the mode of reference of a referring phrase was "*suppositio*". Apparently in origin this is a legal term meaning "going proxy for"; Aquinas and Ockham say quite indifferently that a term has *suppositio* for (*supponit pro*) and that it stands for (*stat pro*) one or more objects. In paraphrasing medieval writers I shall quite often tacitly use "mode of reference" for their "*suppositio*".

40. In discussing the subject-predicate relation, I argued that in any proposition in which a 'purely referential' proper name occurs, we may treat that name as a logical subject to which the rest of the proposition is attached as a predicate. Now for such an occurrence of a proper name a referring phrase can always be substituted without further disturbance of the syntax. So, if we use "$f(a)$" to represent a predicate "$f(\ \ )$" attached to a subject "a", it seems appropriate to say that in "$f(*A)$" we have the same predicable attached to a *quasi subject*, to the referring phrase "$*A$". Similarly in chemistry a complex molecule may have a place that can be occupied either by a single atom or by a radical, e.g. either by the sodium atom Na or by the ammonium radical NH_4, or again either by the chlorine atom Cl or by the cyanide radical CN. This analogy between propositional and molecular structure is important—and so is the way in which, as we shall see later, it breaks down.

Why should I use the grudging term "quasi subject"? Let us use "$f(\ \ )$" and "$f'(\ \ )$" to represent contradictory predicables; then, when attached to any proper name "a" as subject, they will give us contradictory predications; but if "$*A$" takes the place of "a", the propositions "$f(*A)$ and "$f'(*A)$" will in general not be contradictories—both may be true or both false. "Some men can laugh" and "Some men cannot laugh" are both true; "Jemima can lick any dog in town" and "Jemima cannot lick any dog in town" are both false if Jemima can lick one dog but not another; and yet "—— can laugh", "—— cannot laugh" and "Jemima can lick ——", "Jemima cannot lick ——" are contradictory predicables. Thus we cannot regard "some men" or "any dog in town" as genuine subjects, to which contradictory predicates are attachable to get contradictory propositions. "Every man is *P*" and "Every man is not *P*" may indeed very readily be taken as contradictory forms; but only because the latter form would be commonly read as meaning "Not every man is *P*", in which there is not even the appearance of attaching "—— is not *P*" to "every man" as subject.

41. These facts about contradictories led Frege to deny that a referring phrase is an expression at all from a logical point of view. On his view, we should regard "every", for example, as logically going with the grammatical predicate; "Every —— can laugh" and "Not every —— can laugh" will be contradictory predicables, which yield contradictory predications when the blanks are filled with a general term like "man". "Every man" will no more occur in the proposition as a logical unit than "Plato was bald" occurs as a logical unit in "The philosopher whose most eminent pupil was Plato was bald"; the question what it refers to will thus not arise, and attempts to answer it reveal according to Frege a 'superficial', 'mechanical or quantitative', way of regarding the matter.[7]

Frege's analysis is both legitimate and important; but on his own principles the possibility of one analysis does not show that none other is possible,[8] and indeed an alternative analysis could easily be fitted into Frege's general view. Let us use the term "first-level predicable" for the sort of predicable that can be attached to a proper name to form a proposition about what is-named. On Frege's view any such first-level predicable, if well-defined, itself stands for something—for a concept (*Begriff*); and a pair of propositions "Every man is *P*", "Not every man is *P*", would be contradictory predications about the concept for which

[7]Frege (3), p. 93n.
[8]Frege (3), p. 46.

the predicable "―― is *P*" stood. It thus seems natural to regard "every man ――" and "not every man ――" as being likewise predicables—a contradictory pair of *second*-level predicables, by means of which we make contradictory predications about a concept. But of course this is radically different from the sort of theory by which "every man" has a sort of reference to individual men and is a quasi subject to which first-level predicates are attached.

42.   In any event, there is yet another difference between referring phrases and genuine logical subjects. Connectives that join propositions may also be used to join predicables; and the very meaning they have in the latter use is that by attaching a complex predicable so formed to a logical subject we get the same result as we should by first attaching the several predicables to that subject, and then using the connective to join the propositions thus formed precisely as the respective predicables were joined by that connective. "Joe deserted or got killed" is tantamount to "Joe deserted or Joe got killed"; "Jim understands this argument only if highly intelligent and free from silly prejudices" is tantamount to "Jim understands this argument only if Jim is highly intelligent and Jim is free from silly prejudices".

For referring phrases it is quite otherwise: "$f(^*A)$ & $g(^*A)$" may be quite different in force from "$f\&g(^*A)$"; e.g., "Jane loves some boy and Jane hates some boy" is quite different from "Jane loves and (Jane) hates some boy". Similarly "$f(^*A)$ v $g(^*A)$" may be quite different from "f v $g(^*A)$": thus, "Every politician either is cynical or deceives himself" is quite different from "Either every politician is cynical or every politician deceives himself". Neither breakdown of equivalences happens for definite descriptions; but for them it is arguable that there is such a breakdown over "if. . . then"; e.g., the fact that there were two first consuls of Rome makes "The first consul of Rome was, if cruel, then cruel" more open to exception than "If the first consul of Rome was cruel, then the first consul of Rome was cruel", which is surely just an instance of "If *p*, then *p*".

On the other hand, when referring phrases are around, it may not be quite so easy to recognize your instance of "If *p*, then *p*".

For this proposition:

(1) If Jemima can lick *any* dog, then Jemima can lick *any* dog

is not an instance of "If *p*, then *p*", but rather is tantamount to:

(2) If Jemima can lick some dog, then Jemima can lick *any* dog.

We might think this was because of an ambiguity in "*any* dog" (even though the emphasis indicated by the italics, which would give the proposition its intended meaning, would be precisely the same for both occurrences of "*any* dog"); we might think the first occurrence meant "some dog" and the second "every single dog". I think this is the wrong explanation; even in (1) and (2) there is a difference between "*any* dog" at its first occurrence and "some dog", but this difference is compensated for by other differences between the structure of the propositions. This may be brought out by paraphrase:

(1) It is true as regards any dog that, if Jemima can lick him, then it is true as regards any dog that Jemima can lick him

(2) If it is true as regards some dog that Jemima can lick him, then it is true as regards any dog that Jemima can lick him.

The paraphrases show that "*any* dog" meant exactly the same in the antecedent and in the consequent of (1), and again in the consequent of (2).

What we have here been concerned with is what Russell calls *scope*. Let us suppose that a complicated proposition abbreviated as "*f*(* A)" contains a clause "*g*(* A)" as part of itself: then we shall in general have to distinguish between taking a referring phrase "* A" as the quasi subject of the whole of (the context abbreviated to) "*f*( )" and taking it as merely the quasi subject of "*g*( )"; in the latter case we must treat only "*g*( )", not the whole of "*f*( )", as the scope of "* A". For example in (1) the scope of the first "*any* dog" is "if Jemima can lick ——, then Jemima can lick *any* dog"; (1) expresses the supposition that this complex predicable is true of *any* dog. In (2) on the other hand the proposition "Jemima can lick some dog" occurs as the antecedent, and the scope of "some dog" is merely the context "Jemima can lick ———". This difference in scope between "*any* dog" and "some dog" neutralizes the difference between them, so that (1) and (2) come to practically the same.

43.   There is certainly a strong temptation to say: In the context "If Jemima can lick ———, then Jemima can lick *any* dog", "*any* dog" means the same as "some dog", even though they mean different things from each other in other contexts. I think we should resist the temptation. We just cannot infer that if two propositions verbally differ precisely in that one contains the expression E_1 and the other the expression E_2, then, if the total force of the two propositions is the same, we may cancel out the identical parts and say that E_1 here means the same as E_2. I shall call this sort of inference *the canceling-out fallacy*; we shall come across it more than once. A simple example of it would be: the predicables "——— killed Socrates" and "——— was killed by Socrates" must mean the same, because "Socrates killed Socrates" means the same as "Socrates killed Socrates". The expression "In the context of the propositions P_1, P_2, the meaning of E_1, E_2 is the same" is a muddling one: it may mean no more than that P_1, which contains E_1, means the same as P_2, which contains E_2 and is otherwise verbally the same as P_1; or it may seek to explain this by the supposition that here E_1 and E_2 mean the same, though perhaps not elsewhere; and the slide from one to the other just is the canceling-out fallacy.

44.   I now come to the different modes of reference that are ascribed to referring phrases by the medieval and Russellian theories. Russell admittedly does not speak of different modes of reference; on the contrary, he says that "every man" and "a man" have the same denoting relation to different objects; these objects would correspond respectively to a conjunctive list "Socrates and Plato and Aristotle and . . ." and to a disjunctive list "Socrates or Plato or Aristotle or . . .". But even if we could accept Russell's

Realist metaphysics on this matter, the routes from "every man" and from "a man" to Socrates (or Plato) would pass through characteristically different 'combinations' of men; accordingly, for Russell no less than the medievals, "every man" and "a man" would be differently related to any given man, say Socrates, whereas either phrase would be related in the same way to Socrates as to Plato. Russell's disagreement with the medievals lies only in his accounting for this difference by a metaphysical speculation, which we may henceforth ignore as irrelevant to logic.

The simplest applicatives to discuss are "some" and "any". If we may waive difficulties about classes that are either infinite, like numbers, or 'open' toward the future, like dogs, it is easy to state truth-conditions for "f(any A)" and "f(some A)"; assuming, in both cases, that "$f(\ )$" is the whole scope of the referring phrase. Let "a_1, a_2, a_3, . . ." be a complete list of proper names *of* and *for* As, if "A" is a logically simple substantival term; if on the other hand we have 'restricted' applicatival phrases, in which "A" is short for something of the form "B that is P", then let this list be a complete list of the proper names which both are names *of* and *for* Bs and are names of things to which the restriction "P" applies. (By calling the list "complete", I mean that each of the things in question has a proper name and no name is left out.) Then we shall clearly have:

> "f(some A)" is true iff[9] this disjunction is true: "$f(a_1)$ ∨ $f(a_2)$ ∨ $f(a_3)$ ∨ . . ."
> "f(any A)" is true iff this conjunction is true: "$f(a_1)$ & $f(a_2)$ & $f(a_3)$ & . . ."

For example, if "Bingo, Tripod, Towzer" is a complete list of proper names that are names *of* and *for* dogs and are such that the restriction "living in town" is true of each dog so named, then we shall have:

> "Jemima can lick some dog living in town" is true iff "(Jemima can lick Bingo) or (Jemima can lick Tripod) or (Jemima can lick Towzer)" is true.

[9]As is usual in logic books, I spell "if" this way when it has (as in ordinary English it quite commonly has) the biconditional sense of "if and only if".

"Jemima can lick any dog living in town" is true iff
"(Jemima can lick Bingo) and (Jemima can lick Tripod)
and (Jemima can lick Towzer)" is true.

Thus it seems plausible to say that "any dog living in town"
and "some dog living in town" alike refer impartially to Bingo,
Tripod, and Towzer, the first doing so conjunctively and the
second disjunctively. This view was taken by medieval logicians
and by Russell. The medievals called the mode of reference of
"any A" *confused and distributive*, that of "some A" *determinate*. The point of the second epithet is that "*f*(some dog)" will be
true iff some determinate interpretation of "*x*" in "*f*(*x*)" as the
name of a dog makes "*f*(*x*)" true; a blurred awareness of this was
what led to the untenable views that we studied in Chapter One,
about the reference of "some man" to some man. For the epithet
"confused and distributive" I shall generally substitute "distributive". The doctrine of distributed terms is in fact originally a
muddled memory of the medieval *suppositio confusa et distributiva*. Distributive *suppositio* was called "*confused and* distributive" because of a supposed resemblance to another mode of
reference (which we shall come to presently) called "merely confused"; but since I can see no specially important feature common to these two modes of reference rather than any other two, I
shall for simplicity just call them the *distributive* and the *confused* mode of reference or *suppositio*.

45. Confused *suppositio* is always sharply contrasted with determinate *suppositio* in medieval logic. Russell uses to the same
end a distinction often made in ordinary English between "some"
and "a"; "*f*(some A)" and "*f*(an A)" have the common logical
feature that each is true if we can find a true interpretation of
"*f*(*x*)", reading "*x*" as the proper name of something that "A"
signifies; but "*f*(an A)" may be true even if no such true interpretation of "*f*(*x*)" is to be found. For instance, "A United
States citizen is murdered every twelve minutes" may be true
even if for no interpretation of "*x*" as the name of a United States
citizen does "*x* is murdered every twelve minutes" come out true;
"Some United States citizen is murdered every twelve minutes"

would often be taken in the same sense, but it will be convenient for our purposes to take "some" phrases as always having determinate *suppositio*, so that this proposition would be true only if one could ask for the name of the unfortunate victim.

46.   Confused *suppositio* in fact refutes the idea that a referring phrase can be correctly used only if one could in principle supply a namely-rider (as Gilbert Ryle calls it). Such riders can be supplied when there is either determinate or distributive *suppositio*; "Jemima can lick some dog in town—namely Bingo"; "Jemima can lick any dog in town—namely (for example) Bingo". But no namely-rider is called for in order that "Jemima is waiting for a mouse who lives in that hole" should be true: if several mice do, Jemima need not be waiting for one rather than another, and no way of supplying a namely-rider need be correct.

Sentences containing namely-riders are apparent exceptions to our requirement that referring phrases can fill the same places as proper names: for "Jemima can lick some dog in town, namely some dog in town" and "Jemima can lick Bingo, namely Bingo" are alike absurd. The explanation I should offer is that sentences with a namely-rider in them are not (purely) propositional in force; the word "namely" gives a sort of promise, which is not a proposition. "Namely", in fact, commits the speaker to the undertaking of supplying an instance for which his statement is true; and the first of our absurd sentences is so because what the speaker undertakes is not fulfilled, the second, because he undertakes something absurd—there are no instances of Bingo to give. There is nothing wrong with either of the propositions (properly so called) that are here involved, "Jemima can lick some dog in town", "Jemima can lick Bingo"; and for them our requirement is fulfilled.

47.   The nonrequirement of a namely-rider was in effect used by some medieval logicians as their way of explaining confused *suppositio*; but I cannot regard it as a good way—you cannot specify the logical force of an expression just by saying what it is that need not be true when propositions containing the expression are true. A better attempt at explanation is to be found in

Ockham and Russell; Ockham explains confused *suppositio*, and Russell explains "a" phrases as opposed to "some" phrases, in terms of a disjunction, not of propositions, but of proper names. In Russell's example, Miss Smith has two suitors, Brown and Jones: "You must have met a suitor" corresponds to "You must have met Brown or Jones", which is quite different from "You must have met Brown or you must have met Jones"; on the other hand, "Some suitor has won Miss Smith's hand" would correspond to "Brown has won Miss Smith's hand or Jones has won Miss Smith's hand". [10] Similarly, Ockham holds that in "I promise you a horse" "a horse" may be replaced *salva veritate* by a disjunctive list of (present and future) horses, even though this proposition were being so interpreted that no substitution of the proper name of a horse would preserve truth; and this is his criterion for the term's having confused *suppositio*. [11]

To a contemporary logician the idea of a disjunction of proper names may well seem alien; he would naturally try to treat a proposition apparently containing such a disjunction as mere shorthand for one containing a disjunction of propositions or of predicables; e.g., "You must have met Brown or Jones" would be shorthand for "You must (have met Brown) or (have met Jones)". But we must not take a disjunction of proper names to be obviously less intelligible than a disjunction of propositions or predicables. In elementary grammar lessons, we learn that connectives like "and" and "or" may be used to conjoin expressions of like grammatical role into a complex expression which again has that grammatical role; e.g., "Jack" and "Jill" are grammatically alike and so are "went up" and "tumbled down"; so from "Jack went up the hill" we may pass to "Jack or Jill went up the hill", or again to "Jack went up or tumbled down the hill". Contemporary logicians would readily take the "or" of the second proposition as expressing the logical sum of two relations; it may have turned out that to read "or" as combining proper names does not so readily fit into a logical scheme, but one could hardly dismiss this use of "or" in advance as having negligible logical significance.

[10]Russell, sec. 59.
[11]Ockham, c. 72.

Moreover, there are contexts where a disjunction of names cannot very plausibly be reduced to any other sort of disjunction. Suppose a jeweler's shop has two assistants, Bill and Joe, and a valuable ruby is missing: "Only Bill or Joe had opportunity to take the ruby" is quite different from the disjunction of "Only Bill had opportunity to take the ruby" and "Only Joe had opportunity to take the ruby"; and if we want to get the "or" joining a pair of clauses or predicables, we have to construct some such artificial-looking form as "For any x, only if x is Joe or x is Bill had x opportunity to take the ruby". So here "Bill or Joe" seems to be genuinely standing in the place of a proper name; and in the case supposed it can be replaced *salva veritate* by "an assistant", which would therefore presumably have the confused mode of reference. The medievals, who had a curiously strong interest in exclusive propositions, did in fact hold that in "Only an A is P", "an A" had *suppositio confusa*. [12]

We must not, however, too readily assume that we do understand a disjunction of proper names. A child could no doubt be taught the use of a common, shared, name "tripodortowzer" in simple acts of naming—taught to use that name precisely for each of the two dogs Tripod and Towzer. But what would then be meant by the question "Is tripodortowzer eating that bone?"? It looks as though the answer ought to be "Yes" or "No" according as the predicable "eating that bone" (suitably understood from the context of the utterance) did or did not apply to what is named by "tripodortowzer"; but since this name would name either of two dogs, this condition is incurably ambiguous. Thus "Tripod or Towzer is eating that bone", which is not ambiguous if the predicable can be understood from the context of utterance, cannot be taken as an answer to our supposed question; nor, therefore, can its grammatical subject "Tripod or Towzer" be equated with the supposed common name "tripodortowzer". And no other possible way immediately suggests itself of construing a list formed with "or" as a genuine complex subject or quasi subject.

All the same, let us provisionally swallow the notion of proper names' being disjunctively combined; it at least seems to make

[12]See, e.g., Ockham, c. 73 and c. 75.

sense of the distinction between determinate and confused *suppositio*, and this distinction is continually important in both philosophical and nonphilosophical examples. To take a nonphilosophical example: Let Bill have three sisters, Mary, Jane, and Kate. Then "Tom has obliged himself to marry *a* sister of Bill's" would by Russell's convention correspond in truth-value to "Tom has obliged himself to marry Mary or Kate or Jane"—so that the obligation could be fulfilled if he married any one of them. On the other hand "Tom has obliged himself to marry *some* sister of Bill's" would correspond in truth-value to "(Tom has obliged himself to marry Mary) or (Tom has obliged himself to marry Kate) or (Tom has obliged himself to marry Jane)". In this case, the *suppositio* being determinate, there has to be an answer to the question "Which sister of Bill's has Tom obliged himself to marry?", if the proposition is true.

If we do use the distinction between a disjunction of proper names and a disjunction of propositions to explain this distinction between the two modes of reference, then we must allow that there may be cases in which the propositions "*f*(an A)" and "*f*(some A)" absolutely coincide in inferential force. In the context "Tom has obliged himself to marry ———" it makes a difference whether we insert "a sister of Bill's" or "some sister of Bill's"; but it makes no difference at all in the context "Tom has just married ———", since there is no difference whatever in inferential force between "Tom has just married Mary or Jane or Kate" ("*a* sister"), and "(Tom had just married Mary) or (Tom has just married Jane) or (Tom has just married Kate)"—i.e., "Tom has just married *some* sister". Russell accepted this result, but did not infer that in such cases "an A" and "some A" must coincide in meaning; such an inference would have been, in fact, just the canceling-out fallacy, already exposed.

Medieval logicians, on the other hand, did hold that, if in a given proposition the *suppositio* of a term is changed from determinate to confused, the inferential force of the proposition is altered. In some of them, this resulted from their unsatisfactory negative account of confused *suppositio*, in terms of what a proposition exemplifying such *suppositio* does not imply. Since Ockham, however, anticipated Russell's positive disjunction-of-names explanation, I cannot but suspect him of inferring that if in a given case "f(an A)" means much the same as "f(some A)", then here "an A" means "some A", and is thus an instance not of confused but of determinate *suppositio*. This, of course, is the canceling-out fallacy.

There is an amusing paralogism to prove that a cat who watches a mousehole will not catch what she waits for. She cannot but catch some determinate mouse if she has any success at all; but she was waiting just for *a* mouse, not for any determinate mouse. Now, if Jemima catches Minnie, we may say "Jemima was waiting for a mouse from that hole, and Minnie is a mouse from that hole, and Jemima has caught Minnie". But Russell would allow us to analyze "Minnie is a mouse from that hole" as "Minnie is-identical-with a mouse from that hole"[13] and to treat this "a" phrase like others. Accordingly, if m_1, m_2, m_3, are all the mice from that hole, we may *salva veritate* substitute "m_1-or-m_2-or-m_3" for "a mouse from that hole" both times, so as to get: "Jemima was waiting for m_1-or-m_2-or-m_3, and Minnie is identical with m_1-or-m_2-or-m_3, and Jemima has caught Minnie". On this score, Minnie is after all identical with what Jemima was waiting for. We may worry over the expression "Minnie is identical with m_1-or-m_2-or-m_3"; and our worry would be justified if we thought there was disjunction *in rebus*, as Russell did; for Minnie certainly would not be identical with a number of mice nonrelationally combined. But if we are less Realist than Russell was, and are on the other hand willing to exploit his doctrine that "f(an A)" *may* coincide in import with "f(some A)", this worry disappears; "Minnie is identical with *a* mouse from that hole", "with m_1-or-m_2-or-m_3", may very well be taken to coincide in import with "Minnie is identical with *some* mouse from that hole"—"Minnie is identical with m_1 or Minnie is identical with m_2 or Minnie is identical with m_3"— which is comparatively unproblematic.

48. An example of philosophical errors in reasoning that can be easily exposed by the apparatus of *suppositio confusa* and *sup-*

---

[13]Cf. Russell, pp. 54–55n. He of course holds that other analyses are possible.

positio determinata is the inference (apparently) made by Berkeley from the premises:

> (i) A sensible object, e.g. the tree in the Quad, does not depend for its continued existence on being perceived by me, nor, *pari ratione*, by any finite person like me;

> (ii) The tree in the Quad is, however, dependent for its continued existence on being perceived by some person.

Berkeley goes on to what he says follows 'immediately and necessarily', namely:

> (iii) The tree in the Quad depends for its continued existence on being perceived by a nonfinite person, i.e. by God.

The inference would be valid only if the truth of (ii) would warrant the question: "On whose perception, then, does the tree in the Quad depend for its continued existence?"; that is, in medieval language, only if "some person" in (ii) had *suppositio determinata*. But if I said, for example, "This poker game depends for its continuance on some person's going on playing", it cannot be asked which person has to go on playing all the time to keep the game going—any one player may drop out and yield his hand in the game to a newcomer. Here, and in (ii), "some person" would be counted as having *suppositio confusa*; the question "Namely, which person?" need not arise. Similarly, then, if there were a rota of finite percipients, the tree in the Quad might be ensured a continued existence, even though no finite percipient kept his eye on it all the time.

By Russell's convention, of course, "some person" would have *suppositio determinata*; but in (ii), although it reads more natural than "a person", "some person" has *suppositio confusa*. Contrariwise, "*a* nonfinite person" in (iii) reads more naturally than "*some*...", but has *suppositio determinata*. There is no foolproof way of interpreting ordinary language on such points; the price of freedom from fallacy is eternal vigilance.

49.   The difference between "*f*(some A)" and "*f*(any A)" was explained in terms of the difference between a disjunction and a conjunction of propositions; that between "*f*(some A)" and "*f*(an

A)", in terms of the difference between a disjunction of propositions and a disjunction of proper names. This suggests room for another mode of reference, symbolized let us say by "every": "f(every A)" differing from "f(any A)" in a way corresponding to the difference between a conjunction of proper names and a conjunction of propositions. We should thus get the following symmetrical scheme:

> If "a_1, a_2, a_3, . . ." is a complete list of proper names of and for As, then:
> "f(an A)" is true iff "$f(a_1$ or a_2 or a_3 or. . .)" is true;
> "f(some A)" is true iff "$f(a_1)$ or $f(a_2)$ or $f(a_3)$ or. . ." is true;
> "f(any A)" is true iff "$f(a_1)$ and $f(a_2)$ and $f(a_3)$ and. . ." is true;
> "f(every A)" is true iff "$f(a_1$ and a_2 and a_3 and. . .)" is true.

In the last expression, the names conjoined with "and" are not to be read as forming the single subject of a collective predication like "Mary and Jane and Kate together weigh 390 lb." We may get a clear instance of the intended distinction between "any" and "every" if we go back to Tom's relations with Bill's sisters Mary, Jane, and Kate. We have, by our convention:

> "Tom can lawfully marry any sister of Bill's" is true iff "(Tom can lawfully marry Mary) and (Tom can lawfully marry Jane) and (Tom can lawfully marry Kate)" is true;
> "Tom can lawfully marry every sister of Bill's" is true iff "Tom can lawfully marry Mary and Jane and Kate" is true.

The second is a much stronger proposition than the first—it means that Tom can lawfully at once marry Mary and marry Jane and marry Kate. But it is not a collective predication about Mary, Jane, and Kate; codes of law that allow simultaneous polygamy need not therefore treat a man's wives as a corporation and deem that he is married to the corporation. We may call the seemingly distinct mode of reference that "every" phrases like this one have, the *conjunctive* mode.

50.   There was not much medieval recognition of the conjunctive mode as distinct from the distributive. In general, as in our example, "*f*(every A)" is a stronger proposition than "*f*(any A)"; in some examples, the two will coincide in import—e.g., if we take the context "*f*( )" to be "Tom is in love with ——" and "A" to be "sister of Bill's". Thus, if a proposition "*f*(every A)" is erroneously identified with "*f*(any A)", the difference will not force itself on people's attention in the way that it became necessary to distinguish "*f*(an A)" from "*f*(some A)" to prevent fallacious inferences from "*f*(an A)"; for, as a rule, whatever follows from "*f*(any A)" also follows from "*f*(every A)", though not vice versa. On the other hand, the fourfold scheme given above *is* found in Russell.

51.   The explanation of the fourfold scheme that I have given is easily shown to fit almost all the long lists of examples given by Russell even though Russell's professed explanation of his scheme is different from mine.[14] It would take up too much space to discuss these lists in detail: I shall indicate how to check Russell's assertions as to the import of the several items, give the full working-out of some items, and leave the rest as an exercise for the reader.

Russell uses in this passage the following terminology for notions belonging to set theory. "Term of" means "member of"; "belongs to" means "is a member of"; "common part" or "part in common" (of two or more classes) means "common member"; "is contained in" means "is a subclass of, or is the same class with"; "the logical sum of the classes c_1, c_2, c_3, . . ." means "the class having just those members that are either members of c_1 or members of c_2 or members of c_3 or . . .", and "the logical product of the classes c_1, c_2, c_3, . . ." means "the class having just those members that are at once members of c_1 and members of c_2 and members of c_3 and . . .".

Russell uses in his examples the lower-case italic letters "*a*" and "*b*"; his use is rather inexact—he uses the same letter as proxy now for a general term that can have a plural and now for a

---

[14]Russell, sec. 61.

proper name of a class or series. For typographical convenience, I shall use "A", "B", instead of "*a*", "*b*", and shall restrict these letters to the general-term use; thus, where Russell writes "the logical sum of *b*", "any class belonging to *b*", "the series *a*", I shall write "the logical sum of the Bs", "any B", "the series of the As". This seeming pedantry is indispensable to clear thought on the matter; and readers should correct Russell's careless language in this way before checking his results.

The task of checking is considerably lightened by getting the following preliminary results.

Let us use the sign "=" between quoted expressions to express substitutability *salva veritate*. Let "$a_1, a_2, a_3 \ldots$" be a complete list of the As, and "$b_1, b_2, b_3, \ldots$", of the Bs. Then we have:

"term of an A"	= "term of a_1 or of a_2 or (of) a_3 or . . ."
	= "term of the logical sum of a_1, a_2, $a_3, \ldots$"
	= "term of the logical sum of the As".
"term of every A"	= "term of a_1 and (of) a_2 and (of) a_3 and . . ."
	= "term of the logical product of a_1, a_2, $a_3, \ldots$"
	= "term of the logical product of the As".

Similarly:

"belongs to a B"	= "belongs to the logical sum of the Bs".
"belongs to every B"	= "belongs to the logical product of the Bs".

I now give a few cases to show how Russell's interpretations both accord pretty well with the ordinary use of "some", "any", "every", and "a", and also strictly conform to our rules. One further rule is needed to get the right results: If a "some" phrase and an "any" phrase occur in the same proposition, the rule for "some" must be applied before the rule for "any". This rule, we shall see later, is crucial.

(α)(2) "Any A belongs to a B"
= "Any A belongs to the logical sum of the Bs"

  = "The class of all As is contained in the logical sum of
   the Bs"

(α)(3) "Any A belongs to some B" (by the rule for "some")
  = "(Any A belongs to b_1) or (any A belongs to b_2) or
   (any A belongs to b_3) or..."
  = "(The class of all As is contained in b_1) or (the class
   of all As is contained in b_2) or..."
  = "In some B the class of all As is contained":

(γ)(10) "A term of an A belongs to every B"
  = "A term of the logical sum of the As belongs to the
   logical product of the Bs"
  = "The logical sum of the As and the logical product
   of the Bs have a part in common".

(γ)(11) "A term of an A belongs to any B" (by the rule for
   "any")
  = "(A term of an A belongs to b_1) and (a term of an A
   belongs to b_2) and...".

Now:

  "A term of an A belongs to b_1" = "A term of a_1 or (of)
   a_2 or... belongs to b_1"
  = "(A term of a_1 belongs to b_1) or (a term of a_2
   belongs to b_1) or..."
  = "(a_1 has a part in common with b_1) or (a_2 has a part
   in common with b_1) or..."
  = "Some A has a part in common with b_1".

So:

(γ)(11) = "(Some A has a part in common with b_1) and (some
   A has a part in common with b_2) and..."
  = "For any B you take, some A has a part in common
   with it".

We could have reached the same results by applying our rules
first to "an A" and then to "any B".

(γ)(19) "A term of some A belongs to any B" (by the rule for
   "some")
  = "(A term of a_1 belongs to any B) or (a term of a_2
   belongs to any B) or...".

Now:

> "A term of a_1 belongs to any B" (by the rule for "any")
> = "(A term of a_1 belongs to b_1) and (a term of a_1 belongs to b_2) and ..."
> = "(a_1 has a part in common with b_1) and (a_1 has a part in common with b_2) and ..."
> = "a_1 has a part in common with any B".

So:

> $(\gamma)(19)$ = "(a_1 has a part in common with any B) or (a_2 has a part in common with any B) or ..."
> = "(There is) some A (that) has a part in common with any B".

It is laborious, but not difficult, to check through Russell's thirty-two examples—or rather, thirty-eight, if we observe that at $(\alpha)(5)$ and at $(\gamma)(4)$, (5), (6), (16), and (17), we have each time a pair of examples alleged to coincide in import. The result is that in thirty-five out of thirty-eight cases the import worked out by our rules exactly agrees with Russell's. The only exceptions are $(\gamma)(4)$, (5), and (6); in each of these cases Russell assumes "any term of *an* A" = "any term of *some* A", and thus wrongly gives a pair of forms as equivalent. In fact, if we work out the cases by Russell's implicit rules, we get quite a different result. Let "$f(\ )$" represent the context in which the phrase "any term of an A" is embedded; this is in fact "—— belongs to every B" for $(\gamma)(4)$, "—— belongs to a B" for $(\gamma)(5)$, and "—— belongs to some B" for $(\gamma)(6)$. Whichever context "$f(\ )$" is short for, we shall have:

"f(any term of an A)" = "f(any term of any A)".

For let us suppose that the As are just a_1, a_2, a_3, ..., the terms of a_1 are just a_{11}, a_{12}, ..., the terms of a_2 just a_{21}, a_{22}, ..., and so on. Then we shall have:

"f(any term of an A)" = "f(any term of a_1 or (of) a_2 or ...)"
= "$f(a_{11})$ and $f(a_{12})$ and ... and $f(a_{21})$ and $f(a_{22})$ and ... and $f(a_{31})$ and $f(a_{32})$ and ..."

But here we have further:

"f(any term of a_1)" = "$f(a_{11})$ and $f(a_{12})$ and ...",
"f(any term of a_2)" = "$f(a_{21})$ and $f(a_{22})$ and ...",

and so on. So we have:

"f(any term of an A)" = "f(any term of a_1) and f(any term of a_2) and f(any term of a_3) and ..."

But now if we apply Russell's implicit rule for "any" phrases to the context "f(any term of ——)", we have also:

"f(any term of any A)" = "f(any term of a_1) and f(any term of a_2) and f(any term of a_3) and ..."

And thus we have, as I said:

"f(any term of an A)" = "f(any term of any A)".

This result of Russell's implicit rules, like many of his results, is in good accordance with the ordinary English use of the applicatives concerned; his having made "f(any term of an A)" equivalent to "f(any term of some A)" in these three cases is clearly a mere slip.

52.   It is very curious that Russell's professed explanation of the difference between "every" and "any" does not at all agree with the rules that he so carefully observes in practice. As regards "every", he correlates "Every suitor (is paying court to Miss Smith)" with "Brown and Jones are paying court to Miss Smith", which he distinguishes from "Brown is paying court to Miss Smith and Jones is paying court to Miss Smith": so far, all is in order. But it would have been better if Russell had chosen an example in which the proposition containing a conjunction of names differed in inferential force from the corresponding conjunction of propositions; his actual choice of examples leads him to the quite erroneous assertion that, when such a list combined by means of "and" is not read collectively, the proposition containing it is equivalent to a conjunction of propositions—which is not in general true, and if it were true would wipe out again the distinction Russell makes between "any" and "every".

Russell's account of "any" is still more bedeviled by a badly chosen example: "If you met any suitor of Miss Smith, you met a very ardent lover". On the one hand, this will correspond to: "If you met Brown or Jones, you met a very ardent lover"; on the other hand, it will be true iff both "If you met Brown, you met an ardent lover" and "If you met Jones, you met an ardent lover" are true propositions. So Russell says there is 'some difficulty' about the notion of "any suitor", which 'seems half-way between a conjunction and a disjunction'.[15]

If this difficulty arose at all, it would arise already in the propositional calculus, independently of any referring phrase's being used. "If p or q, then r" is equivalent to "(If p, then r) and (if q, then r)"; but this gives no warrant for the idea that the "or" in "if p or q" is a peculiar connective, 'half-way between a conjunction and a disjunction'.

For the rest, Russell's perplexity depends on his ignoring the *scope* of referring phrases. The following three propositions are all equivalent:

(1) If you met a suitor of Miss Smith, you met a very ardent lover.

(2) If you met some suitor of Miss Smith, you met a very ardent lover.

(3) If you met any suitor of Miss Smith, you met a very ardent lover.

But the force of the referring phrase is different in each one; and on the other hand in (1) and (2) the scope of the referring phrase is simply "you met ——", whereas in (3) it is "If you met ——, you met a very ardent lover". In accordance with our rules, the antecedent of (1) corresponds to "You met Brown or Jones", that of (2) to "You met Brown or you met Jones"; thus in the context "you met ——" the difference between "some" and "a" does not affect the import of the antecedent. On the other hand, the import of (3) is as Russell states, precisely because the "any" phrase has a long scope, and because "If p or q, then r" is equivalent to "(If p, then r) and (if q, then r)"; (3) corresponds to

[15]Russell, sec. 59.

a conjunction of the results of inserting "Brown" and "Jones" instead of the "any" phrase in (3). So the example, properly understood, only confirms the correlation we made between "any" phrases and propositional conjunction; there is no warrant for the expression "half-way between conjunction and disjunction". There seems as little warrant for Russell's saying that in 'complicated cases' there is no longer an equivalence between a predication about *any* so-and-so and the conjunction of corresponding predications about the several so-and-so's; at least, he supplies no example, here or elsewhere.

53. Russell's defective explanations do not count against the validity of his distinctions; and the distinction between "every" and "any", like that between "a" and "some", is often important in philosophical, as also in everyday, arguments. In everyday life, it may be, fallacious reasoning (that is likely to take people in) dependent on a confusion of "any" and "every" is not so easily to be found, though perhaps the art of some salesmen and politicians consists in smoothing over the transition from "You can afford any one of these items" to "You can afford every one of these items". The fallacy is naturally more rife in philosophy, where a fallacious inference is not so readily exposed by its yielding a false or improbable conclusion from true premises; an example is the transition from "Any sense perception may be illusory" to "Every sense perception may be illusory".

54. This concludes my treatment of the doctrine of *suppositio*. The reader may well suppose that, in spite of the errors of detail into which Russell and the medievals fell, the theory must be essentially sound—that something on these lines is needed, to deal with definite fallacies. I shall now try to show that the doctrine of *suppositio* is radically inconsistent, though less obviously so than the doctrine of distribution, and that we need to start all over again on new lines. Of course the fallacies which the doctrine of *suppositio* tried to eliminate *are* fallacies, and we shall have to give some account of them; but this no more justifies the doctrine of *suppositio* than the fallaciousness of syllogisms with an 'undistributed middle' is a ground for accepting the doctrine of distribution.

Four

The Shipwreck of a Theory

55.   To state the doctrines of referring phrases discussed in the last chapter, I used the symbol "$f(\ )$" as a schema for a 'context' in which there could stand either a proper name or a referring phrase. This of course presupposed that the context represented by "$f(\ )$" would be a univocal expression in the propositions represented (say) by "$f(a_2)$", "$f(\text{some A})$", "$f(\text{an A})$". There are, however, as we shall see, serious difficulties about this.

   If a context "$f(\ )$" is really univocal, then by our previous explanations it must be a predicable, and will actually be a predicate when supplied with a proper name as its subject. If it is attached to a referring phrase, which, we decided, deserves to be called only a quasi subject, it will not be the predicate of a proposition in which it occurs; but the identity of a predicable, as we said, does not depend on its always being an actual predicate; and if our symbolism, and therewith the theory of referring phrases, is to be justified, a context represented by "$f(\ )$" must be an univocal predicable. For when we were giving truth-conditions for various sorts of propositions schematically representable by inserting a referring phrase in the blank of "$f(\ )$", we used the same letter with the blank filled by a proper name; and in the latter use "$f(\ )$" must represent a predicable; so, if the symbolism is to be justified, "$f(\quad)$" at its other occurrences must also represent the same predicable.

This may seem to work well so far as concerns "some" and "any" phrases. The truth-conditions of "$f(\text{any } A)$" and "$f(\text{some } A)$" are respectively given by a conjunction and by a disjunction of clauses, in each of which clauses "$f(\quad)$" occurs as a predicate with a proper name as its subject. A similar thing holds for phrases formed with "most". Suppose we have a finite complete list of names *of* and *for* As that does not include the same A twice over under different names: then the truth-conditions of "$f(\text{some } A)$", "$f(\text{any } A)$", and "$f(\text{most As})$" are respectively given by a disjunction, a conjunction, and a (certain) disjunction of conjunctions, of the singular propositions in which "$f(\quad)$" is attached to the several names on the list. For example, let "a_1, a_2, a_3, a_4" be our list of As. Then:

> "$f(\text{any } A)$" is true iff "$f(a_1)$ & $f(a_2)$ & $f(a_3)$ & $f(a_4)$" is true.
>
> "$f(\text{some } A)$" is true iff "$f(a_1) \vee f(a_2) \vee f(a_3) \vee f(a_4)$" is true.
>
> "$f(\text{most As})$" is true iff "$[f(a_1)$ & $f(a_2)$ & $f(a_3)] \vee [f(a_2)$ & $f(a_3)$ & $f(a_4)] \vee [f(a_3)$ & $f(a_4)$ & $f(a_1)] \vee [f(a_4)$ & $f(a_1)$ & $f(a_2)]$" is true.

It would be a little troublesome to give a rigorous general formulation of this sort of truth-condition for "$f(\text{most As})$"; but it ought to be intuitively clear that, given an actual list of As, a truth-condition always could be specified by giving such a disjunction of conjunctions. Thus in regard to "$f(\text{any } A)$" or "$f(\text{some } A)$" or "$f(\text{most As})$", it seems entirely plausible to regard "$f(\quad)$" as a predicable attached to a referring phrase—provided that the scope of the referring phrase is the whole of the context "$f(\quad)$".

On the other hand, "$f(\text{a cat})$" and "$f(\text{every cat})$" each have as truth-conditions a single proposition in which the referring phrase is replaced by a list of cats' names combined with "or" or "and" (as the case may be). If we waive our previous difficulties about the logical role of "and" and "or" used like this, we may plausibly suppose that one and the same predicable "$f(\quad)$" may occur in "$f(\text{Jemima and Ahab and Smoky}\ldots)$", or again in "$f(\text{Jemima or Ahab or Smoky}\ldots)$", and on the other hand in "*f*(Jemima)"—this last being a degenerate case of a list, containing only one item. As before, then, we may plausibly suppose that one and the same predicable may be identified in "*f*(a cat)", "*f*(every cat)", and "*f*(Jemima)"—provided that the scope of the referring phrases is the whole of the context "*f*( )".

We shall see, however, that if we do thus regard the contexts of "a" and "every" phrases, we get into difficulties over the *dictum de omni* principle.

56. Concerning the *dictum de omni* there has been an extraordinary amount of confusion; this long preceded the corrupt logical tradition in which, as Descartes already complained in the *Discourse on Method*, 'sound and useful rules' (like the *dictum de omni*) are inextricably mixed up with 'useless or harmful ones' (like the doctrine of distribution). Indeed, in origin the very name of the *dictum de omni* expresses a confusion: it comes from translation of Aristotle's "*kata pantos kategoreisthai*", i.e. "to be predicated (sc. truly predicable) of every one", in *Prior Analytics* 24^{b}28. A little careful reading of the text and context shows that Aristotle was not here enunciating a fundamental principle of syllogistic, nor even formulating a rule at all; Aristotle begins his work by introducing and explaining a number of logical terms of art, and "predicated of every one" has to come in such a list as "universal quantification" must for a modern logician.

We cannot, I think, get any light on the matter by looking at formulations of the dictum in medieval logic; but we can make some steps in the right direction by considering the sort of syllogism that the medieval logicians regarded as validated by the dictum—*boni syllogismi regulati per dictum de omni*. For there is indeed a common principle underlying these syllogisms, and we can see that this is so before we are able to formulate the principle accurately. Given what purports to be such a formulation, it is a matter not of any stipulation on my part, but of hard logical facts, whether this rule will do the job; if it will, then it appears reasonable to appropriate the name "*dictum de omni*" for *this* formulation of the rule, rather than for ones to be found in the literature that are inadequate.

The *boni syllogismi* in question were such as would appear in the notation of section 36 as follows:

Whatever is f is g; $f(^{*}A)$; *ergo* g $(^{*}A)$

where "―― is f" and "$f($ $)$" are just different styles for schematically representing one and the same chosen predicable. The usual interpretations of the asterisk as an applicative would be confined to "every" and "some"; medieval logicians, as we have seen, mostly had nothing corresponding to Russell's distinction of "every" and "any". But clearly validity will be preserved for certain other applicatives as well—"more than one", "all but one", and "most" (or "almost every"), for example. For other applicatives the pattern of inference is invalid: as for example if we take "$^{*}A$" to mean "just one A" or "few As" (where "Few As are so-and-so" = "Most As are not so-and-so but some are").

In order to extract a common principle from these *boni syllogismi*, we must leave it unspecified *which* applicative is used in the minor premise and the conclusion, so long as it is the same in both. How then are we to exclude applicatives for which this syllogistic pattern is invalid? We may of course divide applicatives into *dictum de omni* applicatives and the rest, according as the above syllogistic pattern does or does not turn out valid; but thus far I have merely listed some *dictum de omni* applicatives, and we have no idea how to recognize their common property; a rule that the above syllogistic pattern is valid when there is a *dictum de omni* applicative employed will be vacuous, for validity of the pattern is thus far our only criterion for a *dictum de omni* applicative.

We may gain a better insight, I think, by analyzing a more complicated example, not reducible to syllogistic form:

(A) No man has admired any pig;
　　(Almost) every man has seen a pig;
　　Ergo, (almost) every man has seen, but not admired, something (or other).

(I use this rather stilted form for the conclusion, rather than the more natural ". . . has seen something but not admired it" or ". . . has seen something which he has not admired", in order not to raise at this stage problems about the use of pronouns with antecedents, like "it", "which", and "he" here: they are to be discussed in the next chapter.) Even with the familiar quantifier "every", this argument cannot be put in syllogistic form; and we may see, moreover, that any *dictum de omni* applicative substituted for "(almost) every" both times would likewise make the argument valid. We must therefore not conceive the *dictum de omni* as validating *only* syllogisms.

The key to our problem is to be found if we relate argument (A) to one of simpler structure:

(B) No man has admired any pig;
    The man *a* has seen a pig;
    Ergo, the man *a* has seen, but not admired, something
    (or other).

Here I use "the man *a*" as proxy for a term that is a name *of* and *for* a man. It is easy to establish the validity of (B) itself. From the first premise of (B) we may infer "The man *a* has not admired any pig". So (B) is valid if this argument is valid:

(C) The man *a* has not admired any pig;
    The man *a* has seen a pig;
    Ergo, the man *a* has seen, but not admired, something
    (or other).

And (C) is easily seen to be a valid argument; we need not here analyze it further. So (B) is valid. The question is: how can we get from the validity of (B) to that of (A)?

The transition from (B) to (A) is not one from premises to conclusion, in accordance with a rule whose soundness consists in preserving truth; it is a transition from one argument to another, by a rule whose soundness consists in preserving validity. This brings us to a fundamental distinction between two kinds of logical rules. Even as everybody doing logic learns to distinguish truth and validity, stating and arguing; similarly, everybody ought to learn the distinction between truth-preserving and validity-preserving rules. It will be handy to have labels for the two kinds. For truth-preserving patterns of argument Aristotle's term "schema" is still in use, so I shall here speak of *schematic* rules. Procedures for transforming valid arguments into valid arguments are of course implicitly used very often in Aristotle's *Prior Analytics*, but were brought into the focus of explicit logical consideration only by the Stoics, who spoke of *themata*; following the Stoic precedent, I shall speak of *thematic* rules.

The *dictum de omni* rule justifying the transition from argument (B) to argument (A) must clearly be a thematic rule, so I shall say a little more in general about thematic rules. The simplest thematic rule is the rule that allows us to arrange arguments in a chain: this is so obvious that logic books rarely formulate it explicitly (though I have known one which rejected the general validity of the rule!). Given that "*p, ergo q*" and "*q, ergo r*" are both so interpreted ("*q*" the same way both times) as to come out valid, then the chain of argument "*p, ergo q, ergo r*" will likewise be valid.

In the formulations of logic with so-called introduction and elimination rules, the distinction between thematic and schematic rules is usually not emphasized, although in comparison with this the distinction between introduction and elimination rules is quite superficial. The rules for inferring a conjunction from its two conjuncts as separate premises, for inferring a conjunct from a conjunction, and for inferring a disjunction from either disjunct, are all of them schematic rules, truth-preserving rules; this similarity is far more important than that the first and third rules should be classed together under the heading "introduction rules" and the second be called "an elimination rule". On the other hand, what is called "*vel*-elimination" is a thematic rule, a rule for blending together two valid arguments to make a new valid argument. If we have a valid argument deriving "*r*" from "*p*" (*plus* perhaps some set of further premises S), and another valid argument deriving the same conclusion "*r*" from "*q*" (*plus* perhaps some further premises S'), then we may frame a new valid argument deriving "*r*" from "*p vel q*" (plus any further premises in S and S' that were used in getting "*r*" by the original arguments). This rule is utterly different in character from the other three; it is validity-preserving, not truth-preserving; and it cannot be applied directly to premises, but only when we already have a pair of valid arguments to plait together. The specious symmetry and system obtained by presenting these four rules as the elimination-rule and the introduction-rule for each of the two connectives "and" and "*vel*" can only obscure the logical powers of the rules.

The transition from (B) to (A) is also legitimated by a thematic rule; and the thematic rule that we shall need is one that will also validate the medievals' *boni syllogismi*, as transformations of the simpler syllogism:

(D) Whatever is f is g; $f(a)$; *ergo* $g(a)$.

I propose, as I said, to appropriate the term "*dictum de omni*" as a name for the thematic rule that is required. If we compare this syllogism with the syllogism:

(E) Whatever is f is g; $f(^*A)$; *ergo* $g(^*A)$

a simple solution may perhaps suggest itself. If the major premise of syllogism (D) is valid, then whatever the predicable "$f(\quad)$" applies to the predicable "$g(\quad)$" also applies to. Now "$f(^*A)$" is a true proposition iff "$f(\quad)$" applies to whichever As the phrase "$^*A$" is being used to refer to; but by the major premise "$g(\quad)$" applies to whatever "$f(\quad)$" applies to; so if both "$f(^*A)$" and the major premise shared by (D) and (E) are true, the predicable "$g(\quad)$" will apply to whichever As the phrase "$^*A$" is being used to refer to. But this last clause gives the truth-condition of "$g(^*A)$"; and thus the validity of (E) is established.

Simple and convincing as this reasoning may seem, it is entirely fallacious. Any referring phrase "$^*A$" can be used to refer, in its fashion, to each and every one of the things called "A"; in giving truth-conditions for propositions containing such a phrase, as we saw in the last chapter, if the things in question can be actually listed then we must mention each one of them on a par with all the others. If another applicative phrase were being used, say "$\dagger A$", we should still be referring to the same things, namely to each and every A. So we cannot speak *distinctively*, as the above argument made it appear that we could, of the As that the phrase "$^*A$" is being used to refer to; nor is it apparent why we may not pass from a minor premise "$f(^*A)$" to a conclusion "$g(\dagger A)$", since the same As are referred to in both. The whole argument is really based on the error discussed in Chapter One, the error of making "every dog" refer to *every* dog and "some dog" only to *some* dog. We easily slip into this error unawares: the exploration of this false trail in our search for the *dictum de omni* principle will have been worthwhile if it helps us to detect and avoid the error, which might otherwise mar our understanding of the dictum.

We shall get a clearer view of how the *dictum de omni* works if we slightly modify the arguments upon which it works and those to which it leads. Suppose we start from an argument from "$f(a)$" (plus perhaps some set of extra premises S) to "$g(a)$", "a" being taken as a name *of* and *for* an A. We want to show that, if we use the right sort of applicative, "$f(^*A)$" (plus any premises in S used in the original argument) will yield the conclusion "$g(^*A)$". To do this we first transform the original argument to make it a chain argument: from "$f(a)$" (and any needed premises in S) we are first to infer "$f(a)$ & $g(a)$", and then from this conclusion to detach "$g(a)$"; clearly this chain of reasoning is valid iff the original argument is valid. In parallel to this, we shall first show that for a rightly chosen applicative we may pass from "$f(^*A)$" (and the needed premises in the set S) to "$f(^*A)$ & g(the same A)", and then that from this conclusion we may infer "$g(^*A)$".

I argued in the last chapter in favor of the view that (in certain contexts at least) a general term like "elephant" may be regarded as a name and as a possible logical subject: "elephant" in such uses would name each and every elephant, a proper name "Jumbo" just one elephant. I further hold that with *certain* applicatives (not with all: e.g., obviously not with "no" or "alone") we may take "$f(^*A)$" as predicating with respect to the subject-name "A" precisely what is predicated with respect to the subject-name "a" in "$f(a)$". Though I am disagreeing with Frege about the status of common nouns, I am accepting his view, already mentioned in section 41, that in a proposition of the form "$f(^*A)$" the applicative *may* be taken to go rather with the predicable represented by "$f( )$" than with the noun represented by "A". (In various natural languages the applicative would appear as an adjective agreeing with "A" in gender, number, and case; grammar thus suggests a reference to some proper or improper subclass of the As; but grammar is here gravely misleading.) And thus we may regard "$f(*A)$" and "$f(a)$" as making the same predication, though in relation to different logical subjects.

A puzzle may arise here: it may be that with two different applicatives, represented say in "$f(\dagger A)$" and "$f(*A)$", we each time get a predication concerning the subject-term "A" which is the same as that made concerning "a" in "$f(a)$"; how then can the star and the dagger differ in sense? The temptation here is once more a temptation to the canceling-out fallacy. In the degenerate case where there is but one thing called by the common name "A", "$f(*A)$" and "$f(\dagger A)$" will indeed both come out true iff the predicable "$f(\quad)$" is true of that one A; but since it is no part of the sense of either proposition to say how many As there are, the two predications will not have the same sense, even in this case; still less need they have even the same truth-value when there are several As. What I am, however, implying is that when we replace "A" by "a", a name *of* and *for* an A, whose sense requires that it does not name several As, then "$f(a)$" and "$f(\dagger a)$" and "$f(*a)$" will all have the same sense. But to suppose that therefore "$f(\quad)$" and "$f(\dagger\quad)$" and "$f(*\quad)$" all have the same sense, regardless of which common or proper name is inserted into these contexts, just is the canceling-out fallacy.

Some of the considerations in the last paragraph may be reminiscent of the way that textbooks propagating distributionist logic will assimilate the singular form "S is P" to "Some S is P" or "Every S is P" (there is a certain hesitation here between "some" and "every"). But the underlying rationale is quite different. For me it is nonsensical to ask which individuals a phrase "every S" or "some S" refers to, and on the contrary the applicative shows how "—— is P" latches onto the subject "S"; for the distributionist logicians on the other hand the reason why assimilation of the forms is justified when we have a singular subject-term is that then "S" and "every S" and "some S" all have the same reference. So the agreement on this point between these writers' view and mine arises only from their making a double error about the (supposed) reference of applicatival phrases, an error which cancels out and conceals itself as in a wrong addition of a column of figures.

I remarked in section 34 that the continued reference made in telling a tale by repetition of proper names could also be effected by phrases of the form "the same A". In fact, if "*a*" is a name *of* and *for* and A, "*f*(*a*) & *g*(*a*)" will have just the same sense as "*f*(*a*) & *g*(the same A)": what is important for the sense is the continued reference intended to one and the same A, but this intention is equally well fulfilled in either way of speaking. (Of course this does *not* mean that in the context "*f*(*a*) & *g*(——)" the phrase "the same A" has the sense of the name "*a*": that inference would once more be the canceling-out fallacy.)

Now for certain applicatives, I have argued, we may rewrite "*f*(*a*)" as "*f*(* *a*)"—thus showing that what is predicated in relation to "*a*" in "*f*(a)" is what is predicated in relation to the common name "A" in "*f*(* A)". If we are considering some applicative whose sense allows us to rewrite "*f*(*a*) & *g*(*a*)", or its equivalent "*f*(*a*) & *g* (the same A) as "*f*(* *a*) & *g* (the same A)", then given a valid inference from "*f*(*a*)", or equivalently "*f*(* *a*)", to "*f*(* *a*) & *g*(the same A)", we may construct another valid inference from "*f*(* A)" to "*f*(* A) & *g*(the same A)". —If the inference we start from requires extra premises from some set S besides "*f*(*a*)" to warrant the conclusion, then the new inference will require these same extra premises besides "*f*(* A)".—As we saw in section 34, the continued reference effected by "the same so-and-so" does not require the use of a proper name even initially; if I tell a tale, true or false, about the cat Tibbles and the river Arrow, then a hearer who is not destined ever to encounter Tibbles or the Arrow even in discourse ever again would have lost nothing if I had begun the story with "A cat was sitting by a river" instead of "Tibbles was sitting by the river Arrow". The same principle is involved here as there.

There is one important restriction upon this generation of a new valid argument: the name "*a*" must not occur either in the set of extra premises S or in the predicables used to interpret the schematic letters "*f*", "*g*"; otherwise our procedure will not be validity-preserving. For example, "any" is an applicative fulfilling our condition; but if we took the set S to have the single member "*g*(*a*)", the validity of the inference from this and "*f*(*a*)" to "*f*(*a*) & *g*(*a*)", or equivalently "*f*(any *a*) & *g*(the same A)" does *not* warrant us in regarding as valid the inference from "*g*(*a*)" and "*f*(any A)" to "*f*(any A) & *g*(the same A)". Similarly, if interpretations of "*R*" and "*g*( )" are so chosen as to make valid the inference from "*a* is R to/*a*" to "(*a* is R to/*a*) and *g*(the same A)", it does not follow that we may regard as valid the inference from "*a* is R to any A" to "(*a* is R to/any A) & *g*(the same A)". (I have used the mark "/" here merely in order to help readers to pick out the predicable "*a* is R to ——", not as a logical sign.)

No such perils, however, attend our inferring "*g*(* A)" from "*f*(* A) & *g*(the same A)". Obviously we could not treat the clause represented by "*g*(the same A)" as an independently significant conjunct that could also occur as a freestanding proposition; the reference to the As in this clause is borrowed from the previous clause "*f*(* A)", and the applicative represented by the asterisk has precisely the role of showing *how* the predicables represented by "*f*( )" and "*g*( )" are being supposed to latch onto the As when one asserts or assumes "*f*(* A) & *g*(the same A)" as a premise. So what we may detach from the premise as a conclusion is not "*g*(the same A)" but "*g*(* A)".

Now at last we are in a position to formulate the *dictum de omni* principle.

Let the asterisk represent an applicative such that, for any predicable that "h( )" may stand in for, "h(*A)" predicates in relation to the name "A" just what "h(a)" predicates in relation to "a", where this is a name of and for an A. Suppose we have a valid inference "p; f(a); ergo g(a)", in which neither the premise "p" nor the predicables "f( )" and "g( )" may be taken to contain occurrences of the name "a". Then the inference "p; f(*A); ergo g(*A)" will also be valid.

The restriction of the name "*a*" to being a name *of* and *for* an A may seem unnecessary, but in fact it does not make the principle less general. For under the stated conditions, the derivation of "*g*(*a*)" from "*p*" and "*f*(*a*)" would be valid iff "*a*" were uniformly replaceable by any other name *of* and *for* an A; but if the proof would remain valid *whatever* proper name took the place of "*a*", it would clearly remain valid for a more restricted class of replacement; so all is in order.

The *dictum de omni* in its general form is difficult to grasp accurately; but once it is thoroughly understood, it ought to appear obvious. Exceptions to it can only be apparent exceptions. To guard against fallacy and see that the thematic rule has been rightly applied, it is often wise to take two bites at a cherry and check first whether the transition from "p; $f(a)$; *ergo* $f(a)\&g(a)$" to "p; $f(^* A)$; *ergo* $f(^* A)\&g$(the same A)" has been correctly carried out, and then whether we have a proper instance of the inference from "$f(^* A)\&g$(the same A)" to "$g(^* A)$".

It is easy to see how the *dictum de omni* principle will take us from valid references to valid inferences when the asterisk is taken to mean "any" or "some" or "most", at any rate if we confine our attention to cases where the As can actually be (nonrepetitively) listed in a finite list. For the necessary and sufficient truth-condition for "$f(^* A)$" or "$g(^* A)$", if the asterisk means "any", or "some", or "most", will then be given by a certain truth-function of propositions formed by attaching the predicable "$f(\ \ )$" or "$g(\ \ )$" to the several items of this list of As: the truth-function in question is a disjunction for "some", a conjunction for "any", and a (certain) disjunction of conjunctions for "most", as we saw in section 55. If now we have a premise "p" such that "p;$f(a_n)$; *ergo* $g(a_n)$" comes out valid—I assume here that the previously mentioned restriction is observed for occurrences of the name "a_n"—then from "p" and such a truth-function of propositions "$f(a_n)$" we may infer as a conclusion the exactly corresponding truth-function of propositions "$g(a_n)$". So in view of what we just now saw about necessary and sufficient truth-conditions, in these finite cases "p; f(some A): *ergo* g(some A)" and "p; f(any A); *ergo* g(any A)" and "p; f(most As); *ergo* g(most As)" will all come out valid.—Of course this line of reasoning will not work when the As cannot in fact be exhaustively and nonrepetitively listed by names existing in the language we are using; but all the same this may help toward an intuitive grasp of the principle.

57. The application of the *dictum de omni* to "most" phrases clears up a puzzle that exercised logicians while the doctrine of distribution prevailed. From the premises "Most As are *P*" and "Most As are *Q*" there clearly follows the conclusion "Something is both *P* and *Q*". But on the doctrine of distribution *no* conclusion ought to follow from such premises, since the middle

term "A" is not distributed—a horrid sin against the laws of distribution.

Sir William Hamilton, and others who came after him, attempted to generalize the laws so as to cover the case: the middle term need not be distributed in either premise separately, so long as it was *ultratotally* distributed in both premises together. That is, as De Morgan puts it: "It is enough that the two premises taken together affirm or deny of more than all the instances [!] of the middle term".[1] De Morgan's expression is intentionally absurd: the argument is that the two premises between them would refer to more than all the As there are, unless some As were referred to in both premises. For each premise refers to most As, i.e. to more than half the As; so if they referred to entirely separate sets of As, they would between them refer to more As than the whole class of As, which is absurd. So on pain of this absurdity, some of the As which are *P*, referred to as "most As" in one premise, must be the same as some of the As which are *Q*, referred to as "most As" in the other premise. Therefore, the premises imply that something is both *P* and *Q*.

This *reductio ad absurdum* is a tortuous argument and is invalidated by two of the fundamental mistakes of distributionist logicians: the assumption that "most" As" refers to a set of As containing most As, just as "some As" is held to refer to some As; and the assumption that which As are referred to in "Most As are *P*" depends on which As the predicable "*P*" is true of. We have seen that the truth-condition of "Most As are *P*" relates symmetrically to each of the things called "A", not only to a majority of them or to such of them as are *P*.

There is a further defect in De Morgan's reasoning. Suppose there are infinitely many As, for example as many As as there are natural numbers; for this case we may take "Most As are *P*" to mean "All As, with at most finitely many exceptions, are *P*". We now still have the valid inference that puzzled Hamilton and De Morgan; but we cannot now justify it by saying that if the majority of As that are *P* were an entirely separate class from the majority of As that are *Q* then the two premises between them

---

[1] De Morgan, p. 127: cited in Keynes, p. 377, cf. also p. 104.

would refer to more than the total class of As; for two denumerably infinite classes taken together make only a class as numerous as each one of them.

Applying the *dictum de omni*, we may clear up the puzzle very
simply and naturally. To show that "Something is both *P* and *Q*"
follows from "Most As are *P*" and "Most As are *Q*" it will be
enough to show that this triad of propositions is an inconsistent
one: (1) "Whatever is *P* is non-*Q*" (2) "Most As are *P*" (3) "Most
As are *Q*". Now (1) and "*a* is *P*" of course yield "*a* is non-*Q*", for
arbitrary reading of "*a*" as a proper name. So, by the *dictum de
omni*, (1) and (2) yield (4) "Most As are non-*Q*", which is inconsistent with (3). So from (2) and (3) as premises, contrapositively,
we may derive the contradictory of (1), i.e. "Something is both
P and *Q*".

58.   As I have said, exceptions to the *dictum de omni* principle
can be only apparent. It is not even an apparent exception that,
given premises that warrant us in passing from "*f*(*a*)" to "*g*(*a*)",
we cannot pass from "*f*(no A)" to "*g*(no A)"; for it is at the least
intuitively odd to take "no A" as a way of referring to the things
called "A"; and if we look at the stages of derivation, "*f*(no A),
ergo f(no A) and *g*(the same A)" is absurd, and so is "*f*(no A) and
g(the same A), *ergo g*(no A)". But we likewise cannot pass from
"*f*(just one A)" to "*g*(just one A)", or from "*f*(few As)" to "*g*(few
As)": yet here it is not easy to see what is wrong with the intermediate steps of inference:

> *f*(just one A); *ergo f*(just one A) and *g*(the same A); *ergo*
> *g*(just one A).
> *f*(few As); *ergo f*(few As) and *g*(the same As); *ergo g*(few
> As).

The explanation, I think, is that a proposition of the form
"*f*(few As) & *g*(the same As)" is a portmanteau proposition into
which two distinct propositions are packed, and the added clause
"*g*(the same As)" hangs on to only one of these two. For example
"Few M.P.s spoke against the Bill, and they were Tories" un-
packs as: "Most M.P.s did not speak against the Bill; but some
M.P.s did speak against the Bill, and they were Tories". Here the

pronoun "they" takes the place of "the same M.P.s"—the use of pronouns is to be further discussed in the next three chapters. From this, according to the method of inference we used in expounding the *dictum de omni*, we can infer only the trivial conclusion "Some M.P.s were Tories"; "Few M.P.s were Tories" is again a portmanteau proposition, and part of what we get by unpacking it is "Most M.P.s were not Tories", which was not packed into the premise.

Similarly for "f(just one A)". "Just one man broke the bank at Monte Carlo" expands into "Never has more than one man broken the bank at Monte Carlo; but a man once did (break the bank, etc.)". If we now add on the clause "and he (sc. that same man) has died a pauper", this attaches only to the second clause of the expanded proposition; and we can infer only, trivially, "A man has died a pauper". "Just one man has died a pauper" would have as part of its own unpacking "Never has more than one man died a pauper", which was not packed up into the premise.

The last paragraph may well strike some people as vitiated by the same misunderstanding of referring expressions as Russell's theory of definite descriptions. Surely, if the sentence "Just one man broke the bank at Monte Carlo" were not just a logician's example, but were being actually used to make a statement, the context of utterance would show whom the phrase "just one man" referred to; and then in the added clause "and he has died a pauper", "he" carries on the reference of this phrase.[2] Very well: if the context of utterance does make "just one man" refer to just one man, and "he" carries on this reference, why could not the principal do the job of the proxy—why could we not go on "and just one man has died a pauper"? Philosophers who warn us not to asimilate other sorts of words to proper names may themselves be guilty of just such assimilation in thinking that a phrase like "a man", or "just one man", refers to a man, or just one man, as "Socrates" refers to Socrates, or that, as Strawson says, the pronoun "he" takes up a reference to a definite person indefinitely made by the phrase "a man".[3]

[2]Strawson, pp. 187, 194.
[3]Strawson, p. 187.

59.   Let us turn from these apparent exceptions to phrases of the form "most As". To these, as we saw, the *dictum de omni* does apply. But here too we get apparent exceptions—cases in which, even given premises that would warrant our passing from "*f*(*a*)" to "*g*(*a*)", we seem to get "*f*(most As)" true and "*g*(most As)" false. For example, consider the proposition "Each boy admires most girls". (In the next few paragraphs I shall use "each" instead of Russell's "any", to avoid some linguistic awkwardnesses.) Now let it be the case that the predicable "Each boy admires ———" is true only of those whom some other predicable "*g*( )"—say "envied by most girls"—is true. We now nevertheless cannot pass from "Each boy admires most girls" to "*g*(most girls)", nor even to "*g*(some girl)". For the predicable "*g*( )" need not, in the case supposed, be true of any girl at all, unless the predicable "Each boy admires ———" is true of her; but the premises could be true even if there were not one girl whom each boy (without exception) admired. Now we may clearly choose the predicable "*g*( )" so that it does genuinely occur in "*g*(most girls)" and "*g*(some girl)"; and we cannot plausibly suppose that the source of trouble is an ambiguity in "most". Our conclusion must therefore be that the reason for the apparent breakdown of the *dictum de omni* is that in "Each boy admires most girls" the predicable "Each boy admires ———" does not genuinely occur.

Similarly, this predicable does not genuinely occur in the proposition "Each boy admires a girl". For even if most girls are sure to envy anyone there may be whom each boy admires, and each boy admires a girl, it does not follow that most girls envy a girl. To play fair in appraising this inference, we must be careful to pass through the steps of inference that our account of the *dictum de omni* would apparently warrant: "(1) Each boy admires a girl; (2) *ergo*, each boy admires a girl, and most girls envy her (sc. that same girl); (3) *ergo*, most girls envy a girl". In the first two steps "a girl" would be an instance of *suppositio confusa*, so that the question "Which girl?" would be out of place; nevertheless we can see that, if the first step warranted the second, "a girl" in the conclusion could have *suppositio determinata*. For from:

Each boy admires a girl, and most girls envy that same girl

we can go down to the singular instance ("Smith" being the proper name of a boy):

Smith admires a girl, and most girls envy that same girl

from which again follows "Most girls envy a girl", in the sense in which it is proper to ask "Which girl?"—i.e., rather, "Most girls envy *some* girl". This conclusion plainly is not warranted by the original premises.

Moreover, even the weaker conclusion "Most girls envy *a* girl", with "a girl" understood as an instance of *suppositio confusa*, would still not be warranted on these premises. This reading of "Most girls envy a girl" would mean that, for each one out of a majority of girls, there is a girl whom she envies; and this would imply "Some girl or other is envied". But this implication is not warranted by the premises; the premises tell us only that whoever there may be that each boy admires is sure to be envied (by most girls)—they do not tell us that there is any such person. Here too, then, we must conclude that the predicable "Each boy admires ——" does not genuinely occur in the premise "Each boy admires a girl".

Of course, if "Mary" is a proper name corresponding in its sense to a correct use of "the same girl", then from "Each boy admires Mary" we can infer "Each boy admires a girl"; yet this inference appears to be vitiated by a fallacy of ambiguity, unless "Each boy admires——" occurs univocally in the premise and in the conclusion. We can, however, explain the validity of this inference. The proposition "Each boy admires Mary" can be analyzed in two ways: as the result of attaching the predicate "Each boy admires ——" to the subject "Mary", and as the result of attaching the predicable "—— admires Mary" to the referring phrase "each boy". Moreover, "Each boy admires a girl" can certainly be analyzed as the result of attaching the predicable "—— admires a girl" to the quasi subject "each boy"; and this predicable will be true of whomever the predicable "—— admires Mary" is true of. So, by the *dictum de omni*, we may pass from "Each boy/admires Mary" to "Each boy/admires a girl"—provided we show that we can pass from "*a* admires Mary"

to "*a* admires a girl", where "*a*" is an arbitrary proper name. This
we can certainly do, given the sense we have assumed for
"Mary", if we read "*a* admires/Mary" and "*a* admires/a girl" as
containing the common predicable "*a* admires ———". But now
we may also regard the same pair of propositions as formed by
attaching two predicates to the common subject "*a*"; and then we
may use the *dictum de omni* to show that just as we may pass
from "*a*/admires Mary" to "*a*/admires a girl", so we may pass
from "Each boy/admires Mary" to "Each boy/admires a girl".
And thus we have validated this last inference without needing to
recognize the predicable "Each boy admires ———" as occurring
in premise and conclusion. On the other hand, we have here
made essential use of the way certain propositions admit of more
than one analysis into a predicable and a subject or quasi subject;
in such cases no change of sense goes with the transition from
one analysis to the other.

Let us now consider propositions which on the face of it result
from attaching predicables to "every" phrases. Let us again take as
examples propositions about the polygamous Tom: "Tom married every sister of Bill's" and "Tom always remembers the anniversary of the day when Tom married every sister of Bill's". In
either of these, if we go by our present account of "every"
phrases, "every sister of Bill's" is replaceable *salva veritate* by a
conjunctive list of Bill's sisters, say by "Mary and Jane and Kate".
If we had had "any" instead of "every" in these two propositions,
then to make sure of getting propositions of the same truth-value
we should need to form the conjunctions of the results of replacing "any sister of Bill's" by the several names "Mary", "Jane",
and "Kate". This would conform to our distinction between
"any" and "every". "Tom married every (any) sister of Bill's"
would of course be a degenerate case, in which substituting "any"
for "every" makes no effective difference to the truth-conditions;
but there is a considerable difference if we take "Tom always
remembers the anniversary of the day when Tom married every
sister of Bill's". (In this example, "Tom . . . any sister of Bill's"
would perhaps not be an entirely appropriate expression unless
Tom had other wives whose wedding anniversaries he kept less
solicitously; but this sort of inappropriateness is logically

irrelevant—a logician need no more take account of it than he need consider whether an expression is polite, obscene, striking, or cacophonous.)

These examples thus perfectly fit our previous Russellian account of the difference between "any" and "every"; but in fact we cannot regard our nondegenerate case of an "every" proposition as formed by attaching the predicable "Tom always remembers the anniversary of the day when Tom married ——" to "every sister of Bill's". For here too, if we could recognize an occurrence of this predicable, the *dictum de omni* would admit of exceptions. Even if this predicable were true of each of Tom's wives, i.e. of everybody of whom "Tom married——" was true, we could nevertheless not infer from "Tom married every sister of Bill's" to "Tom always remembers the anniversary of the day when Tom married every sister of Bill's"; for though plurally married to Bill's sisters, Tom need not have married them all on one day.

Given a little ingenuity, I think it could be shown that wherever the Russellian theory seeks to distinguish, and apparently can distinguish, between "f(some A)" and "f(an A)", or again between "f(any A)" and "f(every A)", the occurrence of the predicable "$f($ $)$" in connection with the "a" or "every" phrase is disqualifiable, by the *dictum de omni* test that I have illustrated. Thus at least that part of the theory of modes of reference which relates to "every" and "a" phrases will have proved untenable.

60.   A further problem arises about what we may call *two-place* predicables. We get a two-place predicable by removing the two proper names from a proposition like "Tom loves Mary"; the resulting expression "—— loves . . ." is, as Frege put it, doubly in need of completion, and may be completed into a proposition by inserting in the blanks a pair of referring phrases such as "every boy" and "some girl". Now at first sight the class of propositions formed in this way give excellent support to the theory of referring phrases. Let us simplify the matter by considering a small community in which there are just two boys, Tom and John, and just two girls, Mary and Kate. Let us then work out by our rules— waiving the *dictum de omni* difficulties—the difference between "Some girl is loved by every boy" and "A girl is loved by any

boy". The first, by our rule for "some", corresponds to:

> "(Mary is loved by every boy) or (Kate is loved by every boy)".

And from this, by applying the rule for "every" to the two clauses of the disjunction, we get:

> "(Mary is loved by Tom and John) or (Kate is loved by Tom and John)".

If we had begun by applying the rule for "every" to the original proposition, we should have got: "Some girl is loved by Tom and John", from which, by applying the rule for "some", we should have reached the same final result. Now let us take "A girl is loved by any boy" and apply first the rule for "any"; the result is:

> "(A girl is loved by Tom) and (a girl is loved by John)"

from which, by applying the rule for "a" phrases, we should get:

> "(Mary or Kate is loved by Tom) and (Mary or Kate is loved by John)".

If we had applied the two rules in the reverse order, we should have got in the first place "Mary or Kate is loved by any boy"; this is not quite ordinary language, but if we mechanically apply the rule for "any" we finally get the same result as before.

The Russellian theory thus seems to give a clear and coherent account of the difference between pairs of propositions mutually related like "Some girl is loved by every boy" and "A girl is loved by any boy". The doctrine of distribution is impotent here, as elsewhere; "some girl" and "a girl" would alike be undistributed, "any boy" and "every boy" alike distributed. The distinction was obliterated four centuries ago by the fools who, in devising the doctrine of distribution, cut out from the medieval theory of *suppositio* what they took to be useless subtleties.

It is interesting to observe that one case of this distinction corresponds very closely to an example given independently by Walter Burleigh[4] and by Russell,[5] namely the distinction between the two propositions:

[4]Burleigh, p. 37.
[5]Russell, sec. 60.

Shipwreck of a Theory

An instant of time precedes any instant of time

and

Some instant of time precedes every instant of time.

If we construe the second proposition one way, it is self-contradictory, since it would imply that we can specify an instant that precedes every instant including itself; and if we take "every instant" to mean "every other instant", then the second proposition is almost the exact opposite of the first, since it would then be to the effect that there is a first instant of time, whereas according to the first proposition there is no first instant without a predecessor. In either event the two propositions are wholly different.

61.   Let us now, however, see how our rules apply to a case like "Any boy loves some girl". If we first apply the rule for "any" phrases, we get (assuming as before our miniature community):

John loves some girl and Tom loves some girl

from which again we get, applying the rule for "some" phrases to the two conjuncts:

(1) (John loves Mary or John loves Kate) and (Tom loves Mary or Tom loves Kate).

If on the other hand we first apply the rule about "some", we get:

Any boy loves Mary or any boy loves Kate

from which again we get, applying the rule about "any" to the two alternative clauses:

(2) (John loves Mary and Tom loves Mary) or (John loves Kate and Tom loves Kate).

It is obvious that (1) and (2) are not logically equivalent: if John loves Mary but not Kate, and Tom loves Kate but not Mary, then (1) is true and (2) is false. So, although our rules for "some" and "any" phrases do not raise the same difficulties as "every" and "a" phrases do—we have no puzzles as to interpreting conjunctions and disjunctions of proper names, nor as to the *dictum de omni*—a serious difficulty does arise as soon as we insert one phrase of each sort in the blanks of a two-place predicable

"$f($——$, \ldots)$". (I owe to Strawson this elegant proof that inserting one phrase of each sort always, not just for some instances, generates a difficulty for the theory of *suppositio*.)

62.   Both medieval logicians and Russell seem to have divined this difficulty. One way of evading it would be to forbid the awkward class of propositions by a suitable set of formation rules. This, in effect, was what the medievals did: they ruled that any predicable whose (quasi) subject had distributive *suppositio* might itself contain only a term with confused *suppositio*, not one with determinate *suppositio*.[6] This is tantamount to this formation rule: *In a context formed by filling up one blank in a two-place predicable with an "any" phrase—a context of the type "f(any A, . . .)"—the remaining blank may not be filled up with a "some" phrase, though it may be filled up with an "a" phrase.* They would for example have ruled that in "Any boy loves some girl", "some girl" must be read as an instance of confused *suppositio*—i.e., on Russell's convention it ought to be "a girl". Of course if we go down to the particular cases that come under "Any boy loves some girl", we get "John loves some girl and Tom loves some girl"; and in each conjunct "some girl" has determinate *suppositio*; but to infer from this that "some girl" has determinate *suppositio* in the original proposition is, for medieval logicians, to commit the fallacious transition 'from many determinates to one' (*a pluribus determinatis ad unum determinatum*).[7]

This restrictive formation rule would, of course, require another: *In a context formed by filling up one blank in a two-place predicable with a "some" phrase—a context of the form "f(*——*, some B)"—the remaining blank may not be filled up with an "any" phrase, though it may be filled up with an "every" phrase.* This is just the other side of the first rule; but nothing like this comes into ordinary medieval logic, because few medieval logicians made a distinction of kinds of *suppositio* corresponding to Russell's distinction between "any" and "every" phrases.

[6]Ockham, c. 73.
[7]Burleigh, c. 5; Kretzmann (1), p. 118.

Shipwreck of a Theory

Russell, as I observed in the last chapter, allowed propositions containing both a "some" and an "any" phrase, and had a tacit rule for construing them: in working out their import, the rule for "some" phrases was always to be applied before the rule for "any" phrases. I gave some instances of this in the last chapter. Another example: what Russell gives us in contrast to "A moment precedes any moment" is not "Some moment precedes every moment", but "Some moment does not follow any moment";[8] he is plainly reading this as saying of some specifiable moment that it does not follow any moment; and this corresponds to reading "Any boy loves some girl" as saying of some specifiable girl that *any* boy loves her—i.e., it corresponds to the reading (2) above, obtained by applying the rule for "some" before the rule for "any".

63. These rules of formation or interpretation need only be clearly formulated to make it obvious how artificial and awkward they are. Moreover, the sort of rule that was tacitly used by Russell cannot even be formulated for a proposition that results from filling up the blanks of a two-place predicable with two phrases of the same sort. We might well think that for such a proposition no trouble could arise; and indeed there is no trouble if we apply our rule for "any" phrases, or for "some" phrases, twice over to "f(any A, any B)", or to "f(some A, some B)". But what about propositions of the form "f(most As, most Bs)"? A rule of the medieval type, forbidding us to frame such a proposition, would be ridiculously arbitrary; and a rule of the Russellian type, telling us which sort of phrase to deal with first, cannot even be formulated for cases like this. Yet here we can easily show that two equally justifiable readings of the proposition exist.

Let us suppose that a, b, c, d, and e are electors to certain university posts. The rules for the election provide that at the first ballot each elector may vote for at most three candidates. As it happens, there are five candidates, u, v, w, x, and y; and the voting at the first ballot goes in as Table 1 (see following page). A medieval logician might take this as the *casus*, situation, in

[8]Russell, sec. 60.

Table 1

	u	v	w	x	y
a	×	−	×	−	−
b	−	×	×	−	−
c	×	−	×	×	−
d	−	−	×	×	×
e	−	×	−	×	×

which we have to determine the truth or falsity of this puzzling proposition (*sophisma*): "Most of the electors voted at the first ballot for most of the candidates". The *probatio*, or proof that the *sophisma* is true, would run thus: Most of the electors, in fact three out of five (*c*, *d*, and *e*), voted for three (out of five), i.e. for most, of the candidates. The *improbatio*, or proof that the *sophisma* is false, would run thus: Only for two out of five candidates (in fact, for *w* and *x*) did three or more electors out of five give their vote at the first ballot; so for most of the candidates most of the electors did not vote; i.e., the *sophisma* is false.

"What of it? Ordinary language just is ambiguous and has no such precise logic as you are perversely looking for." Well, I do not think we need resign ourselves to drawing impressionistic pictures of an irregular landscape; let us first see what a little triangulation of the terrain will effect in the way of map making.

64. We might after all very naturally say: There are two ways of taking this *sophisma*: either as saying of most electors that they voted at the first ballot for most candidates, or as saying of most candidates that at the first ballot most electors voted for them. The truth-condition will be, in the first case, that the predicable "—— voted at the first ballot for most of the candidates" shall be true of each one out of a majority of the electors; in the second case, that the predicable "Most of the electors voted at the first ballot for ——" shall be true of each one out of a majority of the candidates. As regards the proposition "All of the electors voted for all of the candidates", there is similarly a notional distinction between two truth-conditions: that "—— voted at the first ballot for all of the candidates" shall be true of each one of the electors,

and on the other hand that "All of the electors voted at the first ballot for ——" shall be true of each one of the candidates; but here the distinction is purely notional, and in fact does not affect the force of the proposition. Our *sophisma*, on the other hand, is really not one proposition but two, and in the *casus* imagined the two would have different truth-values.

The distinction made here is readily generalized. Suppose we are to form a proposition by putting the referring phrases "$*A$" and "$†B$" into the first and second blanks respectively of the two-place predicable "$f(——, \ldots)$": then we shall not in general get a single unambiguous proposition "$f(*A, †B)$". The proposition obtained by first inserting "$*A$" into the first blank so as to get the one-place predicable "$f(*A, \ldots)$", and then inserting "$†B$" into the remaining blank, will in general be quite different from the one obtained by first inserting "$†B$" into the second blank so as to get the one-place predicable "$f(——, †B)$", and then inserting "$*A$" into the remaining blank. (Even when the symbols "$*$" and "$†$" both stand in for one and the same unambiguous applicative, there may be two propositions distinguishable in the way just stated—as we saw in the last paragraph, concerning "most".) And if there are two such distinct propositions, then we must hold that the one-place predicable "$f(*A, \ldots)$" simply does not occur in the proposition formed by attaching the one-place predicable "$f(——, †B)$" to the quasi subject "$*A$".

With this apparatus at our command, we can explain the difference between "Some girl is loved by every boy" and "A girl is loved by any boy" without recourse to the distinctions between "some" and "a", or between "any" and "every". For there is a vast difference between saying of some girl that she is loved by every boy, and saying of every boy that some girl is loved by him: we might express this by parentheses, writing "Some girl (is loved by every boy)" for the first and "(Some girl is loved by) every boy" for the second. In either case, the words within parentheses form a predicable, which does not occur at all in the other proposition; this predicable is attached to a referring phrase as a quasi subject. And my use of "every" rather than "any" in this example is a mere concession to idiom.

Reference and Generality

It may here be asked: Can our rules for "some" and "any" phrases be applied to occurrences of these phrases imprisoned within such parentheses? By those rules, "*f*(some girl)" would be true, in regard to our miniature community, iff "*f*(Mary) or *f*(Kate)" were true; but by what we have just said, "(Some girl is loved by) every boy" is not of the form "*f*(some girl)"—to treat it so it would amount to wrongly seeing in this proposition an occurrence of the predicable "—— is loved by every boy".

The solution, however, is easy. Let us say that the one-place predicable "*f*(some girl, . . .)" is true *of* any given thing iff the disjunction of one-place predicables "*f*(Mary, . . .) or *f*(Kate, . . .)" is true *of* that same thing; e.g., "Some girl is loved by . . ." would be true of any given individual iff "Mary is loved by . . . or Kate is loved by . . ." were true of him. Similarly, the use of an "any" phrase within a one-place predicable would be subject to a rule that that predicable is true *of* anything iff a certain conjunction of one-place predicables is true *of* that same thing. This natural extension of our theory of truth-conditions from propositions, which are merely true or false, to predicables, which are true or false *of* individuals, is I think sufficient to remove the difficulty as raised; we shall have to reconsider the whole theory, however, at a later stage.

At this point the analogy we drew earlier between propositional and chemical structure breaks down. If in a complex molecule we can replace a sodium atom by an ammonium radical and a chlorine atom by a cyanide radical, then, so long as the rest of the chemical bonds are undisturbed, it will not matter which substitution is made first—we shall get the same molecular structure either way. But when we pass from "Kate / is loved by / Tom" to "Some girl / is loved by / every boy", it does make a difference whether we first replace "Kate" by "some girl" (so as to get the predicable "Some girl is loved by ——" into the proposition) and then replace "Tom" by "every boy", or rather first replace "Tom" by "every boy" (so as to get the predicable "—— is loved by every boy" into the proposition) and then replace "Kate" by "some girl". Two propositions that are reached from the same starting point by the same set of logical procedures (e.g. substitutions) may nevertheless differ in import because these procedures are taken to occur in a different order. This principle has application to other procedures than the insertion of referring phrases.

65.   It is tantalizing to see how a great medieval logician had this solution between his finger tips only to let it drop. William of Sherwood remarks that the proposition "Every man sees every man" may be viewed in two different ways, according as we take the first or the second "every man" to have got into the proposition first, the other one 'arriving later' and 'finding the first already there'. This metaphor of phrases' racing to get into propositions expressed the same thought as my speaking of an order of procedures; the phrase that got in first was the one used to make the predication concerning every man—that he sees every man, or that every man sees him, as the case may be. To use my way of writing: In "Every man (sees every man)", the second "every man" is taken to have got into the proposition first (so as to form the predicable "—— sees every man"); and the other way round for "(Every man sees) every man".[9]

In this case, there is, as William himself observes, no difference made to the force of the proposition by taking it in one way or the other, *sive sic sive sic*. But in another example this does make a difference: viz., "Every man sees every donkey except Brownie". William and his contemporaries had a curious interest in such 'exceptive' propositions. (It perhaps compensated for not having a treatment of definite descriptions; for "Every A except a_1 is P" is, as they interpreted it, tantamount to "a_1 is the one and only A that is not P".) Now the question is whether we take "every man" or "every donkey except Brownie" to be the phrase that, as William here puts it, embraces (*includit*) the other—which in his language is the same thing as the other's having 'got in first'. If "every donkey except Brownie" embraces "every man", the proposition will be read according to the grouping "(Every man sees) every donkey except Brownie", and will be true iff the predicable "Every man sees ——" is false of Brownie but true of every other donkey, i.e., iff not every man sees Brownie but every man does see every other donkey. If on the other

[9]O'Donnell, p. 53; Kretzmann (2), p. 37.

hand "every man" embraces "every donkey except Brownie", the proposition will be read according to the punctuation "Every man (sees every donkey except Brownie)", and will be true iff it holds good of every man that he does not see Brownie but does see every other donkey. These are clearly different truth-conditions; one implies that not every man sees Brownie, the other that no man does.[10]

William thus fully grasped the difference made by a different order of logical procedures; unhappily, he used the idea only to solve particular *sophismata*, and never got beyond this *ad hoc* use to the formulation of a general principle. His theory of *suppositio* is quite on the usual lines; and he most likely never suspected that the principle he used but did not formulate would make the distinction between confused and determinate *suppositio* entirely superfluous. This illustrates what Peirce called 'the damnable particularity' of medieval logicians—that tendency to develop *ad hoc* solutions, as opposed to general theories, which did so much to make their genius sterile.

66. The difficulties about the *dictum de omni* can now be cleared up. The proposition, for example, "Tom always remembers the anniversary of the day when Tom married every sister of Bill's" is, as we suspected, not analyzable as a predicable attached to a quasi subject "every sister of Bill's"; rather, this referring phrase has its scope confined to the "when" clause; and this clause is replaceable *salva veritate* by "when Tom married Mary and Tom married Jane and Tom married Kate", or for short by "when Tom married Mary and Jane and Kate". On the other hand, the truth-condition of the proposition:

> Tom always remembers the anniversary of the day when Tom married any sister of Bill's

is given by the conjunction of the results of supplying the predicable:

> Tom always remembers the anniversary of the day when Tom married ——

[10]O'Donnell, pp. 62–63; Kretzmann (2), p. 67.

with "Mary", "Jane", and "Kate" as subjects. We can thus analyze this proposition as the result of attaching this predicable to the quasi subject "any sister of Bill's". The difference between the "any" and "every" phrases is simply that the "any" phrase has a larger scope. The obscure notions of a conjunctive list of names, and of different modes of reference, have turned out quite needless for our explanation; we need only the notion of a referring phrase's having a scope, a notion in any case indispensable.

With a little ingenuity, all the examples that gave plausibility to the distinctions between "any" and "every", between "some" and "a", can be explained by differences of punctuation or scope. Thus, we may explain "Jemima is waiting for *some* mouse from that hole" and "Jemima is waiting for *a* mouse from that hole" as being respectively equivalent to two ways of construing the sentence:

> Jemima is waiting till some mouse shall emerge from that hole

namely, according as we take the scope of "some mouse" in this to be the whole of the rest of the sentence or to be restricted to the "till" clause. The first reading would signify that as regards some mouse or other it is the case that Jemima is waiting till *it* shall emerge from that hole: the second, that Jemima is waiting till it shall have happened that some mouse or other emerges from the hole.

Similarly, "The tree in the Quad depends for its continued existence on being perceived by *some* person"—"... by *a* person"—may be construed as respectively equivalent to two different ways of taking the words:

> It is necessary that, if the tree in the Quad continues to exist, the tree in the Quad shall be perceived by some person

namely, according as we take the scope of "some person" to cover the whole of the rest of the sentence or to be confined to the clause "the tree in the Quad shall be perceived by some person". In the first case, it is supposed as regards some person or other that it is necessary for the tree's continued existence that it should be perceived by *him;* in the other case, what is supposed to be necessary for the tree's continued existence is just that it should be perceived by some person or other.

67.   People may wonder at my spending such pains on a clumsy vernacular explanation of what is set forth so perspicuously in the modern notation of quantifiers and bound variables. But before we can be confident of rightly translating propositions from the vernacular to the modern notation and back, we need to grasp the rationale of the notation; and I think my sort of investigation serves to bring out this rationale, by showing what logical requirements the notation had to meet.

Let us see how the quantifier-and-variable notation would show the difference between "Every boy (loves some girl)" and "(Every boy loves) some girl". I shall here use the restricted quantifiers "for any boy x" and "for some girl y". It is commonly held that restricted quantifiers can be got rid of by reducing them to the unrestricted "for any x" and "for some y"; "for any boy x" would become "for any x, if x is a boy, then...", and "for some girl y" would become "for some y, y is a girl and...". I shall use restricted quantifiers without prejudging the legitimacy of this reduction; at the least, they will make our work easier to survey. The predicable "—— loves some girl" will then be represented by "for some girl y, —— loves y"; and "Every boy (loves some girl)" will come out as:

(1) For any boy x, for some girl y, loves y.

The predicable "Every boy loves ——" will on the other hand be represented by "for any boy x, x loves ——"; and "(Every boy loves) some girl" will then come out as:

(2) For some girl y, for any boy x, x loves y.

The order of the quantifiers, which is all that distinguishes (1) and (2), thus corresponds to William of Sherwood's idea of one phrase's getting into a proposition and another's arriving later to find it already there. The typographically first quantifier corresponds, however, to the phrase that gets there second, and vice versa, which shows the importance of knowing the rationale of the notation. The role of the variables "x" and "y", which are 'bound to' the restricted quantifiers, is to show what is shown in the vernacular by the choice of which referring phrase we shall insert into which blank of the two-place predicable "——— loves...."; thus, the difference between (2) and:

(3) For some girl y, for any boy x, y loves x

is the difference between "(Every boy loves) some girl" and "Some girl (loves every boy)". But in both (2) and (3) we first form a one-place predicable by filling up one blank in "——— loves..." with "every boy" or "for any boy x, ... x ..."; and then we fill up the remaining blank with "some girl" or "for some girl y, ... y ...", which is a quasi subject of the one-place predicable.

When I speak of filling up a blank in a two-place predicable with "for any boy x, ... x ..." or "for some girl y, ... y ...", what I mean is that the variable "x" or "y" that is 'bound to' the quantifier shall be inserted in the blank, and then the quantifier shall be prefixed to the result. But this way of drawing a parallel between symbolic and ordinary language requires us to divide up the symbolism in a very unnatural-looking way: e.g., "For some man x, Jim killed x" would divide up not at the comma but into "For some man x, ... x ..." and "Jim killed ———". There is nothing really objectionable about this: but in the next chapter we shall study another way of drawing the parallelism, which is far more natural and gives us important insights into the role of bound variables.

Five

Pronominal Reference:
Relative Pronouns

68.   In this chapter and the next I shall examine certain theories that ascribe reference to pronouns. Some philosophers, following the suggestion of grammar books, have held that, when a pronoun has an antecedent, its role is to carry on the reference of that antecedent; and again, the so-called indefinite pronouns, e.g. "anything" and "something", have been supposed to refer in some way to things in general. I shall try to show that both views are mistaken.

The two sorts of pronoun that I have just mentioned are closely connected with the modern quantifier-notation. The indefinite pronouns would be a natural means of rendering quantifiers into the vernacular—"anything" or "everything" being used for the universal, and "something" for the existential, quantifier; and pronouns with antecedents strictly correspond to the letters used as bound variables.

Let us consider the following formula:

$$(1) \; (x) \, ((y) \, (y \text{ hurts } x \supset x \text{ hurts } y) \supset x \text{ hurts } x)$$

We assume the universe of discourse to consist of persons, so that the indefinite pronoun answering to a universal quantifier will be "anybody" rather than "anything"; thus (1) might be rendered in the vernacular as follows:

(2) If there is anybody who, if there is anybody who hurts him, hurts him in turn: then he hurts himself.

The pieces of (2) and (1) stand in strict mutual correspondence. The two occurrences of the phrase "there is anybody . . ." correspond to the two universal quantifiers "(x)" and "(y)". The four pronouns whose antecedent is the first "anybody"—viz., the first "who", the first "him", "he", and "himself"—correspond to the four occurrences of the variable "x", which are bound to the quantifier "(x)"; and the two pronouns whose antecedent is the second "anybody"—viz. the second "who" and the second "him"—correspond to the two occurrences of the variable "y", which are bound to the quantifier "(y)". (The role of "in turn" is simply to emphasize the changed antecedent of the second "him".)

The quantifiers "(x)" and "(y)" would be said to have different *scopes*—the scope of a quantifier being here indicated by the pair of parentheses whose opening member immediately follows that quantifier. Thus, the scope of "(x)" runs to the end of (1), whereas that of "(y)" does not go beyond "$(y$ hurts $x \supset x$ hurts $y)$". Now this also has something strictly corresponding to it in the logical structure of (2). Just as I said in Chapter Three that in the proposition:

If Jemima can lick any dog, then Jemima can lick any dog

the scope of the first "any dog" is the complex predicable:

If Jemima can lick ——, then Jemima can lick any dog

the proposition being true iff this predicable is true of any (and every) dog; so analogously we may say that the scope of the first "(there is) anybody (who)" in (2) is the complex predicable:

If ——, if there is anybody who hurts him, hurts him in turn: then he hurts himself.

For (2) is true iff this complex predicable is true of anybody (and everybody)—i.e. iff the insertion of a proper name of a person in the blank always yields a true proposition. Thus the scope of the first "anybody" runs right to the end of (2), like the scope of "(x)". And similarly we should say that in:

> James, if (there is) anybody (who) hurts him, hurts him in turn

the scope of "(there is) anybody (who)" runs to the end of the proposition, since the proposition is true iff the complex predicable

> James, if —— hurts him, hurts him in turn

is true of anybody and everybody. Analogously, we should also say that in (2) the scope of the second "(there is) anybody (who)" runs to the end of the clause

> who, if there is anybody who hurts him, hurts him in turn

but does not extend any further than that. This clause corresponds to "$(y) (y$ hurts $x \supset x$ hurts $y)$" in (1). Just as the symbolic expression is not a proposition, since it contains, instead of a name, a variable bound to the quantifier "(x)"; so the corresponding relative clause has "who" instead of a name like "James", and "who" looks back to the first "anybody".

Let us now discuss a class of case mentioned in the last chapter. The difference between:

> (3) For any boy x, for some girl y, x is crazy in regard to y

and:

> (4) For some girl y, for any boy x, x is crazy in regard to y

may be clearly brought out in the vernacular as follows:

> (5) It holds good of any boy that there is some girl in regard to whom he is crazy.

> (6) There is some girl in regard to whom it holds good of any boy that he is crazy.

The pieces of (5) and (6) stand in strict reciprocal correspondence to those of (3) and (4); and in each pair of propositions, as was explained before, we have the same pieces put together in a different way. The phrases "it holds good of any boy that" and "there is some girl" respectively correspond to the restricted quantifiers "for any boy x" and "for some girl y", and the pronouns "he" and "whom" respectively correspond to the bound variables "x" and "y" in "x is crazy in regard to y"; and as before, a variable's being bound to a quantifier is what corresponds to a pronoun's having an antecedent.

In symbolic logic we get bound variables, not only with quantifiers, but also, for example, in the notation for classes and in definite descriptions. Here also we have in the vernacular a strictly corresponding use of pronouns with antecedents. For example, the symbolic expressions "$\hat{n}(n^2 > 2n)$" and "$(\imath n)(n > 0 \cdot n^2 = 2n)$" respectively become in the vernacular "the (class of) numbers whose square is greater than their double" and "the number that is greater than zero and whose square equals its double"; and here the pronouns "whose", "their", "that", "its", whose antecedent is "the number(s)", correspond to the bound variable "n".

This important relation between pronouns in the vernacular and variables was well understood by Frege, who applied to both sorts of sign the description "indefinite indicator" (*"unbestimmt andeutend"*). (Frege disliked the term "variable" because of the muddles historically associated with it.) More recently, Quine has repeatedly drawn attention to the matter, and has rightly been unmoved by criticisms, which are based on mere misconception; it is very desirable that young students of symbolic logic should grasp this relationship between pronouns in the vernacular and variables.

For the philosophical theory of reference, then, it is all one whether we consider bound variables or pronouns of the vernacular. I shall attend to the latter; my aim is not to explore the labyrinth of idiom, but to bring out some logically important features of the use of pronouns, and consequently of variables too, which a familiarity with symbolic manipulations may make people overlook.

69.   Among the pronouns that have grammatical antecedents, relative pronouns are conspicuous; but not all such pronouns are

relative pronouns, and those of them that are relative pronouns have nothing logically special about them—at least as regards their relation to their antecedents. In our previous example, "the numbers whose square is greater than their double", the pronouns "whose" and "their" have exactly the same relation to their antecedent "the numbers"; just as the two bound variables in the parentheses in "$\hat{n}(n^2 > 2n)$" have exactly the same logical relation to "$\hat{n}$". I shall therefore do as the medieval logicians did, and break Priscian's head by calling any pronoun with an antecedent a relative pronoun; the narrower sense of "relative pronoun" may be distinguished, when necessary, by prefixing the adverb "grammatically".

We must recognize, however, that a pronoun's being grammatically relative does sometimes make a certain difference to its logical role. Compare the obviously equivalent propositions:

(7) Any gentleman who is so grossly insulted must send a challenge.

(8) Any gentleman, if he is so grossly insulted, must send a challenge.

It is clear that "who" and "he" bear the same relation to the antecedent "any gentleman"; but "he" cannot simply take the place of "who"—"who" is a portmanteau word into which were packed up the pure relative pronoun "he" and the connective "if". In other instances there may be a different conjunction latent with a grammatically relative pronoun. Thus, in the proposition:

(9) The Old Guard was now brought up against the enemy position by Napoleon himself, who was forty years old that very day

"who" is replaceable by "and he"; had the clause run "who realized the danger to his right flank", "who" would be replaceable rather by "because he". It remains true, however, that there is no special relation that a pronoun bears to its antecedent merely in virtue of being grammatically relative; what does specially characterize a grammatically relative pronoun in these examples is that it is replaceable by a combination of a pronoun and a connective, but there is nothing special about it strictly qua pronoun.

70. It may well appear, however, as though there were a different relation of pronoun to antecedent in a *defining* and in a *qualifying* relative clause. This difference, which is grammatically very well marked in English, certainly does correspond to a logical difference, in most instances; because it is not so well marked in Latin, medieval logicians had to be at some pains to expose this source of equivocation. Thus the proposition:

(10) Just one man, who has recently died a pauper, broke the bank at Monte Carlo

becomes quite a different proposition if we omit the commas around the relative clause. Their presence shows that the clause is a *qualifying* one; their absence would show that it was a *defining* one. In (10) as it stands we might replace "who" by "and he"; we plainly could not do the like to (10) with the commas omitted.

An explanation of the difference that suggests itself is that a defining relative clause goes along with its antecedent to form a complex general term; e.g., we may substitute the complex general term "man who has recently died a pauper" for "A" in the schema "Just one A broke the bank at Monte Carlo". It may well seem that in this formation of a complex general term 'by restriction' (to use the terminology of Chapter Three) we have a quite special relation of pronoun to antecedent; though even so not only grammatically relative pronouns would stand in the relation, because in the complex general term (say) "man whom any woman affectionately remembers if he has made love to her", the pronouns "whom" and "he" relate to the same antecedent in the same way.

We may seem to have here quite a good working explanation of the difference between defining and qualifying relative clauses. It is a point in favor of this explanation that it can deal with cases where the same relative clause may indifferently be taken as a defining or as a qualifying one. For example, inserting commas around the relative clause in:

(11) A Manchester man who has recently died a pauper broke
     the bank at Monte Carlo

makes no difference to the import of the proposition; and this fact
is quite in accord with the explanation. For, on the one hand, in
(11) we may replace the relative clause by "— and he has
recently died a pauper —", just as we could in (10); this
suggests that (11) like (10) contains a qualifying relative clause.
On the other hand, (11) is equally the result of substituting the
complex general term "Manchester man who has recently died a
pauper" for "*B*" in the schema "A *B* broke the bank at Monte
Carlo"; and this was our criterion for the defining relative clause.

71.   What, then, is the logical structure of a phrase "*A* that is *P*"
formed from a substantival term "*A*" and a predicable "——— is
P"? On the face of it, this structure is logically posterior to the
predicational structure "*A* is *P*", and must be analyzed in terms
of it. Lewis Carroll admittedly had odd Bradleian doubts as to the
intelligibility of such a predication, e.g. of "Pigs are pink" (how
can a thing, like a pig, *be* an attribute, like pink?); he sought to
resolve his doubts by a rule of construction: "The Substantive
shall be supposed to be repeated at the end of the sentence", e.g.,
"Pigs are pink pigs".[1] But "pink pigs" means "pigs that are pink";
and this depends for its intelligibility on "Pigs are pink", not vice
versa.

We may thus expect that the analysis of a proposition containing the complex term "pink pigs" should contain the predication
"... pigs are pink". But need such analysis contain a part that
can be picked out and identified as the analysis of the phrase
"pink pigs"? I do not see that this is necessary. Suppose we
analyze "Some pink pigs squeal" as "Some pigs are pink and the
same pigs squeal". This analysis does contain the predication
"... pigs are pink", but no part of it can be picked out as the
analysis of the phrase "pink pigs". If we deleted from the analyzed
proposition the words "some" and "squeal", the remaining words
would not form a logical unit at all; and this may rouse our
suspicion as to whether we should recognize complex terms, like
"pink pigs" or "pigs that are pink", as genuine logical units.

[1] Lewis Carroll, *The Game of Logic* (London: Macmillan, 1887), p. 2.

This suspicion may be confirmed if we look at examples (7) and (8) above. Whereas in (7) "gentleman *who* is so grossly insulted" looks like a logical unit, the string of words in (8) "gentleman, *if he* is so grossly insulted" has no such look at all. Nor need we rely on mere intuition at this point; to take such a string of words as forming a complex term that can be substituted for "A" in "any A" demonstrably leads to paralogisms, of medieval vintage. "Only an animal can bray; *ergo*, Socrates is an animal, if he can bray. But any animal, if he can bray, is a donkey. *Ergo*, Socrates is a donkey". Thus we clearly cannot take "animal, if he can bray" as a complex term that is a legitimate reading of "A" in "Socrates is an A; any A is a donkey; *ergo* Socrates is a donkey." Of course "(—— is an) animal, if he can bray" is a perfectly good unambiguous predicable; but there is not in the other premise a corresponding use of "animal, if he can bray" as part of an "any" phrase that is a quasi subject.

72.   We could of course validly draw the conclusion "Socrates is a donkey" from the premises "Socrates is an animal *and he* can bray" and "Any animal, *if he* can bray, is a donkey"; and these are respectively equivalent to "Socrates is an animal that can bray" and "Any animal that can bray is a donkey". This suggests that the phrase "animal that can bray" is a systematically ambiguous one, so that we must divine from the context which connective is packed up along with "he" into the portmanteau word "that". But we cannot count this as proved, because there is a risk of the canceling-out fallacy. If in some proposition the phrase "animal that can bray" is replaceable by "animal, if he can bray" without changing the total force of the proposition, it does not follow that the one phrase is really an expansion of the other; so if in another proposition "animal that can bray" is replaceable by "animal, and he can bray", it likewise cannot be safely inferred that "animal that can bray" is ambiguous.

We may, however, confirm the suggestion of ambiguity by considering another sort of medieval example. In the pair of propositions:

(12) Any man who owns a donkey beats it

(13) Some man who owns a donkey does not beat it

"man who owns a donkey" has all the look of being a complex term, replaceable by the single word "donkey-owner"; yet if we do make this replacement, (12) and (13) become unintelligible. It may seem as though this happened only because "it" is deprived of an antecedent. Perhaps "—— beats it" and "—— does not beat it" get a special sense in their respective contexts because "it" is looking back to "a donkey"; if so, we might overcome the difficulty by rewording (12) and (13) so as to supply this sense without having a pronoun that refers back to part of the term "man who owns a donkey".

A plausible rewording would run as follows:

(14) Any man who owns a donkey owns a donkey and beats it.

(15) Some man who owns a donkey owns a donkey and does not beat it.

It looks as though the context would supply the same special sense for "—— beats it" and "—— does not beat it" as it did in (12) and (13), because of the reference back from "it" to "a donkey"; and accordingly the transitions from (12) to (14) and from (13) to (15) are on the face of it instances of the valid patterns of inference:

(16) Any A that is P is Q; *ergo*, any A that is P is P and Q.

(17) Some A that is P is R; *ergo*, some A that is P is P and R.

And in (14) and (15) we should no longer have any difficulty over replacing "man who owns a donkey" by "donkey-owner". Incidentally, both (16) and (17) are obviously convertible inference-patterns; so it looks as though (12) and (14), (13) and (15), were equivalent pairs.

It may look like that, but it is not so. Whereas (12) and (13) are contradictories, their supposed equivalents (14) and (15) are not; for both would be true if each donkey-owner had two donkeys and beat only one of them. Medieval logicians would apparently have accepted the alleged equivalences; for they argued that a pair such as (12) and (13) could both be true (viz. in the case in which we have seen that (14) and (15) would in fact both be true) and were therefore not contradictories. But plainly (12) and (13), as they would normally be understood, are in fact contradictories; in the case supposed, (13) would be true and (12) false.

We might have another shot at rewording (12) and (13) so as to keep "man who owns a donkey" as a term; we should have to try to get them into the form "Any *A* is *P*—Some *A* is not *P*", with "*A*" read as "man who owns a donkey" or "donkey-owner", and "(—— is) *P*" conveying the sense that the context is supposed to give to "—— beats it". But I think this would be waste of effort; for we can surely see that the right rewording is got by our old dodge of splitting up a grammatically relative pronoun:

(18) Any man, if he owns a donkey, beats it.

(19) Some man owns a donkey and he does not beat it.

This rendering is quite unforced, and does give us a pair of contradictories, as it ought; but now the ostensible complex term has upon analysis quite disappeared.

I maintain, then, that the complex term "*A* that is *P*" is a sort of logical mirage. The structure of a proposition in which such a complex term appears to occur can be clearly seen only when we have replaced the grammatically relative pronoun by a connective followed by a pronoun; when this is done, the apparent unity of the phrase disappears; moreover, the context alone can determine which connective (e.g. whether "if" or "and") has to be introduced into the analysis. "Only an *A* that is *P* is *Q*" is an interesting case; here, the connective required in expounding the pronoun "that" is "only if"—"an(y) *A* is *Q* only if it is *P*". Sometimes, though, a proposition of this form is a portmanteau proposition, into which is packed up the further implication "Only an *A* is *Q*".

73.   In the rather stilted English that logic books use, the grammatically relative pronoun that stands at the beginning of a defining relative clause is very often replaced by "such that" followed by the appropriate inflection of "he, she, it, they"; e.g., "a number that is greater than zero and whose square is greater than its double" would be replaced by "a number such that it is greater than zero and its square is greater than its double". To have used this locution would have saved me the trouble of

dealing with two sorts of relative pronouns—those that are, and those that are not, grammatically relative; my reluctance to resort to this was on account of the scruples others have felt about "such that". Russell, when he regarded "such that" as an indispensable logical constant, had nothing better to say about its role than that it was *sui generis*.[2] And some Oxford philosophers have argued that "such that" raises problems not raised by the familiar relative pronouns: "such that" means something like "of a nature having the consequence that", and use of the phrase would thus always raise the problems what the 'nature' in question is and how the 'consequence' follows from it.

We need not treat these Oxonian scruples with much respect. They seem to be based on the etymology of "such that", and on vague memories that in Latin the "that" clause following "such" would be what is called a consecutive clause, a clause of consequence. People who write letters to the papers may appeal to the etymology of an expression as showing its 'correct' meaning; philosophers need not. For logical purposes, "such that" is best treated, regardless of its etymology, as one single word. It is a rare, and would often be a clumsy, construction in English to form a relative clause with an invariable prefatory word followed by one or more (logically) relative pronouns; but this construction is the regular Hebrew idiom, the analogue of "such that" being "*asher*"; e.g., "man whose brother I killed" would be "man *asher* I killed his brother".

What then is the logical role of "such that" or "*asher*"? If we accept the view that a defining relative clause shows its logical character clearly only when we have replaced the grammatically relative pronoun by a connective followed by a pronoun—the context determining which connective is needed—then "such that" or "*asher*" is an all-purpose connective, a sort of universal joint, which goes proxy for whichever connective—"and", "if", "only if", etc.—may be required by the context. No wonder Russell was puzzled when he tried to find a fixed sense for "such that".

[2]Russell, secs. 1, 23, 33, 80.

Relative Pronouns

74.   At this point a reader may protest that my theory is inconsistent with the definitions that can be given for general terms. Surely "rhombus" can be defined as "parallelogram that has equal sides", or in some such way; yet on my theory the two expressions cannot have the same sense, for "parallelogram that has equal sides" has not even syntactical coherence and moreover must be expounded differently in different contexts. "Any parallelogram that has equal sides is a rhombus" comes out as "Any parallelogram, *if it* has equal sides, is a rhombus"; but "*Only* a parallelogram *that* has equal sides is a rhombus" comes out as the conjunction of "*Only* a parallelogram is a rhombus" with "*Only if it* has equal sides is a (sc. any) parallelogram a rhombus" (see the end of section 72); and "Any rhombus is a parallelogram that has equal sides" comes out as "Any rhombus is a parallelogram *and (it)* has equal sides".

The first reply to this natural objection is to distinguish kinds of definition. A definition may be conceived as a rule for expanding a shorter expression, the *definiendum*, into a longer expression, the *definiens*; as we saw over the nonreplaceability of "man who owns a donkey" by "donkey-owner" in (12) and (13), this sort of definition does not give the actual linkage between a common name "*A'*" and an "*A* that is *P*" phrase in ordinary language. Of course there could be a rule in some artificial modification of English that e.g. "donkey-owner" and "man who owns a donkey" are always interchangeable *salva congruitate*, without any further consequential changes in the sentences concerned; but no such rule obtains in English as we have it, and the abbreviative style of definition is quite unsuitable to show how a name "*A'*" and a phrase "*A* that is *P*" are related.

We ought rather to hold that e.g. "rhombus" and "parallelogram that has equal sides" are related by an explanatory definition, a proposition in which the two expressions occur not in quotes: something of this style:

> Any rhombus is a parallelogram that has equal sides, and any parallelogram that has equal sides is a rhombus.

Or again:

Any rhombus, and only a rhombus, is a parallelogram
with equal sides.

We have already seen how to paraphrase away the "A that is P"
phrase in these contexts; the use of such explanations does not
commit us to the view that "rhombus" is synonymous with any
such phrase.

The exact form of explanatory proposition that will be needed
depends on solutions for logical problems that we have not yet
attacked, in particular upon our view of the relations between the
common name "A", the predicable "——— is an A", and the
relational expression "the same A as". We shall revert to these
matters in Chapter Seven. But there is no reason to doubt that we
could supply explanatory propositions whose use as extra premises would logically justify the replacement of "rhombus" by
"parallelogram that has equal sides", or vice versa, in all cases
where this is logically legitimate.

Frege's view on the definability of proper names is of some
interest in this connection. On the one hand, he insisted that the
definiendum must be simple, and that for a sign like "2" we must
supply one elucidation, not a number of elucidations of its use in
different contexts; on the other hand, he regarded a simple proper
name as short for a complex sign (which also would be for him an
Eigenname, i.e. a proper name). Now there is no reason at all
why an abbreviation should be syntactically simple; and if several
abbreviations all contain the mark "2", there need not be one
single rule for expanding them into an unabbreviated form
(though no doubt it is neater, more elegant, to have a single rule);
all that is logically requisite for an abbreviation is that one shall
be able to construct the unabbreviated expression from it in a
unique way. On the view I have been advocating, "2" must be
syntactically simple if it is a name, and a name must be introduced once for all by an elucidation that warrants our using it in
all available contexts; and so far this agrees with what Frege says;
on the other hand, no name can on this view be an abbreviation
for anything. We should observe here that the definitional equa-
tion by which Frege introduces a simple *Eigenname* always has
the role of a substantive proposition in which the name is used for

the first time. Frege makes no such distinction as we find in *Principia Mathematica* between "=" and "=Df"; on the contrary, he says that the sign of equality, just because it is used in all definitions, cannot itself be defined.[3]

The importance of our result is only philosophical; nothing has been established as to what terms may be introduced 'by definition', but only as to how the 'definition' of a term should be regarded. Still, the result has quite considerable importance for philosophy. For Wittgenstein was surely right in saying that a name cannot be dissected by a definition.[4] A name relates directly to what it names; a complex sign cannot bear a direct relation to the thing signified—the relation must be mediated by the constituent signs of the complex. So a name, as Aristotle already said, must have no parts that signify separately;[5] and equally, a name cannot be an abbreviation for a complex expression, for then also it would be related to the thing signified only via the signs in the complex expression.[6] We have independently established that in using a phrase "A that is P" to elucidate a term "A'", we are not introducing the term as an abbreviation for the phrase; so such an elucidation does not disqualify "A'" as a name. The elucidation has in fact the form of a proposition in which "A'" is used.[7] If we have other reason to treat substantival general terms as names, we now see that their 'definability' in no way counts against this.

75.   In the rest of this chapter it will be unnecessary to give special consideration to grammatically relative pronouns, whether they occur in defining or in qualifying clauses; it is always easy to get rid of them by a small verbal change. This means, in particular, that no special importance attaches to definite descriptions of the form "the (one and only) A that is P". We can always turn a proposition ostensibly of the form "f(the A that

---

[3]Frege (3), p. 80.
[4]Wittgenstein, 3.26.
[5]*De interpretatione*, 16a 20–21.
[6]Cf. Wittgenstein, 3.261.
[7]Cf. Wittgenstein, 3.263, where we must remember that for him "name" and "primitive sign" are coextensive.

is *P*)", one where the definite description seems to take the place of a proper name, into the form "just one A is *P*, and *f*(that same A)"—a form which we had occasion to discuss in the last chapter, when expounding the *dictum de omni*. The change of form is great only under the aspect of surface grammar; logically, all that we have done is to expand the portmanteau word "that" into the connective "and" and the relative pronoun "that same". A phrase of the form "A that is *P*" never constitutes a single term, a logical unit; and a phrase of the form "the A that is *P*" likewise cannot constitute one.

Predicative occurrences of definite descriptions are not instances of the schema "*f*(the A that is *P*)". The predicable "——— is *the* A that is *P*" is analyzable as "——— is *an* A that is *P* and only ——— is an A that is *P*". Here "is an A that is *P*" is in turn analyzable as "both is an A and is *P*"; the role of "only" will be discussed in Chapter Seven, section 108.

A proper name can never be an abbreviation for a definite description; though we may of course introduce a proper name as a name for the object described by such a description. A natural way of effecting such an introduction would be to enunciate a proposition with the proper name as subject and the definite description as predicate: "Neptune is the planet of the Solar System next out from Uranus." If we have no other way of identifying the object named than is supplied by the definite description, it may be natural to think of the proper name as short for the description; but this would be wrong.

Even if a substantival term "A'" can be satisfactorily linked to a phrase "A that is *P*" by the sort of explanatory or elucidatory proposition that we have considered, we are still left with the problem how to explain applicatival phrases "*(A that is *P*)" where "*" is a *dictum de omni* applicative. We seem to understand these phrases straight off, given that we know the applicatives and the way they work with syntactically simple substantival terms; similarly, we seem to understand e.g. "every sister of Bill's" straight off, without needing to connect "sister of Bill's" with some simple common name "A" introduced ad hoc, such that every A, and only an A, will be a sister of Bill's. And it appears awkward also that the connection of "*f*(every A that is *P*)" with

"f(every A$'$)" works out differently from that of "f(some A that is P)" with "f(some A$'$)", as I have argued it does; nor is it at all apparent how on similar lines we could deal with the prefixing of "most" or "almost every" to an "A that is P" phrase, since "Almost every A that is P is Q" is not equivalent either to "Almost every A, if P, is Q" or to "Almost every A is P and Q". The intuitive objections are to my mind unimportant; intuitions as to which bits of a sentence go together to form a unified expression are often demonstrably wrong, as we have seen. The difficulty about our not having a uniform account of the way each of the *dictum de omni* applicatives goes with an "A that is P" phrase is one that we shall see in Chapter Seven not to be insuperable.

76. If defining relative clauses are paraphrased away in the manner here recommended, the resulting proposition will still contain a relative pronoun, in the logical sense of the term. The relative pronoun within a phrase "A that is P" did not look as if it had any referential force of its own; on the contrary, its role seemed to be that of binding the phrase into a unity, and it was this logical unit that seemed to have a reference. But other relative pronouns, including the ones introduced by the sort of paraphrase just mentioned, do appear to have a referential role— that of picking up a reference made elsewhere (*recordatio rei antelatae*, as medieval logicians would say). Can such a role be coherently ascribed to relative pronouns?

Let us begin by noticing that sometimes a pronoun may be eliminated from a proposition, without changing the force of the proposition, by a repetitious expression. When such pronouns have no point beyond variety, perhaps elegance, of expression, they might well be called "pronouns of laziness". Thus, in "His sudden elevation to the peerage was a surprise to Smith", it would apparently be only a stylistic alteration if I wrote "Smith's", or in journalistic fashion "His (Smith's)", instead of "His".

Not all relative pronouns can thus be treated as pronouns of laziness. Consider these two propositions:

(20) Just one man broke the bank at Monte Carlo, and
       he has recently died a pauper.

(21) Smith broke the bank at Monte Carlo, and he has recently died a pauper.

In (21) the pronoun "he" is apparently one of laziness, but "he" in (20) is not replaceable by "just one man" or "a man" without essentially altering the force of the proposition. The reason is not that a pronoun of laziness can go proxy only for a proper name; in the sentence I wrote just now, "In (21)'the pronoun . . . one of laziness", the word "one" is a pronoun of laziness going proxy for "a pronoun". But in (20) it is quite impossible to find any noun or noun-phrase for which "he" goes proxy; "he" is indeed replaceable by "that man", but here again "that" is a relative pronoun, and has the apparent role of referring back to an antecedent, just as "he" had.

When a relative pronoun is not a pronoun of laziness, it is in general quite absurd to treat it as a 'singular referring expression' and ask what it refers to. It is, for example, quite absurd to ask which man is meant or referred to by the pronoun "he" in (20).

Here as elsewhere, we must remember that if a term in a proposition has reference there must be some way to specify this reference regardless of that proposition's truth-value. To be sure, "Smith" has as its reference the man who broke the bank at Monte Carlo iff "Smith is the man who broke the bank at Monte Carlo" is true; but the reference of "Smith" must be specifiable in some other way that does not depend on whether this proposition is true. For "Smith" must already have a reference before the question "Is Smith the man who broke the bank at Monte Carlo?" can be asked; and its reference in this question cannot depend on which answer is right. Similarly, (20) can be turned into a question, simply by enclosing it in the framework "Is it true that . . . ?"; so if "he" in (20) has a reference, this must be somehow specifiable regardless of whether (20) is true or false, so as to be the same whichever answer to the question is right.[8]

Let us suppose for the sake of argument that (20) is indeed, as on the surface it appears to be, a conjunction of two clauses, with "he" as logical subject of the second clause. Signs are arbitrary,

[8]I have rewritten the two following paragraphs in response to a criticism published by Dr. T. Smiley (*Philosophical Books*, October 1963).

and "he" has a lot of work to do in other connections; so for clarity's sake let us stipulate that the result of inserting the term "*a*" in (20) instead of "he" shall have the same sense as (20). If "he" is a referential term in (20), so will "*a*" be in the modified (20), in (20)' let us say; and (20)' will be the result of attaching to "*a*" as subject the predicable:

> Just one man broke the bank at Monte Carlo, and —— has recently died a pauper;

it is of course irrelevant that (20)' admits also of other analyses. If "Just one man broke the bank at Monte Carlo" is false, this predicable will be false *of* any object whatsoever; but it does not follow that (20)' is then false; unless "*a*" has been given a reference, (20)' will not be false but truth-valueless. The predicable "—— cut off Henry VIII's head" is false of everybody; but if a schoolboy in his history essay exhibits a sheer confusion between Oliver and Thomas Cromwell, "Cromwell" in his use is a name without reference; he simply does not know what he is talking about, and "Cromwell cut off Henry VIII's head", as a sentence in his essay, is not false but truth-valueless.

How then can a reference be supplied for "*a*" in this use? If the first half of (20) and (20)' were true, it would be plausible to take "he" in (20), or again "*a*" in (20)', as referring to the one and only man who broke the bank at Monte Carlo. But if that first half is false, this way of specifying reference fails; so unless some other is provided, a way that will work whether the first half is true or false, (20)' will be truth-valueless in the case of the first half's falsehood; but (20), which we stipulated was to share the same sense, is in this case not truth-valueless but false. So it appears that we cannot coherently assign reference to "*a*" in (20)', nor therefore to "he" in (20). (We saw in Chapter One the futility of saying that the reference of a term is somebody the speaker had in mind; so we need not consider any attempt to specify a reference for "he" in that way.) It is simply a prejudice or a blunder to regard such pronouns as needing a reference.

77. The idea of a pronoun's picking up an earlier reference is more plausible as regards a sort of quasi syllogism mentioned by

Reference and Generality

Strawson.[9] Let us consider this dialogue:

> A: A man has just drunk a pint of sulphuric acid.
>
> B: Nobody who drinks a pint of sulphuric acid lives through the day.
>
> A: Very well then, *he* won't live through the day.

It is very tempting to take "he" in A's second remark as picking up the reference of "a man" in A's first remark. We could then describe A's procedure as follows: A accepts a major premise from B, and then, in accordance with the *dictum de omni*, he passes from predicating "—— has just drunk a pint of sulphuric acid" of a certain person to predicating of the same person "—— will not live through the day" (sc. "after his drinking a pint of sulphuric acid"). But let us not forget the arguments deployed in Chapter One against the view that "a man" ever refers to a man (ever conveys, as Strawson puts it, 'a reference to a definite person, indefinitely made'[10]). Even if A is under quite a false impression as to who has drunk sulphuric acid, this in no way affects the truth of what A says or the correctness of A's inference; so it is quite irrelevant whom A has in mind; and there is no other way of getting out of "a man" a reference to a definite person. And if "a man" makes no such reference, "he" cannot pick up any such reference from "a man".

Let us suppose B to be a deaf-mute, so that the exchange above took place on B's writing tablet. In this case it is plain that "He won't live through the day" is not an independent proposition. B had on his writing tablet first of all the shorter proposition "A man has just drunk a pint of sulphuric acid" and then the longer proposition "A man has just drunk a pint of sulphuric acid—he won't live through the day"; the particle "Very well then" expresses A's inference of the longer proposition from the shorter one. The added clause in the longer proposition is a mere fragment of a sentence, not a conjunct in a conjunctive proposition; it has no truth-value, and "he" has here no reference. It makes no

[9]Strawson, p. 194n.
[10]Strawson, p. 187.

logical difference if the dialogue is spoken and not written. Naturally, the earlier part of the longer proposition will then have perished and exist only in the memory of A and B; but this physical peculiarity of the linguistic medium is logically irrelevant. To treat it as relevant would be as silly as the medieval puzzle: How can a spoken proposition be true, since at no time is it all there to be true?

78.   The unexceptionable class of cases where a pronoun does pick up the reference of its antecedent is supplied by pronouns of laziness. Suppose we have two propositions, P_1 and P_2, which differ precisely in that an expression E occurs twice in P_1 but is replaced by a pronoun of laziness at one occurrence in P_2; then the pronoun of laziness in P_2 has precisely the same import as its antecedent E, and thus it has the same reference as E. But if E occurs twice in P_1 and its second occurrence in P_1 is replaced by a pronoun in P_2, and if P_1 and P_2 have as wholes the same import, it does not follow that this pronoun conforms to the definition of "pronoun of laziness". The pronoun in P_2 occurs in the very same context as the second occurrence of E had in P_1; but it is illegitimate to cancel out the identical context and say that the pronoun in P_2 has the same import and reference as E had in P_1. And only such canceling-out warrants us in saying that the pronoun in P_2 must have the same import and reference as its antecedent E. So the mere fact that a pronoun is thus substitutable for its antecedent does not after all warrant us in thinking it picks up the reference of its antecedent; and if it does not pick it up, then the term "pronoun of laziness" is a misnomer, for the pronoun is not a mere elegant variation for its antecedent.

Let us consider an example:

(22) If any man owns a donkey, he beats it.

(23) If Smith owns a donkey, he beats it.

The pronoun "he" is replaceable by "Smith" in (23) without changing the import of the proposition; it is not thus replaceable by "any man" in (22); so it looks as if it were a pronoun of laziness in (23), but not in (22). All the same, (23) predicates of Smith precisely what (22) predicates of any man; both contain the same unambiguous complex predicable "If —— owns a donkey, he beats it", which is incomplete in sense, not as "—— beats it" was in (12) and (13), but only as any one-place predicable is until it is attached to a subject or quasi subject. On the other hand, the proposition:

(24) If Smith owns a donkey, Smith beats it

contains the completely different predicable "If —— owns a donkey, Smith beats it"; when attached to the quasi subject "any man", this gives us the proposition:

(25) If any man owns a donkey, Smith beats it

which is wholly different in force from (22). Thus the wholly different sense of the predicables "If —— owns a donkey he beats it" and "If —— owns a donkey Smith beats it" shows that even in (23) "he" has a definite logical role of its own, and is not a mere pronoun of laziness—not a mere device for avoiding the repetition of "Smith".

79. Having rejected various views of relative pronouns, I shall now try to give a positive account of my own.

Let us consider the predicable "Either —— does not own any donkey or he beats it". (I think this is very much the same as "If —— owns a donkey he beats it"; but I do not wish to raise a stale and barren controversy about "if"—my concern is not with "if" but with the relative pronouns, whose role is obviously the same in both predicables.) We can twist this predicable around so as to get rid of the relative pronouns: "—— either-does-not-own-or-beats any donkey", where the hyphens are meant to exclude the reading: "—— either does not own any donkey or beats any donkey". The hyphenated expression is a two-place predicable, from which we get the one-place predicable by filling up one blank with "any donkey"; and this two-place predicable is in its turn built out of the two two-place predicables "—— owns . . ." and "—— beats . . .", by means of negation and the connective "either —— or ——". It is easy to see how this use of the connectives is related to their use with propositions: If we use

"A", "B", for proper names, "Either A does not own B or A beats B" (or rather: "Either not: A owns B, or: A beats B") will be true iff "A either does not own or beats B" is true. (Compare my remarks in sections 27 and 42 about the use of negation and connectives with one-place predicables.)

What then is the role of the pronouns "he" and "it" in "Either —— does not own any donkey or he beats it"? They are not merely superfluous: they serve to show how the two two-place predicables are fitted into the framework "either not —— or ——". For it is not enough to say that "—— owns . . ." takes the place of "F" and "—— beats . . ." that of "G" in "either not F or G"; this would be enough if we were considering a pair of one-place predicables, but for two-place predicables there is the further question whether the one that takes the place of "G" is fitted in right side up or upside down relatively to the one that takes the place of "F". Consider the difference between "Either —— does not own any donkey or he kicks it" and "Either —— does not own any donkey or it kicks him"; the difference of word order and inflection between the pronoun pairs "he—it" and "it—him" shows that the place of "G" in "either not F or G" is differently filled in the two cases by the two-place predicable "—— kicks . . ."—in the first case it is so to say right side up, in the second case upside down, relative to the predicable "—— owns . . .", which takes the place of "F". Similarly, if we used variable-letters, we should get a significant difference between "$\sim (x$ owns $y)$ ∨ $(x$ kicks $y)$" and "$\sim (x$ owns $y)$ ∨ $(y$ kicks $x)$"—the order of the letters in the formulas, "x, y, x, y" or "x, y, y, x", is significant as the order of the pronouns was.

We might of course use some quite different logical device to the same end; thus, in *Principia* notation there is the logical constant "Cnv", which turns a relative term into its correlative; and the distinction we are discussing would then be shown by the difference between "$(-$ owns$)$ ∪ kicks" and "$(-$ owns$)$ ∪ $($Cnv'kicks$)$"[11] This incidentally shows how confusing and superficial the ordinary jargon about constants and variables is; the

---

[11] In giving the notation from Whitehead and Russell, I omit the superfluous dots that are used to show that negation and disjunction and conjunction operate upon relative terms.

same logical difference may be shown either by a rearrangement of variables or by insertion of a logical constant; so there is not, as the terminology might suggest, a radical distinction between the roles of variables and constants. And when we see the role of "he" and "it" from this side, it hardly seems worth while to consider any further the idea of their repeating a reference previously made; nobody would wish to say that Russell's "Cnv" had any such job of back-reference.

This sort of role even more obviously belongs to the reciprocal pronoun "each other" or "one another". How empty and useless an account it would be of the reciprocal pronoun to say that in "John and Jane love one another", "one another" refers over again to John and Jane! The right account is plainly that "one another" is an operator forming a new, symmetrical, two-place predicable from a two-place predicable; to be precise, "x and y are R to one another" says that x and y are in the symmetrical relation symbolized in *Principia* notation by "$R \cap \text{Cnv}'R$", i. e. that x bears to y at once the relation called "R" and its converse. In "John and Jane love one another", as in "John and Jane disagree about politics", the role of "and" is to show that we have a symmetrical two-place predicable. With a predicable that is already symmetrical, the insertion of the symmetry-generating operator "one another" is redundant; "John and Jane disagree about politics with one another" is not significantly different from "John and Jane disagree about politics".

80. The reflexive pronoun has quite a different role. By inserting the reciprocal pronoun we turn a two-place predicable into a new one; by inserting a reflexive pronoun, we fill up one place in a two- or many-place predicable, just as if we had inserted a referring phase. There is thus special temptations to treat a reflexive pronoun as having reference—in fact, the same reference as its antecedent. But we shall see reason to resist the temptation.

When the antecedent of a reflexive pronoun is a singular term, it might seem obvious that the reflexive pronoun is simply replaceable by its antecedent, and is accordingly a pronoun of laziness. But we saw that little significance can be attached to a pronoun's being replaceable by its antecedent; for that pronoun may nevertheless be or not be a pronoun of laziness—it will depend upon the sense of the predicable containing the pronoun. In this case, we have the same unambiguous predicable "——— contradicts himself" in "Hegel contradicts himself", where "himself" is a pronoun replaceable by its antecedent "Hegel", and in "Every philosopher contradicts himself", where "himself" is certainly not replaceable by its antecedent "every philosopher". Moreover, it is not even true that when the antecedent is a singular term it can always take the place of the reflexive pronoun; "Only Satan pities himself" and "Only Satan pities Satan" are quite different in their import. But it is quite impossible to say whom "himself" should refer to in "Only Satan pities himself" if it does not refer to Satan; so, surely, we must conclude that here at least the reflexive pronoun is not a referring word at all.

81.   In cases where the antecedent of a reflexive pronoun is a referring phrase (in the sense of Chapter Three), I cannot demonstrate in the same way that the reflexive pronoun does not pick up the reference of the antecedent. Obviously we should get into immediate difficulties if we also held that "every man" has the special role of referring to every man; for then we could hardly distinguish between "Every man loves every man" and "Every man loves himself". But we have long since seen reason to reject the doctrine of distribution; and on the medieval doctrine that "every man" and "some man" alike refer to each and every man, though with different modes of reference, it would be natural to say that "himself" in "Every (Any) man loves himself" also refers to every man, with yet another mode of reference. This line of thought was in fact exploited by Walter Burleigh,[12] who ascribed to the reflexive pronoun in such propositions a peculiar mode of reference, falling somehow in between distributive *suppositio* and confused *suppositio*.

Burleigh describes quite clearly the rather complicated interrelations of these three modes of reference. (I shall here use "any" to translate Burleigh's "omnis", rather than the more literal "every"; as I said, most medieval logicians did not make the Russel-

---

[12]Burleigh, pp. 30–31.

lian distinction between "any" and "every", but their account of distributive *suppositio* corresponded to Russell's account of "any".) (i) From "Any man loves any man" there follows "Any man loves himself", and from this again "Any man loves a man". (ii) If "Socrates" is a proper name corresponding to a correct use of "the same man", then of the two propositions "Any man loves Socrates" and "Any man loves himself", neither follows from the other. (iii) If "Socrates" and "Plato" are such proper names, then "Any man loves himself" is true iff the conjunction of all the propositions "Socrates loves Socrates", "Plato loves Plato", and so on, is true; whereas "Any man loves any man" is true iff the conjunction of all such propositions and also of propositions like "Socrates loves Plato" is true.

What Burleigh failed to notice was that, if we accept the doctrine of *suppositio*, yet another mode of reference would have to be recognized for "himself" in "Some man loves himself"—one intermediate between determinate *suppositio* and (what I suggested could be called) conjunctive *suppositio* (corresponding to Russell's "every"). Even if we ignore the distinction between "any" and "every", which Burleigh did not recognize, there would be a new kind of *suppositio* coming somehow in between determinate and distributive *suppositio*. Thus: (i) From "Some man loves every man" there follows "Some man loves himself", and from this again "Some man loves some man". (ii) If "Socrates" is a proper name corresponding to a correct use of "the same man", then of the two propositions "Some man loves Socrates" and "Some man loves himself", neither follows from the other. (iii) If "Socrates" and "Plato" are such proper names, then "Some man loves himself" is true iff the disjunction of all the propositions "Socrates loves Socrates", "Plato loves Plato", and so on, is true; whereas "Some man loves some man" is true iff the disjunction of all these propositions and also of propositions like "Socrates loves Plato" is true. On his own premises, then, Burleigh would have had to recognize here a further kind of *suppositio*. In fact, some of the points made here are to be found in Albert of Saxony's *Perutilis logica* (Venice, 1518), Tractatus 2,c.9 ('De modo supponendi relativorum').

It seems that we might have to recognize even further varieties;

one essential objection to the doctrine of *suppositio* is the way new sorts of *suppositio* keep on turning up—

Cycle and epicycle, orb in orb.

It is worth while to seek a unified explanation of reflexive pronouns, even at the price of abandoning the superficially simple idea that they pick up the reference of their antecedents.

82.   Can the reflexive pronoun in truth be regarded as filling up one blank in a two- or many-place predicable? When each of the blanks in a two-place predicable is filled with a referring phrase, there are two different ways of analyzing the result as a one-place predicable attached to a quasi subject; sometimes there are also two essentially different propositions, sometimes not. If we italicize the words that are to be taken together as forming a one-place predicable, we shall have on the one hand the essentially different propositions "*Any boy loves* some girl" and "Any boy *loves some girl*", and on the other hand the only notionally distinct pair "*Any boy loves* any girl" and "Any boy *loves any girl*". Now there is no such twofold construction of a proposition containing a reflexive pronoun; no proposition can be correspondingly represented as "*Any boy loves* himself", for the proposition "Any boy loves himself" can be construed only as containing the predicable "—— loves himself", not as containing the predicable "Any boy loves ——". Thus a reflexive pronoun does not fill one blank of a two- or many-place predicable in the way that a referring phrase does.

The denial that "Any boy loves ——" can be taken to occur in "Any boy loves himself" need not be supported by a bare appeal to intuition; it can be supported by consideration of the *dictum de omni*, which I used in the last chapter to disqualify certain ostensible occurrences of predicables.

Suppose, for example, that P is a proposition "Any man is R to himself" and Q is a proposition "Any man is S to himself"; and suppose that we have a premise T warranting the inference from "Any man is R to a" to "Any man is S to a", "a" being a proper name arbitrarily chosen. If the pronoun "himself" has referential force, it will have this in both P and Q; moreover, since its reference will be determined by its antecedent, "himself" will have the same reference and the same mode of reference in *P* and in *Q*. Moreover, the predicable "Any man is *S* to ———" occurs in *Q* iff the predicable "Any man is *R* to ———" occurs in *P*. To make matters clearer, let us rewrite "himself" as "that very man", and call the results of thus modifying *P* and *Q* by the names "*P′*" and "*Q′*". *Q* will be inferable from *P* (on the basis of the premise *T*) iff *Q′* is inferable from *P′*; it will depend on whether we can treat "that very man" as a phrase to which our two predicables are attached and for which the *dictum de omni* can be applied. In fact, given the premises *T* and "Any man is *R* to any fool" (say), the *dictum de omni* would warrant our inferring "Any man is *S* to any fool", since this pair of propositions *can* be regarded as the results of attaching our two predicables to "any fool". Is the inference of *Q′* from *P′* and *T* parallel to this?

It is clear that even given the premise, we are not in fact warranted in inferring *Q′* from *P′*, i.e. "Any man is *S* to that very man" from "Any man is *R* to that very man". (For example: Suppose it is the case that if there is anybody of whom it is true that *any* man—however stupid—has at least as much sense as he, then that person is despised by any man whatsoever—including himself. Then there will be no way of reading "*a*" as a name *of* and *for* a man so that "Any man has at least as much sense as *a*" is true and "Any man despises *a*" is not true. But that does not mean that in this case from the truism "Any man has at least as much sense as that very man" we could infer "Any man despises that very man".) This is of course not an exception to the *dictum de omni*, but a proof that the predicables "Any man is *R* to ———", "Any man is *S* to ———", do not occur in *P′* and *Q′*. And so *P* and *Q* cannot be analyzed as the results of attaching these predicables to a referentially used pronoun.

83. I maintain, then, that it is wrong to regard "himself" as turning a two-place into a one-place predicable by filling up one place; rather, a reflexive pronoun fills up both places of the two-place predicable into which it is inserted, but itself has an incompleteness tantamount to there being one empty place—an incompleteness that appears in grammar as the need of the pronoun

for an antecedent. In passing from "—— admires..." to "——
admires himself" we are not just filling up the second blank with
"himself"; the real logical structure is better brought out by this
sort of diagram:

him-   admires   -self
  └——( )——┘

where the place between the parentheses is to be filled with the
antecedent of "himself".

This account can easily be extended to many-place predicables. Consider the three-place predicable that we need to describe a case of blackmail— "——threatens - - - with exposure
to...". The two-place predicable represented in this diagram:

him-   threatens --- with exposure to   -self
  └————————————( )————┘

would express the relation of A to B if A threatened B with
exposure to A himself—which would be possible if A did his
blackmailing in disguise, as in G. K. Chesterton's Father Brown
story "The Head of Caesar." On the other hand, the two-place
predicable represented in this diagram:

—— threatens him-   with exposure to   -self
        └——( )————┘

would express the relation of A to B if A threatened B with
exposure to B himself—which would be possible if, for example,
A knew of some crime of B's that B had forgotten by amnesia, as
in Graham Greene's story *The Ministry of Fear.*

Again, it has been known that a starving prisoner in a dungeon
fed himself on himself. The italicized predicable is a one-place
one, derivable from the three-place predicable "—— fed - - -
on..." by the following steps. First we form the two-place predicable"—— fed himself on...", representable by the diagram:

him-   fed   -self   on . . .
  └——( )——┘

then from this we form the one-place predicable "—— fed himself on himself", representable by the diagram:

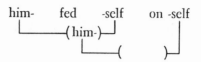

The first "himself", so to speak, hands over its need for an antecedent to the second "himself".

A curious puzzle arises over a previous example of ours. "Only Satan pities Satan" and "Only Satan pities himself" are quite different propositions. Yet we can turn the first proposition, without loss of force, into the form "Satan is pitied only by himself"; and in Irish English, though not in standard English, this could again appear as "Only himself pities Satan". But now there seems to be a difficulty in distinguishing this from "Only Satan pities himself". Surely both could be represented by this diagram:

only him- pities -self
⌐(Satan)⌐

The solution of the puzzle lies in something that our structural formulas cannot be expected to represent adequately—something that, as we have seen before, distinguishes the structure of a proposition from chemical structure. Two propositions that are reached from the same starting point by the same set of logical procedures (e.g. substitutions) may nevertheless differ in import because these procedures are taken to occur in a different order. In the present case we may imagine ourselves starting with the one-place predicable "—— pities Peter", and applying the following logical procedures, in the order in which they are mentioned:

1. Turning a one-place predicable containing the name "Peter" into a two-place predicable by deleting that name. (Result: The two-place predicable "—— pities . . .".)

2. Filling up the two places of a two-place predicable with "himself" so as to get a one-place predicable. (Result: The one-place predicable "—— pities himself".)

3. Operating on a one-place predicable "—— is *P*" to get another one-place predicable, "Only —— is *P*". (Result: The one-place predicable "Only —— pities himself".)

4. Supplying to a one-place predicable the subject "Satan". (Result: The proposition "Only Satan pities himself".)

Suppose we had applied the very same logical procedures to "—— pities Peter", but in the order 3, 1, 2, 4. The application of the procedure 3 to "—— pities Peter" yields the one-place predicable "Only —— pities Peter". From this, by procedure 1, we get the two-place predicable "Only —— pities...", which expresses the relation of A to B when B is not pitied by anyone other than A. From this, by procedure 2, we get the one-place predicable "Only himself pities ——", which is true of a person A iff he bears to himself the relation just mentioned, i.e., iff A is not pitied by anyone other than A. (In this predicable there is no occurrence of the predicable "Himself pities ——", the Irish English for "—— pities himself"; "Only himself pities ——" is not reached from "Himself pities ——" by procedure 3, but formed in quite another way.) Finally, by procedure 4 we got the proposition "Only himself pities Satan".

84. Some readers may think this discussion of complications that arise in the vernacular over the use of reflexive pronouns to be a waste of effort: are not all the complications cleared up automatically by using the notation of quantifiers and bound variables? This objection is superficial. Let us consider the symbolic transcription of "Everybody stands in the relation F to himself"—"For any (person) x, $F(x, x)$". This transcription looks as though it contained occurrences of the one-place predicables "For any x, $F(——, x)$" (i.e., "—— stands in the relation F to everybody") and "For any x, $F(x, ——)$" (i.e. "Everybody stands in the relation F to ——"); each of these predicables is obtained by using "For any x, ... x ..." to fill up one place in one and the same two-place predicable. But this appearance is misleading. Even if neither of our one-place predicables were true of anybody at all—even if there were nobody who bore the relation F or its converse to everybody—even so "For any x, $F(x, x)$" could be true; so this proposition is clearly not in any way a predication of either predicable. Indeed, we cannot coherently describe any logical procedure which, starting with one of these predicables,

would yield the proposition "For any x, $F(x, x)$"—contrast the propositions "For any x, $F(John, x)$" and "For any x, $F(x, John)$". But if both the occurrences of "x" in "$F(x, x)$" are bound to the quantifier "for any x", then each one of them is; and is it not precisely by inserting an "x" bound to "for any x" into one of the empty places in a certain two-place predicable that we obtain an occurrence of the predicable "For any x, $F(x, \text{——})$" or of the predicable "For any x, $F(\text{——}, x)$"?

Frege was well aware of this sort of difficulty. His solution was to deny that a two-place predicable (in his language, *Functionsname*) occurs at all in "For any x, $F(x, x)$"; instead, there is a quite different *one*-place predicable, by attaching which to a name "a" we get the proposition "$F(a,a)$".[13] This solution is clearly insufficient. Of course it is possible to use the letter "F" in writing down either a one-place or a two-place predicable; in that case, although there look to be two argument-places when the one-place predicable is used, as in "$F(a,a)$" or "For any x, $F(x, x)$", the requirement to fill both with equiform signs means that logically the predicable is only one-place. This does not sin against any canon forbidding ambiguous symbolism, for in no context will there be any doubt which sort of predicable, one-place or two-place, the letter "F" is being used to form. The trouble is rather that now it is not clearly shown how this one-place and this two-place predicable are logically connected. On the face of it, the only link is the letter "F" itself, a letter that is being used in two logically different ways; and if for the one-place predicate, with the logically superfluous repetition in the argument-place, we wrote simply "$G(\text{——})$", with no such repetition, then there would no longer be even an appearance of a link.[14]

We can see that there is a puzzle here when once we realize that the repetition of bound variables in "For any x, $F(x, x)$" is essentially different from that in "For any x, Hx and Gx" or again in "For any x, for some y, $F(y, x)$ or $G(x, y)$". As we have already seen, the latter sort of repetitions can be avoided al-

[13]Frege (2), Vol. 1, p. 36.
[14]Cf. Wittgenstein, 3.322, 3.333.

together by joining predicables in a truth-functional way and using the symbol for converse relations: "For any x $(H\&G)x$"; "For any x, for some y, x $(Cnv\,'F \cup G)y$". These devices will not get rid of the repetition in "For any x, $F(x, x)$". We may express self-immolation by calling somebody "priest *and* victim" (assuming these to be correlative terms); but this form of words does not of itself distinguish a self-immolator from

> The priest who slew the slayer
> And shall himself be slain.

What we might well have is a more perspicuous symbolism than "$F(x, x)$" for "x bears the relation F to itself"—a symbolism showing clearly how a one-place predicable is here formed from a two-place one. Let us use the symbol "——; u, v)" for this purpose; this symbol, which may be read (say) as "—— being both u and v", will form a one-place predicable "(——; u, v) $F(u, v)$" from a two-place predicable, "u" and "v" being of course bound variables. And then "For any x, $F(x, x)$" will become "For any x, $(x; u, v)$ $F(u, v)$", in which there are not even apparent occurrences of the predicables "For any x, $F($——, $x)$" and "For any x, $F(x,$ ——$)$". This notation could be easily extended to many-place predicables: thus, instead of "$F(x, y, x)$" we should have:

$$(x; u, v)\ F(u, y, v).$$

It may easily be seen that our new piece of symbolism is a way of transcribing our structural formula illustrating the use of "himself".

Similarly, "$F(z,z,z)$" could be written in the form:

$$(z; y, u, v)\ F(u, y, v)$$

where the prenex operator is to be read as "z being both y and u and v".

Moreover, it is easy to devise a perspicuous way of showing the difference between "Only Satan pities himself" and "Only himself pities Satan". Let us in general symbolize "Only —— is F" by "(only —— w) $F(w)$", where "w" is of course a bound variable; the notation may be read "Only —— is a w for which Fw".

Reference and Generality

Then the formula:

(Satan; *w*, *v*) (only *w u*) (*u* pities *v*)

would say that Satan stood to himself in the relation of *w* to *v* symbolized by "(only *w u*) (*u* pities *v*)", i.e. the relation between *w* and *v* when nobody other than *w* pities *v*. This then would represent "Only himself pities Satan". On the other hand, the formula:

(only Satan *w*) (*w*; *u*, *v*) (*u* pities *v*)

would be true iff the predicable "(——; *u*, *v*) (*u* pities *v*)", i.e., "—— pities himself", were true only of Satan; this would therefore represent "Only Satan pities himself".

I am of course not saying that the conventional way of representing reflexivity by repetition of variables is wrong, only that for certain purposes it is unperspicuous. 'What the signs conceal, their use reveals'; the conventional way of 'identifying variables' requires a number of complicated rules for its working, which it is not at all easy to formulate rigorously. For example, the rules about not letting variables be 'captured' by quantifiers are precisely designed to avoid the sort of misreading by which the proposition "For some *x*, *F*(*x*, *x*)" would contain the predicable "For some *x*, *F*(——, *x*)" or, more specifically, would be derivable from this predicable by our taking it as the "*G*( )" in "*G*(*x*)".[15]

The discussions in this chapter are far from an exhaustive treatment of relative pronouns. I hope, however, that I have said enough to destroy the plausibility of the view that the essential role of a relative pronoun is its picking up the reference of its antecedent. Pronouns of laziness do indeed pick up the reference of the antecedent term, if they merely go proxy for repetition of that term; but most relative pronouns are not pronouns of laziness, and for those that are not the idea of a reference picked up is wholly inappropriate. The roles of such pronouns turn out to be describable in quite different ways; and there is no one role that we have found to be common to all relative pronouns.

[15]See Quine, pp. 147–148.

Six

Pronominal Reference: Indefinite Pronouns

85. The pronouns whose roles are to be discussed in this chapter and the next are all of them called indefinite pronouns; but this fact gives us no clue at all to what their roles are, since the indefinite pronouns of traditional grammar are merely a miscellany of the pronouns left over from the fairly well-marked classes, such as personal, reflexive, possessive, and demonstrative pronouns. The indefinite pronouns we shall be considering in this chapter are the applicatives "any", "every", "some", and their derivatives "anything", "everything", "something"; in the next chapter we shall also consider "the same", "other" (or "else"), and "only" (or "alone").

86. Etymologically, "anything", "everything", "something", are formed by prefixing certain applicatives to the word "thing"; and in various other languages that have a word for "thing" we may form a phrase on the model of "something" that is either the standard expression for "something" (French "quelque chose", Italian "qualche cosa") or at least a tolerable substitute for it (Latin "aliqua res"). We must however reject the idea that these "-thing" pronouns are logically to be regarded as referring

phrases, formed by prefixing applicatives to the general term "thing". For in our account of referring phrases the requirement for the "A" in "*A" to be a substantival term was not arbitrary; an integral part of the account dealt with the logical relations between a proposition "$f(^*A)$" and propositions "$f(a_n)$" in which the referring phrase is replaced by a proper name "a_n"; and here the sense of the name "a_n" had to be connected in a definite way to a use of "the same" either with "A" itself or with some other term "A'" from which "A" was derivable by 'restriction' (cf. section 36). Now if "the same A" is to express a criterion of identity for a nameable object, "A" cannot be read as "thing"; "thing" conveys no criterion of identity, not at least in the widest sense of "thing" which alone is relevant to the "-thing" pronouns.

The word "thing" (or colloquially "thingumajig") is often used as a proxy for some substantival term that a lazy or hurried or forgetful speaker does not find at the tip of his tongue. Again, there is a special use of "thing" as a substantival term in its own right, meaning roughly "piece of matter that moves around with its own proper motion and all together", so that, for example, a watch or a ship or a cat would be a 'thing', but an undetached part of any of them would not count as a distinct 'thing'. But neither of these uses has any bearing on the role of "thing" in its most general sense, or of the "-thing" pronouns; I mention them only to get them out of the way.

87. If "thing" in its most general sense is supplied as the antecedent to the relative pronoun that commences a defining relative clause, the result is grammatically a noun-clause; and a phrase can be formed out of this by prefixing "some" or "any" or other applicatives. This might seem to throw light on some uses at least of the "-thing" pronouns. We might try to analyze, for example, a proposition of the form "Something that is F is G" as formed by supplying to the predicable "—— is G" the quasi subject "Some thing-that-is-F". This quasi subject in its turn would be formed from the applicative "some" and "thing that is F"; "something" would not enter into the analysis as a logical unit. Perhaps all uses of the "-thing" pronouns could be dealt with by working them around into the position of antecedents to

grammatically relative pronouns, and then splitting them up in the way just shown. If so, "-thing" pronouns as such would raise no further problems; the problem would now be as to the structure and logical role of a phrase "thing that is *F*".

This sort of phrase was much used in the pseudo-Aristotelian logical tradition, as a way of turning any arbitrary, naturally occurring, predicable into a 'term' that could occur equally well in subject and in predicate position. An 'Aristotelian' logician could recognize "Peter cut off Malchus' ear" as a predication about Malchus only after it had been twisted into the form "Malchus is a thing whose ear Peter cut off". This whole idea of 'terms' was in any event refuted in Chapter Two; moreover, the internal structure of the supposed predicate-term "thing whose ear Peter cut off" raises just as many problems as that of the proposition "Peter cut off Malchus' ear". The traditional maneuver merely shifts the problems. The exercises in twisting predicables into this 'term' shape seem to me to have been positively harmful; a logician should learn to recognize predicables as they come, just as a botanist must learn to recognize plants that have not been tidied up by a gardener.

The use of a phrase "thing that *F*s" in predicative position—"is a thing that *F*s"—is thus a useless substitute for the plain verb "*F*s". But just because a predicative expression cannot occur in subject position without change of sense, it might be supposed that, when "thing that *F*s" occurs in subject position, "thing that ——" is not redundant, but has the logical role precisely of turning a predicable into something that can occur in subject position. We need not here ascribe separate roles to "thing" and the relative pronoun; "thing that" would be a logically indivisible sign, capable of filling up the empty place in a predicable, as a subject or quasi subject does; but whereas a subject or quasi subject supplied to a predicable turns it into a proposition, the result of using "thing that ——" to fill up the empty place in a one-place predicable would be, not a proposition, but something like a name.

88. A logical sign with some such role as I have here assigned to "thing that ——" may seem to be required in any case by the

double role of substantival general terms. Such terms can verbally occur both in subject and in predicate position; and by our doctrine this must constitute an ambiguity. Obviously, though, the double use of "man" (say) in subject and in predicate position is not a casual ambiguity, like the use of "beetle" for a mallet and for an insect; it is a systematic ambiguity, like the way that a common noun may be used to label either a thing of a given kind or a picture of such a thing, or again like the way that a word may be used to refer to that word itself. These systematic ambiguities are removable by the use of special signs, e.g. the modifying words "picture of a", or quotation marks; and similarly, if we have a logical sign ("thing that ——") by prefixing which to a predicable we generate (something like) a name, then we may eliminate the subject-predicate ambiguity of "man" by taking the predicative use as fundamental and taking subject occurrences of "man" as short for "thing-that is-a-man" (where the copula, I have argued, is logically superfluous).

89. Can we then accept "thing that is F" or "thing that Fs" as a pattern for forming something like a complex name? Some of the reasons given in the last chapter against recognizing complex names of the form "A that is F" would be inapplicable in the present case; for "thing" is not a substantival term that can stand in subject position, as we made "A" do when we analyzed away "A that is F"; and again, we are supposing that "thing that ——" may be a logically simple sign, filling up an empty place in a predicable, so that the account we gave of the role of relative pronouns would appear irrelevant.

But there remain, I believe, insuperable objections to regarding "thing that is F" or "thing that Fs" as anything like a name. A name relates directly to the thing(s) it names; the expression "thing that is F" or "thing that Fs" would relate to things only indirectly, in that a predicable "—— is F" or "—— Fs" would be true of them. Again, we should have to say that "thing whose ear Peter cut off" *does* relate to Malchus iff "thing whose ear Peter is cutting off" *did* relate to Malchus (precisely as the predicable "Peter cut off ——'s ear" *is* true of Malchus iff "Peter is cutting off ——'s ear" *was* true of Malchus); but the relation of a name to what it names is tenseless. Again, the use of a name involves a criterion of identity, whereby we can make sure of naming the same thing on different occasions; but in general a predicable will not supply such a criterion of identity; and we can scarcely say that when "(is) *F*" supplies no such criterion, "thing that is *F*" is ill-formed.

We must therefore reject the view I have been sketching, by which "thing that" would be a logically simple sign with the power of turning one-place predicables into something like names. The view had its attractions; for one thing, it seemed to explain plausibly the systematic subject-predicate ambiguity of substantival general terms. But since the supposed sort of complex name appears chimerical, as names of the form "*A* that is *F*" turned out to be, we shall have to seek another account of this ambiguity.

90.   How can we explain phrases of the forms "anything that is *F*", "something that is *F*", if we are not to regard them as the result of prefixing "any" or "some" to "thing that is *F*"? It is quite easy to eliminate the grammatically relative pronoun "that", in much the same way as it was eliminated in the last chapter: e.g., "Anything that is *F* is *G*", "Something that is *F* is *G*", would respectively become: "Anything is, if *F*, then *G*"; "Something is both *F* and *G*". But since "anything" and "something" are not referring phrases constructed out of "thing", as "any *A*" and "some *A*" are from the substantival term "*A*", the case is not perfectly analogous to the way we eliminated phrases of the form "*A* that is *P*"; and we are left with the roles of "anything" and "something" still unexplained.

91.   The sort of explanation we should like to get is one that will show the relation between "-thing" pronouns and the corresponding applicatives. We have failed in our attempts to explain "anything" and "something" in terms of "any" and "some"; is the converse sort of explanation feasible? Many logicians have thought so; it is a standard procedure in modern textbooks of formal logic to reduce "any *A*" and "some *A*" to "anything that is *A*" and "something that is *A*", and then eliminate the relative

pronoun "that" in the way just explained. And since (the term represented by) "A" has no naming role when it occurs in predicate position, the whole burden of referring to the things called "A" would be shifted from the referring phrases to the pronouns "something" and "anything"—which would of course not refer specially to the things called "A", but to things in general.

This view is perhaps most familiar to modern readers from Quine's writings; it was also maintained with great insistence by Frege. Few modern logicians wholly agree with Frege and Quine on this matter; they rather insist that the quantifiers must be interpreted in relation to a Universe of Discourse, whose membership is delimited once for all. (I shall later return to this question of delimited Universes.) Where Quine differs from Frege is in holding the view that proper names also are theoretically dispensable, so that the unrestricted quantifiers could take over the whole burden of reference. I need not discuss this special view; for I have already argued that, both in acts of naming and within propositions, use for example of "cat... the same cat... the same cat..." closely corresponds in its referential force to repeated use of the proper name "Jemima"; I hold that recognition of proper names as logical subjects stands or falls with recognition of an irreducible subject role for substantival general terms. I shall therefore take issue here with Quine, not about proper names, but about the treatment of referring phrases like "some A".

Let us suppose that the recently ennobled Lord Newriche has been visiting the Heralds' College to consult the heralds about his coat of arms. The papers of his case are on the desk of Bluemantle; "Bluemantle" is a name *for* a herald, in official language, and is grammatically a proper noun. If Lord Newriche saw Bluemantle at the Heralds' College on Monday and Tuesday, then on Tuesday it would be true to say:

(1) Lord Newriche discussed armorial bearings with some herald yesterday and discussed armorial bearings with the same herald again today.

The Frege–Quine view would treat this as equivalent to:

(2) Something (or other) is a herald, and Lord Newriche discussed armorial bearings with it yesterday and discussed armorial bearings with it again today.

Or again, if we use 'bound variable' letters, (1) would come out equivalent to:

(3) For some x, x is a herald, and Lord Newriche discussed armorial bearings with x yesterday and discussed armorial bearings with x again today.

Now by parity of reasoning we may analyze:

(4) Lord Newriche discussed armorial bearings with some man yesterday and discussed armorial bearings with the same man again today

as equivalent to:

(5) Something (or other) is a man, and Lord Newriche discussed armorial bearings with it yesterday and discussed armorial bearings with it again today

or again to:

(6) For some x, x is a man, and Lord Newriche discussed armorial bearings with x yesterday and discussed armorial bearings with x again today.

(I use the neuter pronoun "it" in (2) and (5), because it suits the antecedent "something" and the idea of a quantification ranging over things animate and inanimate alike.)

Let us now introduce the further premise "Whatever is a herald is a man" or "For any x, if x is a herald, then x is a man". This premise is surely true; we need not discuss whether the "is" used here is tenseless, as Quine would hold, or rather is 'omnitemporal' as Strawson says;[1] it is anyhow clear that with this additional premise we may pass from (2) or (3) to (5) or (6). But the premise would certainly not warrant us in passing from (1) to

---

[1] W. Van O. Quine, "Mr. Strawson on Logical Theory," *Mind*, LXXII (1953), 442; Strawson, p. 151.

(4); (1) could be true and (4) false; for with a change of personnel in the Heralds' College, Lord Newriche might have seen a different *man* on Monday and Tuesday but the same *herald*, namely Bluemantle, and his papers could have remained on Bluemantle's desk. Hence the above analyses of (1) and (4), which stand or fall together, must be rejected.

It is easy to see what has gone wrong. (5) or (6) tells us that Lord Newriche discussed armorial bearings with something or other on two successive days, the same by some criterion or other, and this something-or-other *is* a man, whether tenselessly or omnitemporally. This does indeed follow from (2) or (3), and therefore from (1), by way of our additional premise: but it is a much weaker proposition than (4). "The same something-or-other, which is a man" does not boil down to "the same man".

92. Frege has clearly explained that the predication of "one endowed with wisdom" ("*ein Weiser*") does not split up into predications of "one" and "endowed with wisdom" ("*weise*").[2] It is surprising that Frege should on the contrary have constantly assumed that "*x* is the same *A* as *y*" does split up into "*x* is an *A* (and *y* is an *A*)" and "*x* is the same as (*ist dasselbe wie, ist gleich*) *y*". We have already by implication rejected this analysis; for it would mean that "the same *A*" always made sense, for any predicable term "*A*"; and in introducing the notion of substantival terms we explicitly denied this view, which would make all predicable terms substantival.

Frege's explanation of "as many as" in terms of one-one correspondence therefore stands in need of correction. Frege says that the relation 'being *R* to' is one-one (*beiderseits eindeutig*) iff we have:

(i) If *d* is *R* to *a* and *d* is *R* to *e*, then *a* is the same as *e*,

(ii) If *d* is *R* to *a* and *b* is *R* to *a*, then *d* is the same as *b*,

whatever *a*, *b*, *d*, and *e* may be.[3] We ought rather to say that a correlation of *A*s to *B*s by the relation 'being *R* to' is one-one iff

[2] Frege (1), p. 40.
[3] Frege (1), p. 84.

Indefinite Pronouns

we have:

(i) If d is an A and e is a B and d is R to e, then whatever d is R to is the same B as e

(ii) If d is an A and e is a B and d is R to e, then whatever is R to e is the same A as d.

We must here interpret "is an A" and "is a B" as predicative occurrences of substantival terms, for only then will "the same A" and "the same B" be intelligible in our formulas.

The purport of this modification is that it restricts our license to apply Frege's definition of "as many as". Frege says, in effect, that there are just as many Fs as Gs iff, for some R, each F is R to some G, and for each G there is some F that is R to it, and 'being R to' is a one-one correlation.[4] Now if we replace Frege's account of one-one correlation by our modified account, we cannot apply this definition unless "F" and "G" are taken either themselves to be, or to be derived by 'restriction' (section 55) from, substantival terms "A" and "B" such as are schematically represented in our account of one-one correlation. Thus, we could apply this definition to decide whether there were as many human beings as chairs in this room; but there would be no question of telling whether there were as many red things in this room as nonred things; for there is no telling what is or is not the same red thing, there being no criterion of identity, and this is still more obvious for nonred things. On such cases, as we saw, Frege cagily remarks that the (concept signified by the) predicable determines no finite number;[5] but the trouble is not that we cannot make an end of counting in these cases, but that we could not even begin to set up a one-one correlation of the things counted to numerals.

93.   We cannot, then, accept Frege's or Quine's reduction of restricted quantification in (4) to the unrestricted quantification of (5) or (6). How are we to interpret unrestricted quantification? Many applications of quantification theory do not require that we

[4]Frege (1), pp. 83–85.
[5]Frege (1), p. 66.

should have any way of interpreting an absolutely unrestricted quantification; it suffices to read the quantifiers as restricted to a 'universe' delimited by some substantival term like "man" or "(natural) number". But I am not going to argue that unrestricted quantification is uninterpretable; there is nothing wrong with our taking the quantification in (5) or (6) to be absolutely unrestricted. Only, in that case, (5) and (6) will give us much less information than (4); they will each tell us that the same something-or-other both is a man and had Lord Newriche discussing armorial bearings with it yesterday and again today. That is to say, (5) or equivalently (6) is true iff:

(7) Some A is a man, and Lord Newriche discussed armorial bearings with that (same) A yesterday, and Lord Newriche discussed armorial bearings with the same A today

is true for *some* interpretation of A as a substantival term.

I shall further maintain that we may accordingly rewrite (5) or (6) as:

(8) For some A: some A is a man, and Lord Newriche discussed armorial bearings with that (same) A yesterday, and Lord Newriche discussed armorial bearings with the same A today.

The two occurrences of "some A" at the beginning of (8) have quite different roles. In the "some A" that follows the colon, "some" is an applicative, as it manifestly has to be in (7); but "for some A" is a quantifier, whose force is such that (8) is true iff there is some interpretation of "A" as a substantival term that would make (8) minus the quantifier, i.e. (7), to be a true proposition.

I must now explain what view of unrestricted quantifiers this use of "for some A" implies: a view that I believe underlies the doctrine of 'formal concepts' in Wittgenstein's *Tractatus*. We first explain the *category* of a (syntactically simple or complex) sign S in a language L as the class of all those signs S' of L such that S' may take the place of S in any proposition of L without the result's being no longer a proposition of L: *salva congruitate*,

as medieval logicians would say. For example, all propositions of
L will belong to one category; all proper names in L will belong
to one category; all substantival terms in L will belong to one
category; predicables with the same number of empty places, to
be filled by subjects belonging to the same category, themselves
belong to the same category; and so on.

This explanation would need provisos and saving clauses to
make it foolproof; but it will do for present purposes. In applying
it, we need to recognize when there is only apparent occurrence
of one expression as part of another. For example, the predicable
"Some boy admires ——" does not occur in "Some boy admires
himself"; rather, this proposition is obtained by first forming the
predicable "—— admires himself" and then supplying this with
the quasi subject "some boy" (cf. section 82). Again, the proposition "Some philosopher smoked and drank whisky" is not formed
by any logical procedure from the proposition "Some philosopher
smoked"; it is got by supplying the quasi subject "some
philosopher" to the predicable "—— smoked and drank whisky",
whereas the shorter proposition is got by supplying the same quasi
subject to "—— smoked". In both these cases there is only a
spurious occurrence of an expression within a proposition.

Corresponding to a given category we introduce an alphabet of
letters schematically representing (going proxy for) the signs of
that category. We may now go on to interpret the occurrence in
the context "for some ——" of a letter from any such alphabet.
The proposition beginning with such a quantifier will be true iff
the proposition minus this quantifier could be read as a true
proposition by taking the occurrence(s) of the letter 'bound to' the
quantifier as occurrence(s) of an actual expression belonging to
the appropriate category.

94.   Let me illustrate this by a much controverted sort of example. Let us suppose that Johnson is acquainted with a social
figure, Ralph de Vere, and a shopkeeper, Jenkins; unknown to
Johnson, Ralph de Vere and Jenkins are one and the same man.
(Perhaps Ralph de Vere is an impostor; or perhaps he has a taste
for keeping a shop, which he can indulge only in secret; or what
you will.) Now Johnson may be quite incredulous when told that

Ralph de Vere is a shopkeeper. In that case, we can find an interpretation of "*x*" in the category of proper names such that the formula:

> (9) *x* is a man, and Johnson disbelieves that Ralph de Vere is a shopkeeper and does not disbelieve that *x* is a shopkeeper, and *x* is the same man as Ralph de Vere

becomes a true proposition when "*x*" is read thus. On our hypothesis this is obviously the case; for (9) will come out true if we read "*x*" as "Jenkins". Accordingly, the following proposition will also be true:

> (10) For some *x*, *x* is a man, and Johnson disbelieves that Ralph de Vere is a shopkeeper and does not disbelieve that *x* is a shopkeeper, and *x* is the same man as Ralph de Vere.

Quine, as is well known, would reject propositions like (10) as ill formed. His reason for doing this is as follows. If (10) were well formed, (10) would be validly inferred from:

> (11) Jenkins is a man, and Johnson disbelieves that Ralph de Vere is a shopkeeper and does not disbelieve that Jenkins is a shopkeeper, and Jenkins is the same man as Ralph de Vere.

Quine would admit (11) to be well formed. On the other hand, he would say, (10) is equivalent to:

> (12) For some man *x*, Johnson disbelieves that Ralph de Vere is a shopkeeper and does not disbelieve that *x* is a shopkeeper, and *x* is the same man as Ralph de Vere.

And obviously in the case supposed there could be no man *x* such as to make (12) true. Only Ralph de Vere is the same man as Ralph de Vere; and it is not the case that Johnson both disbelieves that Ralph de Vere is a shopkeeper and does not disbelieve this. But if (10) is well formed, (10) and therefore (12) must be true propositions if (11) is true. Since in fact (11) could be true whereas (12) could not, (10) and (12) cannot be well-formed propositions: a quantifier outside an *oratio obliqua* clause cannot bind a variable within the clause.

Quine refuses to explore such escape routes as Carnap's—making "Ralph de Vere" and "Jenkins" relate to different intentional objects but nevertheless to the same man. Carnap's idea is to assume different modes of reference, so that, whereas the intentional objects referred to in the one mode are different, the man referred to in the other mode is one and the same.

I have here deliberately chosen the spelling "intentional"; in recent writing the spelling of this word, and of the corresponding adverb in "—ally" and abstract noun in "—ality", oscillates irregularly between a form with "—tion" and one with "—sion", and in fact Carnap prefers the latter spelling. But in this use the adjective goes back to medieval Latin; and for medievals the *intentio* of a term was what was intended by the mind in the use of the term, *quod anima intendit*. The old spelling persists in the expressions "first intention" and "second intention". Sir William Hamilton had a muddled idea that terms had an associated intensive magnitude, greater according as they expressed more concurrent attributes, and to bring this out he introduced an English form of the Scholastic term for intensity, "*intensio*"; from his day onward, "intension" and its compounds have tended to oust "intention" and its compounds; the spelling of "extension" has no doubt furthered this process. Recent interest in Brentano's doctrine of intentionality has however led to a revival of the old "—tion" spelling.

On my own view of identity I could not object in principle to different As' being one and the same B; conceivably, two intentional objects could be one and the same man, as different heralds may be one and the same man (Norroy is historically a different herald from Ulster, but at the present time they are the same man). Quine would however object that unlike the term "herald" or "man" the term "intentional object" fails to supply *any* criterion of identity. This sort of objection is not decisive: we can recognize, discriminate, and reidentify human voices, although we could not put into words the criterion of identity answering to "the same voice". But it is better to go as far as we can in our theorizing without the introduction of intentional objects.

For all that, I think Quine's rejection of (10) is misconceived. On my specification as to the use of "for some x", the question "For which entity x?" will not arise at all. For unrestricted quantifiers construed as I suggest, there will be no question which entities they 'refer to' or 'range over'; such questions seem appropriate only because we wrongly assimilate the use of quantifiers now under discussion to the use of quantifiers when they are tacitly restricted to some 'universe', which will be delimited by some substantival term (cf. the examples at the beginning of Chapter Five). Quine would of course think the force of (10) must be unaltered by writing "For some man x" instead of "For some x, x is a man, and"; and if this were so, all his difficulties would indeed arise. But since, for reasons independent of the present issue, I reject his account of restricted quantifiers like "for some man x", this risk of trouble is surely averted; (12) indeed could not be true, but (12) is not inferable from (10).

I do not want to say that all the troubles of indirect-speech constructions and quantifications that reach into them can now be lightly dismissed. For example, if we regard (10) as a well-formed proposition, we can nevertheless not take it to be of the form "For some x, $F(x)$", where "$F(\quad)$" represents an ordinary one-place predicable. Although the context:

(13) —— is a man, and Johnson disbelieves that Ralph de Vere is a shopkeeper and does not disbelieve that —— is a shopkeeper, and —— is the same man as Ralph de Vere

always yields a proposition when we insert the same proper name in all three blanks, we cannot take it as an ordinary one-place predicable; for then it would have to be a predicable that applied to Jenkins but not to Ralph de Vere, which is *ex hypothesi* ruled out. However these complications may have to be unraveled, (10) is certainly, on our interpretation, a well-formed proposition. We have specified its truth-conditions, and therefore its sense; its sense, as Frege would say, is the sense of: Such-and-such conditions are fulfilled.

95. ˙From this intentionally difficult example, let us go back to the easier task of interpreting:

> (8) For some A: some A is a man, and Lord Newriche discussed armorial bearings with that (same) A yesterday, and Lord Newriche discussed armorial bearings with the same A today.

As I said, (8) will be true iff there is some interpretation of "A" as a substantival term that would make (7), i.e. (8) minus the quantifier, into a true proposition; in particular, (8) will be true if we get a true proposition by taking "A" in (7) to mean "herald"; and accordingly (8) follows from (1), if we assume that a herald is always a man. The interesting question is whether, as I alleged, (8) is tantamount to:

> (6) For some *x*, *x* is a man, and Lord Newriche discussed armorial bearings with *x* yesterday and discussed armorial bearings with *x* today.

On our general view of unrestricted quantifiers, it is fairly easy to show this—if we assume that the use of "*x*" in (3) corresponds to the category of proper names. For (6) will in that case be true iff the formula:

> (14) *x* is a man, and Lord Newriche discussed armorial bearings with *x* yesterday and discussed armorial bearings with *x* today

comes out as a true proposition for some reading of "*x*" as a proper name. But in view of the connection in sense between any proper name and some substantival term or other, this condition can be fulfilled iff the formula:

> (7) Some A is a man, and Lord Newriche discussed armorial bearings with that (same) A yesterday, and Lord Newriche discussed armorial bearings with the same A today

comes out as a true proposition for some interpretation of "A" as a substantival term. Suppose for example that (14) comes out true when we read "*x*" as short for "Bluemantle", which as we saw is a name *of* and *for* a herald. Then (7) will come out true when we take "A" to stand in for the substantival term "herald". The truth-conditions for (8) will be fulfilled iff (7) comes out as a true proposition for *some* such reading of "A" as a substantival term. But this last is precisely the truth-condition for (8); i.e., (6) and (8) have equivalent truth-conditions. Q.E.D.

Quine would not regard (6) and (8) as amounting to the same thing; the "*x*" in (6) would 'range over' concrete entities, and the "A" in (8) over abstract entities corresponding to general terms like "man" or "herald"; so there would be a different existential commitment. I think this is quite wrong. Proper names and the corresponding substantival general terms relate to the very same entities; the difference is that a substantival term may name many things, and a proper name (accidental ambiguities apart) names just one thing, of a given kind.

I have said that a proposition beginning with a quantifier "For some ——" is true iff the proposition minus this quantifier could be read as a true proposition by taking the occurrence(s) of the letter 'bound to' the quantifier as if there were occurrence(s) of an actual expression belonging to the appropriate category. I do not mean here that the language we are using must already contain an actual expression, of the appropriate category, which, if substituted for the bound variable in the proposition minus the quantifier, would give us a true proposition; it is sufficient that we could coherently add such an expression to our language. For example, the truth value of:

(15) For some *x*, *x* is a pebble on the beach at Brighton

does not depend on anybody's having given a proper name to such a pebble; it is enough that we could coherently add to our language a proper name of such a pebble.

To find out what expressions could coherently be added to a language we need not rely on vague intuitions, or plunge into a labyrinth of modal logic; we can appeal to the proof procedures that work in a given language. It would, for example, be entirely useless for Quine to protest that, since he uses a symbolic language from which all proper names are eliminable, the "*x*" in a proposition of the form "For some *x*, *F*(*x*)" is not a proper-name variable; for this symbolic language contains methods of proof in which a conclusion is treated as inferable from a premise "For some x, $F(x)$" because it is inferable from a line "$F(x)$", and here "x" is handled as an *ad hoc* proper name. Moreover, Quine frequently refers to interpretations of letters like "x" and "y", and surely assigning an object to a letter as its interpretation differs only nominally from treating the letter *pro hac vice* as a proper name of the object.[6] Indeed, in the first of the passages just cited, when speaking of assigning an object to a letter as its interpretation, Quine uses the actual expression: "'x' is reinterpreted as a name of that object". In the circumstances, Quine's thesis that names are theoretically dispensable is pretty well empty.

96.   What are we to say of Quine's slogan: "To be is to be the value of a variable"? It is clear that he means this to imply that the quantifier "for some x" can always be read as "there is an entity x such that . . .". This, however, could at best only apply to proper-name variables; only if "x" is a proper-name variable does the suggested reading of "for some x" make any sense. As we saw, we may introduce quantifiers that bind variables of other style, without thereby pooling the corresponding category with the category of proper names. Moreover, even among formulas beginning "For some x", where "x" is a proper-name variable, there can be found some, like (10) above, which are perfectly construable, but for which Quine's reading of "for some x" is provably wrong.

Verbally at least, Quine's slogan involves what Frege would have called a confusion between concepts of different level and would have regarded as almost the grossest that could be committed.[7] "There is a square root of 4" is true iff, for a suitable language L, "a square root of 4 is a value of a variable in L" is true. But although "a square root of 4" is the grammatical subject of both the sentences just quoted, its logical roles differ. Of the number 2, which is a square root of 4, we may truly say: "2 is a value of a variable in L". But we cannot say "There is 2"; the gap in "There is ——" used this way (in the sense of French "il y a"

[6]Quine, pp. 121, 129, 151, 211.
[7]Frege (3), p. 126.

and German "es gibt") can be filled only by a predicable expression, not by a proper name. "Is a value of a variable in L" is predicable of objects, "there is" is not; it is easy to see how these expressions should come to be thought coextensive predicables, but almost equally easy to see that it is wrong to think so.

I am afraid that there is a genuine confusion in Quine's doctrine, not merely an inaccuracy for the sake of rhetorical effect. For in discussing the problem of existential propositions, Quine nowhere tries to draw a sharp distinction between propositions of the types "There is (not) such a thing as a winged horse" and "There is (not) such a thing as Pegasus". On the contrary, he wishes to assimilate "Pegasus" to general terms. Keeping this example, I should follow Frege in holding that "There is such a thing as a winged horse" is true iff "(—— is a) winged horse" is truly predicable of something or other; whereas "There is such a thing as Pegasus" relates to (and does not exemplify) a certain use of "Pegasus" as a proper name, its purport being that "Pegasus" in that use does indeed name something.

With Frege, I believe that there is no place for empty proper names in scientific discourse, or in any discourse aimed simply at conveying the truth. When an astronomer discovered that he had failed to identify an intra-Mercurian planet under the style "Vulcan", he dropped "Vulcan" from his vocabulary; when the university authorities discover that a name on their records answers only to a fraudulent pretense on the part of an undergraduate clique that there is a person so named, they erase the name. On the other hand, there is no call to erase a description from our language because we conclude that nothing answers to it.

97. This view of vacuous proper names raises a difficulty over the occurrence of proper names in oblique contexts, such as the following:

(16) The heathen believed that Jupiter dethroned his father

(17) The examiners believe that Joe Doakes is worthy of an A grade.

We may suppose (16) to be asserted by a Christian, and (17) by one to another of the undergraduate clique through whose concerted action a fictitious undergraduate named "Joe Doakes" has got put on the university's records. If we adopt Frege's rule that when a proper name is empty, clauses containing it are no longer propositions with a truth-value, then it should seem that (16) and (17) could not be consistently asserted in the supposed circumstances.

Frege's own solution, as is well known, is that "Jupiter" and "Joe Doakes" and other proper names each have an oblique or indirect reference (whether or not they also have an ordinary reference, i.e. actually do name something or other) and that this is what propositions like (16) and (17) are about. But we need not go so far; as Aquinas is wont to say about the more dubious utterances of the Fathers, (16) and (17) ought to be charitably interpreted rather than imitated.

One way of charitably construing (16) and (17) would be:

(18) The heathen intended to use "Jupiter" as a name for a god who dethroned his father

(19) The examiners believe that there is an undergraduate named "Joe Doakes" who is worthy of an A grade

(18) being so read that all the words following "The heathen intended" fall within an indirect-speech construction. In some instances it may be disputable whether an indirect-speech construction really gives us a fair report of what was said, thought, meant, and so forth; however, these ways of expounding (16) and (17) fall well within the limits of fair reporting. For although the heathen, or the examiners, would no doubt normally use "Jupiter", or "Joe Doakes", as (if it were) a proper name, the truth of (16) or (17) implies that they would reply affirmatively to a suitable question in which the name was not used as a name but quoted, a question such as the following:

(20) Do you use "Jupiter" as a name for a god who dethroned his father?

(21) Is there an undergraduate named "Joe Doakes" who deserves an A grade?

And if we replace (16) by (18) or (17) by (19), we no longer have a proposition that even seems to commit those asserting it to the use of a proper name which they themselves would regard as naming nothing.

This technique of interpretation is called for only in cases where an ostensible proper name is used in indirect speech to report the words or attitudes of people who regard it as a name of something, whereas the reporter does not so regard it. No such technique is called for in dealing with propositions like:

(11) Jenkins is a man, and Johnson disbelieves that Ralph de Vere is a shopkeeper and does not disbelieve that Jenkins is a shopkeeper, and Jenkins is the same man as Ralph de Vere.

For somebody who asserted (11) would be committed, no less than Johnson himself whose beliefs are reported, to using both "Jenkins" and "Ralph de Vere" as names; so the problems raised by (11) are quite different from those raised by (16) and (17). The trouble over (11) is that what we get by removing the occurrences of "Jenkins", viz.:

(13) ——— is a man, and Johnson disbelieves that Ralph de Vere is a shopkeeper and does not disbelieve that ——— is a shopkeeper, and ——— is the same man as Ralph de Vere

is not a predicable; at any rate, not a *Shakespearean* predicable—not one which is true of whatever it is true of by any other name, as "smells sweet" is true of a rose. For this reason, although the result of 'existentially' quantifying (13), viz.:

(10) For some *x*, *x* is a man, and Johnson disbelieves that Ralph de Vere is a shopkeeper and does not disbelieve that *x* is a shopkeeper, and *x* is the same man as Ralph de Vere

is clearly interpretable (cf. section 94), we may not take the truth-condition of (10) to be that (13) shall be true of something or other.

98.   In most of this work we have been wholly concerned with Shakespearean predicables. Even in the intentional examples of

Chapter Three, the predicables that were involved, such as "Tom has obliged himself to marry ——" and "Jemima is waiting for ——", are Shakespearean ones; they apply or do not apply to a girl or mouse under whatever name. In the present section the schematic letter "*F*" will be used to represent an arbitrary Shakespearean predicable.

With this restriction, we may assert that "For some *x*, *x* is *F*" has exactly the same truth-condition as "Something or other is *F*" or as "There is something that is *F*"—namely, that the predicable represented by "*F*" should be true of something or other. For "For some *x*, *x* is *F*" will be true iff "*x* is *F*" is true for some interpretation of "*x*" as a proper name; and since "*F*" is a Shakespearean predicable, this will be the case iff "*F*" is true of an object namable by some proper name.

It makes absolutely no logical difference whether we say "There is something that is *F*" or "There exists something that is *F*"; "exists" is merely a shade more formal than "is". It ought not to be necessary to say this; but it is necessary, in view of the things some Oxford philosophers say about "exists". Some of these— e.g. that "exist" does not occur often in ordinary language, that it is a word of philosophical provenance—besides happening to be false, could not possibly be philosophically relevant. As for the idea that "There exists an even prime" commits us to an objectionably metaphysical assertion that the number 2, which is an even prime, *exists*—this is again Frege's 'grossest of all possible confusions' (cf. section 96). The purport of the quoted proposition is that "is an even prime" is true of something, not that "exists" is true of something. (Russell has repeatedly pointed this out; but these Oxford philosophers despise Russell and do not read him.)

A problem arises, however, over propositions of the form "An A that is *F* exists" or "There is an A that is *F*". Are we to read such a proposition as a variant of "Something or other is an A that is *F*" (where "that" goes proxy for "and"—cf. section 74), or as a variant of "Some A is *F*"? We cannot say "both", like the children's answer to "Which hand will you have?" for the two readings are importantly different. If we take "A" to be "man" and the predicable "—— is *F*" to be "Lord Newriche discussed armorial bearings with —— yesterday and discussed armorial bearings with —— again today", then "Some A is F" and "Something or other is an A and is F" spell out respectively as follows:

(22) Lord Newriche discussed armorial bearings with some man yesterday and discussed armorial bearings with him again today

(5) Something (or other) is a man, and Lord Newriche discussed armorial bearings with it yesterday and discussed armorial bearings with it again today

which are certainly not equivalent (cf. section 91). Now it is clear that many ordinary-language propositions of the form "There is an A that is F" are merely variants of the "Some A is F" form; and indeed I cannot myself think of a plausible example where the other reading, "Something or other is an A and is F", is demanded. For a full treatment, then, of existential propositions, we must discuss the form "Some A is F". This brings us to the topic of our next chapter.

Seven

The Logic of Lists

99. I think the best way to understand applicatives like "some", "every", "most", and the like, is to consider first their use in harness, not with substantival general terms, but with lists of proper names. An expression of the form "one of a_1, a_2, . . .", where "a_n" is a proper name, can be substituted without incongruity for a substantival general term in the singular that goes with an applicative; and when we have an applicative like "most" or "all" that goes with a plural term, "of a_1, a_2, . . ." can be substituted for that plural term. If "a_1, a_2, . . ." is a list of all the things called "A", then these substitutions can be made for "A" not only *salva congruitate* but also *salva veritate* (so long as we are concerned with Shakespearean predicables, a qualification that will henceforth often be tacitly required).

It is natural to take "one of a_1, a_2, . . ." as relating in an impartial distributive way to the several objects named by the proper names "a_n". This way for an expression to relate to objects is not so direct as the way that a syntactically simple name relates to what it names; for the relation is here mediated by the names on the list. But the relation of a list to the objects listed in it is near akin to the name-relation, as we may see from the fact that (even according to the ordinary acceptation of the word "list") a single proper name may itself count as a one-item list. The need to preface a list with "one of" or "of" in order to preserve normal syntax has of course no bearing upon its mode of significance; it is logically no more interesting than the fact that we say "the river Thames" but "the City of London". In schematic representations of propositions containing lists, I shall henceforth omit these formative words, and write, for example, "F(some a_1, a_2, . . .)" instead of "F(some one of a_1, a_2, . . .)"; readers with a schoolboy fear of grammarians may think of this as shorthand.

100.   In some contexts a proper name and a list of several names are mutually replaceable *salva congruitate*. For example, this holds good for contexts of the form "F(only ——)"; it is equally congruous to say "Only Bill can have opened the safe" and "Only Bill, Tom, John, can have opened the safe". (The "or" that would be inserted between the items of the list in spoken English has no logical significance.) But there is apparent incongruity if we insert a one-item list, a single name, in a context, for example, of the form "F(every ——)" or "F(most ——)". And there is a demonstrable incongruity if we try to make a list, say "Tripod, Towzer", into the subject of a predicate like "wants a bone" or "is outside in the corridor"; for the truth-condition of the predication—that the predicate be true of what the subject stands for—becomes essentially indeterminate if the subject relates to a number of things in an impartial distributive way. This latter incongruity suggests as the role of certain among the applicatives that they can remove this indeterminacy of truth-conditions.

What sort of truth-condition must a proposition "W(*Tripod, Towzer, Fido)" have, in order that we may reasonably count this condition as a way of making definite the vague condition that "W( )" shall be true of what is named in the list "Tripod, Towzer, Fido"? First, it seems natural to require that this proposition shall have the same truth-value as some truth-function of "W(Tripod)", "W(Towzer)", and "W(Fido)". Secondly, this truth-function must be unaffected by shuffling around the names in the list; otherwise our proposition would have been assigned an inconsistent truth-condition; such permutations of the names must give us always an equivalent truth-function of the same propositions. The need for this second condition is easily shown. Suppose for example we said that "W(*Tripod, Towzer, Fido)" is true iff "W(Tripod) **v** (W(Towzer) & W(Fido))" is true. Then by parity of reasoning "W(*Towzer, Tripod, Fido)" is true iff "W(Towzer) **v** (W(Tripod) & W(Fido))" is true. Now suppose we have "W(Tripod)" true and each of "W(Towzer)" and "W(Fido)" false. Then "W(Tripod) **v** (W(Towzer) & W(Fido))" will be true, because its disjunct "W(Tripod)" is true; but "W(Towzer)" and "W(Tripod) & W(Fido)" will both be false, so that "W(Towzer) **v** (W(Tripod) & W(Fido))" will be false. Thus, on our present supposition as to truth-conditions, "W(*Tripod, Towzer, Fido)" will be true and "W(*Towzer, Tripod, Fido)" will be false; but this is absurd, for changing about the names in a mere list can make no odds. Hence there is no applicative "*" such that the truth-conditions of predications using it could be specified in the way here supposed.

Thirdly, given a premise to the effect that "G( )" is true of whatever "W( )" is true of, we must be able to infer "G(*Tripod, Towzer, Fido)" from "W(*Tripod, Towzer, Fido)". This may be called the *dictum de omni* requirement, and applicatives that satisfy this as well as the first requirement may be called *dictum de omni* applicatives. (Cf. sections 57, 82. The second condition must be fulfilled by any that fulfills the first, on pain of inconsistency, and so needs no further separate consideration.) It is perfectly possible for an applicative not to be a *dictum de omni* applicative; neither "only" nor "no" is one; but if the applicative "*" is not a *dictum de omni* applicative, then the truth-condition for "W(*Tripod, Towzer, Fido)" cannot reasonably be regarded as a matter of having the predicable represented by "W( )" holding true of what the list in subject position stands for; and equally we cannot say that here the same predications are made with the list as subject as are made of the several dogs in propositions like "W(Towzer)" and "W(Tripod)".

From these requirements we can easily derive a fourth one: our truth-function of the propositions about Tripod, Towzer, and Fido separately must be a disjunction of conjunctions (or equivalently a conjunction of disjunctions) of these singular propositions. For, in general, a truth-function of a given set of propositions can be expressed as a disjunction of conjunctions of the given propositions *and/or their negations.* Suppose now we take as one premise a disjunction of conjunctions in which there essentially occur negations of our three propositions "W(Tripod)", "W(Towzer)", and "W(Fido)", and have also a second premise that would warrant us in passing from "W(*a*)" to "G(*a*)" if "*a*" were read as a name *of* and *for* a dog. From this pair of premises we are in general not warranted in passing to a conclusion that is the corresponding truth-function of the three propositions "G(Tripod)", "G(Towzer)", and "G(Fido)": unless the disjunction of conjunctions works out as a tautology or contradiction by truth-tables, it is always possible to assign to the singular propositions predicating "W( )" and "G( )" of Tripod, Towzer, and Fido such truth-values as make the conclusion false when the premises are both true. We could for example find an assignment of truth-values for these six propositions such that given the premise:

$$(W(\text{Tripod}) \quad \& \quad \sim W(\text{Towzer})) \quad v \quad (W(\text{Towzer}) \quad \& \quad \sim W(\text{Fido})) \ v \ (W(\text{Fido}) \ \& \ \sim W(\text{Tripod}))$$

and also the premise "If W(any dog) then G(that dog)" we cannot infer the conclusion:

$$(G(\text{Tripod}) \ \& \ \sim G(\text{Towzer})) \ v \ (G(\text{Towzer}) \ \& \ \sim G(\text{Fido})) \ v \ (G(\text{Fido}) \ \& \ \sim G(\text{Tripod})).$$

So this truth-function does not fulfill the *dictum de omni* requirement. On the other hand, any disjunction of conjunctions of the singular propositions *without any of their negations* will fulfill the *dictum de omni* requirement.

We can now see that the role of certain applicatives is to show which particular truth-function of the singular propositions, among the functions satisfying our requirements, gives the truth-condition for a proposition with a list as subject. "W(every (one of) Tripod, Towzer, Fido)" is true iff "W(Tripod) & W(Towzer) & W(Fido)" is true; "W(some (one of) Tripod, Towzer, Fido)" is true iff "W(Tripod) v W(Towzer) v W(Fido)" is true. (These truth-functions fulfill our requirements in a degenerate way; if the term "disjunction of conjunctions" is stretched to cover cases where we have conjunction or disjunction of a proposition with itself, it is easily seen that our requirements are fulfilled.) And "W(most(of) Tripod, Towzer, Fido)" is true iff "(W(Tripod) & W(Towzer)) ∨ (W(Towzer) & W(Fido)) ∨ (W(Fido) & W(Tripod))" is true.

101.   Now suppose "*" to be an applicative satisfying the *dictum de omni* requirements, as "every" and "some" and "most" do: how are we to interpret "$F(*a_1)$", i.e. the result of inserting a single-item list in the blank of "$F(*$ ———)"? The natural thing would be to take it that "$F(*a_1)$" has the same truth-value as a disjunction of conjunctions of "$F(a_1)$" with itself, i.e. the same truth-value as "$F(a_1)$". The applicative thus becomes in this case redundant; I think this fully accounts for our feeling of incongruity over the use of such applicatives with a proper name. (Not all applicatives are thus incongruous; as we saw, "only" goes with a proper name quite happily.)

This interpretation of "$F(*a_1)$" has the consequence that "$F(*a_1, a_2, a_3, \ldots)$" will be true iff a certain truth-function (disjunction of conjunctions) of propositions "$F(*a_n)$" is true. Thus our reasoning comes full circle. We began by intuitively laying down requirements to which the truth-conditions of "$F(*a_1, a_2, a_3, \ldots)$" must conform if we are to be justified in holding that with this proposition, as with "$F(a_n)$", truth is a matter of having the predicate "$F(\ )$" apply to what the subject stands for. We then find that if these requirements are fulfilled, "$F(*a_n)$" is true iff "$F(a_n)$" is true—that there is a predicate "$F(*$ ———)", attachable to lists of arbitrary length, which when attached to a proper name coincides with the plain "$F(\ )$". And this shows that if our requirements are satisfied, we can indeed hold that "$F(*a_1, a_2, a_3, \ldots)$" and (a proposition tantamount to) "$F(a_n)$" result from attaching the same predicate to different subjects. All this, of course, holds good only if "*" is an applicative of the *dictum de omni* sort.

102.   Although with a predicate like "——— wants a bone" the effect of modifying it to "Every ——— wants a bone" or "Most ——— want a bone" may seem to be the removal of the ambiguity

that would otherwise occur when the predicate was attached to a list, really this effect is only incidental. Our account of the relations between predications with a list as subject and singular predications did not in the least involve that the predicates in the latter would, if unmodified, be ambiguous as attached to lists; it carries over equally well if we consider a predicate "$F(\quad)$" that has no such ambiguity and can already take a list as subject; and we have seen that, for any predicate that has such ambiguity, we can construct a predicate (in fact, more than one) that coincides with it in singular propositions but can be attached to lists of arbitrary length. This means that a language need not contain two categories of predicables, respectively attachable to proper names (one-item lists) only and to lists of arbitrary length; the latter category is theoretically sufficient.

103.   We are now able to clear up one of our puzzles in the discussion of *suppositio*. The example (section 47) was of a jeweler's shop with two assistants, Bill and Joe. Then we have to distinguish between these two propositions:

(1) An assistant alone had opportunity to steal the ruby.

(2) Some assistant alone had opportunity to steal the ruby.

The truth-condition of (2) is given by a disjunction of singular propositions about Bill and Joe:

(3) Either Bill alone had opportunity to steal the ruby or Joe alone had opportunity to steal the ruby.

On the other hand the truth-condition of (1) seems to require a disjunction of proper names:

(4) Only Bill or Joe had opportunity to steal the ruby.

This was in accordance with Ockham's way of distinguishing between determinate and confused *suppositio*, and in fact medieval logicians generally held that the subject-terms of exclusive propositions like (1) were instances of confused *suppositio*. We were, however, unable to make any good sense of disjunctions of proper names.

The Logic of Lists

In fact, the "or" in (4) is quite inessential; we might just as well have had "and". The suggestions of "or" and "and" in this context are indeed different; "or" suggests that if Bill had opportunity, Joe had not, whereas "and" suggests that Bill and Joe alike had opportunity. The actual information given in (4) is, however, merely that nobody other than Bill and Joe had opportunity—and this whether "and" or "or" is used. Really, neither connective has any special significance here; (4) should be construed as the result of attaching the predicable "Only —— had opportunity to steal the ruby" to the list "Bill, Joe" as subject. On the other hand, in the proposition:

(5) Some (one of) Bill, Joe, alone had opportunity to steal the ruby

the equivalent predicable "—— alone had opportunity to steal the ruby" is not directly attached to the list "Bill, Joe", but is modified by the applicative "some"; and (3) supplies the truth-condition of (5), according to our general rule about "some". We then account for the difference between (1) and (2) by taking them as obtained by substituting "(an) assistant" for the list "Bill, Joe" in (4) and (5) respectively; by the principle laid down at the beginning of section 99, these substitutions can be made *salva congruitate*, and in the supposed circumstances *salva veritate* too.

Here as elsewhere, there is no need to suppose that there is any variety in the impartial distributive way that a list has of referring to the several things listed. "$F(\text{every } a_1, a_2, \ldots)$" and "$F(\text{some } a_1, a_2, \ldots)$" differ not because the list "$a_1, a_2, \ldots$" has different manners of reference to things listed, but because the predicable "$F(\ )$" is modified so as to form two different predicates attached to the list as subject: the difference of import between these predicates comes out in the different truth-functions of singular propositions with predicate "$F(\ )$" that have to be used in stating truth-conditions. Wittgenstein spoke of separating the truth-function from the concept *all*;[1] and that is what we too

---

[1] Wittgenstein, 5.521.

need to do. As we have seen, Ockham used the idea of a disjunction of singular terms to explain *suppositio confusa*; and Russell thought that in "$F(a_1$ and a_2 and...)" and "$F(a_1$ or a_2 or...)" we had to do with two different nonrelational ways of combining the objects a_1, a_2.... But in some cases, as we have just seen, the difference between joining the items with "or" and with "and" is not a logical difference at all, but only a matter of idiom and suggestion; and where a difference is made, we can 'separate the truth-function' from the 'all', the list, by turning "$F(a_1$ and a_2 and...)" into "F(every a_1, a_2,...)" and "$F(a_1$ or a_2 or...)" into "F(some a_1, a_2,...)".

104.   There are certain complications that arise when it is a matter of filling up an empty place not in a one-place predicable (so as to get a proposition) but in a many-place predicable. These complications can however be dealt with by the technique sketched in section 64. Just as "F(every a_1, a_2,...)" is true iff "$F(a_1)$ & $F(a_2)$ & ..." is true, so "G(——, every a_1, a_2...)" is true *of something* iff "G(——, a_1) & G(——, a_2) & ..." is true *of that thing*, i.e. iff each of the predicables "G(——, a_1)", "G(——, a_2)",... is true of it. And so in other cases.

Thus far we have actually stated the truth-conditions for propositions of the form "$F(^*a_1$, a_2,...)", where "*" is an applicative satisfying the *dictum de omni* requirement, only for lists with certain particular numbers of items; we clearly need a general formulation of the truth-conditions, regardless of the number of items. The method that commends itself is a recursive one—to supply a rule that reduces the truth-conditions when the list has n + 1 items to those for an n-item list; since we know that "$F(^*a_n)$" reduces to "$F(a_n)$", this procedure would suffice for lists of any finite length.

This method works easily enough for "F(every ——)" or "F(some ——)". Let "a_1, a_2,..." represent an $(n + 1)$ itemed list, and let "a_2,..." represent the same list short of the item "a_1". Then "F(every a_1, a_2,...)" is true iff "$F(a_1)$ & F(every a_2,...)" is true; and "F(some a_1, a_2,...)" is true iff "$F(a_1)$ ∨ F(some a_2,...)" is true.

The recursive truth-condition for "F(most ——)" is only a

little more complicated. First, for simplicity's sake let us suppose that the list supplied as subject to "$F(\text{most} \underline{\quad})$" is nonrepetitive—does not contain two items that name the same thing.[2] We may now reach our rule by some common-sense reflections about majorities. Consider a motion on which all M.P.s present will certainly vote one way or the other, and on which each M.P. has his mind unshakably made up. Then if there is a majority in favor among those present, there is no (one) M.P. whose absence would have turned this into a majority against. On the other hand, if there is not a majority in favor among those present, then there is certainly some M.P. in whose absence there would have been (or perhaps would still have been) a majority against. (For, if the votes were evenly divided, the lack of one favorable vote would mean a majority against; if only a minority voted in favor, then in the absence of one of that minority there would still have been a vote against; and if nobody voted in favor, there would still have been an adverse vote if any one M.P. had been absent.) We may thus lay down the truth-condition for "$F(\text{most } a_1, a_2, \ldots)$" as follows. Let "$F'(\quad)$" be the contradictory of "$F(\quad)$". Then "$F(\text{most } a_1, a_2, \ldots)$" is true iff a false proposition is obtained by any insertion in the blank of "$F'(\text{most} \underline{\quad})$" of a list got by dropping *one* item from the (nonrepetitive) list "$a_1, a_2, \ldots$".

A simple example will show how this works. The truth-condition for "$F(\text{most } a_1, a_2, a_3)$" will be that "$F'(\text{most } a_1, a_2)$" and "$F'(\text{most } a_2, a_3)$" and "$F'(\text{most } a_1, a_3)$" shall all be false. Since a majority out of two means two, this condition reduces to the requirement that we must have the following proposition true:

$$\sim(\sim F(a_1) \ \& \ \sim F(a_2)) \ \& \ \sim(\sim F(a_2) \ \& \ \sim F(a_3)) \ \& \\ \sim(\sim F(a_1) \ \& \sim F(a_3))$$

i.e., "$(F(a_1) \vee F(a_2)) \ \& \ (F(a_2) \vee F(a_3)) \ \& \ (F(a_1) \vee F(a_3))$". This result is easily seen to be correct. We thus have an effective

---

[2] By what criterion 'the same thing'? If the list has been introduced as a list of things called "A", where "A" is a substantival term, the relevant criterion is given by "the same A"; no two items must name the same A (cf. sec. 55). Other cases will not concern us.

mechanical procedure for writing down the truth-function of singular propositions that corresponds to "$F(\text{most } a_1, a_2, \ldots)$".

105.   When the things called "A" can actually be listed in a finite nonrepetitive list "$a_1, a_2, \ldots$", then this substantival general term "A" and the list "$a_1, a_2, \ldots$" are mutually substitutable *salva veritate* in the context of a predicable modified by an applicative, "$F(*$ ——$)$"; this holds good whether or not this applicative conforms to the *dictum de omni* requirement (so long as "$F(\ )$" is a Shakespearean predicable); and even when the things called "A" cannot be so listed, this substitution is still possible *salva congruitate*. This fact, together with the views we have reached concerning lists, guides us to a full acceptance of Frege's view about referring phrases (cf. section 41). We should read "$F(\text{every } A)$" and "$F(\text{some } A)$" as got by attaching the different predicates "$F(\text{every} $ ——$)$" and "$F(\text{some} $ ——$)$" to "A", not by attaching the predicable "$F(\ )$" to two different quasi subjects "every A" and "some A", which refer to the things called "A" in two different ways. For "A" refers, as the list "$a_1, a_2, \ldots$" refers, to things called "A"; and just as it was unnecessary to assume different modes of reference for the list, so this assumption is unnecessary as regards the general term.

On the other hand, we shall disagree with Frege on another issue. Frege denied that a general term "A" ever referred to the individual things called "A"; the reference of a general term was always to something nonindividual—a *Begriff*, a concept. It would take us too far to discuss Frege's doctrine of *Begriffe*, on which I have written more than once; it is enough to remark here that for Frege it would be logically impossible that a univocal predicate should be significantly predicable both of an individual thing and of a *Begriff*. Now if for the sake of argument we accept this, then it follows that, for example, "an assistant" in "Only an assistant can have taken the ruby" does not stand for a *Begriff*; for "Only —— can have taken the ruby" is significantly predicable of an individual, say Bill; and when we come to state the truth-conditions of an exclusive proposition, we shall find that this possibility of predication is not due to any equivocal use of words.

The defect in Frege's reasoning, it appears to me, was his

unquestioned assumption that a name—if we ignore casual equivocation—cannot name more than one thing and that in consequence a general term is not a name but is essentially predicative. The logic of lists, which has led us to a different view, was completely ignored by Frege. So far from following Frege in the view that a word following an applicative is thereby shown to be a word for a *Begriff* and not a logical subject standing for individual things, we shall hold that a general term in such a position has the role of a name, of a logical subject. But I must emphasize that in "F(every man)" it is "man", not "every man", that is the logical subject; and if we count applicatives as parts of the predicate, there are no considerations that should force us to call "man" by the grudging appellation "quasi subject", as we felt obliged to call "every man" when we were trying to regard this as a referring phrase (cf. sections 40, 42).

Our view of general terms has something in common with the views of Aquinas. Aquinas distinguished between a general term that is taken (*tenetur*) *materially* and one that is taken *formally*. The term "fish", say, taken materially is a subject of predication and relates to the objects (*supposita*) called "fish"—e.g. in the sentence "A fish swims in the sea"; but the same term taken formally or predicatively relates not to individual fishes—if I say "A dolphin is not a fish", my proposition relates to no individual fish—but rather to the *nature* of fish.[3] And to the applicatives "some", "every", "only", and the like, Aquinas assigns the role of showing the way the predicate goes with the subject, *ordinem praedicati ad subjectum*.[4] Like Frege, Aquinas will have no truck with the idea that the applicative goes along with a general term to form a quasi subject, to which the predicate is then attached.

This way of putting things diverges from my own only because of the distinction I have marked with the terms "predicate" and "predicable". I think it is best not to call "—— swims in the sea" the predicate of the proposition "Some fish swims in the sea", but rather to regard this proposition as the result of attaching "Some —— swims in the sea" to "fish"; the predicable "—— swims in

[3] Cf. e.g. Aquinas, Ia, q. 13, art. 12. For the terms "*suppositum*" and "nature" as used here, cf. Ia, q. 29, art. 4, ad 1um.

[4] Aquinas, Ia, q. 31, arts. 3, 4.

the sea" genuinely occurs in the proposition, but not as its predicate. Still, it is all right to say that "some" shows how "——
swims in the sea" latches on to "fish".

106. We now have to consider propositions with a subject-term
"A" that cannot be replaced by a list of things called "A".

There are several distinct cases here. First, there may be no
such thing as As. Secondly, the As may be finite in number but
may chance not to have been named in our language (cf. section
95). Finally, it may be in principle impossible to list all the As,
because the class of As is infinite like that of prime numbers or
open toward the future like that of cats.

In the case where the general term "A" is empty, our previous
way of stating truth-conditions has no natural extension. The
ideas of conjunction and disjunction are easily extended from the
case of several propositions to the case of one, because we can
form the conjunction or disjunction of a proposition with itself,
which is of course simply equivalent to the proposition. But
where we have no propositions to start with, we cannot form a
disjunction or conjunction. And so if there are no As we cannot
state the truth-conditions of a proposition "$F(*A)$" in terms of
some truth-function of singular propositions "$F(a_n)$", where
"a_n" is a proper name corresponding to a correct use of "the same
A"; for no object will be identifiable and reidentifiable as the
same A, so there will be no such proper names and no such
singular propositions.

It might be argued that in this case the relevant class of propositions is null; and by appealing to the alleged properties of such a
class someone might try to show what truth-value a disjunction or
conjunction of its members would have. But since a null class
has no members, there can exist no such disjunction or conjunction to have a truth-value. Admittedly, a proposition may have a
truth-value at a time when it does not physically exist; the proposition "No language exists" could be true only when it did not
physically exist. But it is another matter to suppose a truth-value
can be assigned to a proposition whose existence would involve a
contradiction; and the idea of a conjunction or disjunction where
there are no propositions to be conjoined or disjoined is plainly

The Logic of Lists

self-contradictory. Only the sort of sophistical persuasion that makes students swallow the fallacies commonly employed to introduce the null class could make logicians blind to this contradiction.

Faced with these difficulties, some philosophers have ruled that if an empty general term occurs in subject position, then no predication at all, true or false, has been made: a ruling similar to the line I have taken about ostensible proper names that turn out to be vacuous. This ruling, however, does not work out very happily. One would, I think, naturally wish to say that, since there are no dragons, someone who says assertorically "I have a sword that will kill any dragon" or "Most dragons are cannibals" or "A dragon has just chased me down the road" has uttered a falsehood, not merely failed to assert anything; at least, the circumstances in which one would count him as not having uttered a falsehood when he said one of these things in an assertoric way are like the circumstances in which one might count a man as not having uttered a falsehood in saying "The Earth is flat"—e.g. that this was part of a stage-play—and have nothing to do with the emptiness of the term "dragon".

Let us consider the relation between an empty general term, say "dragon", and an ostensible proper name tied to that general term, say "Fafner". In their use outside propositions, to express simple acts of identification and reidentification, "Fafner" and "dragon" are on a level: "Fafner... Fafner... Fafner again" could be correctly used for simple naming of a present object only if "dragon... the same dragon... the same dragon again" could be so used—and in fact neither word can thus be correctly used. We might suppose, then, that the same held good for the use of these words in subject position. Surely the uses of "Fafner... Fafner... Fafner..." in acts of identification and reidentification and in telling a story are related in just the same way as are the uses of "dragon... the same dragon... the same dragon..." for these two purposes (cf. section 34). And since the identification and reidentification supposed would be incorrect, does it not follow, as regards the use of either word in subject position, that the predication attempted is simply of no effect—as one neither hits nor misses if there is no target?

There is, however, a difference between "Fafner" and "dragon" in subject position. In using a word in a sentence as a proper name, one claims the ability (or at least one claims acquaintance, direct or indirect, with somebody who had the ability) to identify and reidentify an object under that name. If we suppose "Fafner" to be tied to "dragon", then, since there are no dragons, this claim as regards "Fafner" is unwarranted; and so predications with "Fafner" as subject are only pseudo predications, and are neither true nor false, being based on a presupposition that is not fulfilled. But in using "dragon" as a subject of predication a speaker does not claim that he or anyone else is or was able to identify and reidentify an object under the style "dragon . . . the same dragon . . . the same dragon . . ."—he claims only that somebody would be able to identify a dragon if confronted with it; and this claim may be warranted even if Nature grudges us dragons to identify.

It may be asked: Of what then are the predications made when the subject is an empty general term? When an ostensible, but really empty, proper name is used as a subject, the speaker (supposing him to be speaking seriously) literally does not know what he is talking about. But not to know what—i.e. which individual thing—you are talking about is no bar to the use of a general term as a subject of predication; to suppose otherwise is just part of the confusions I have long since exposed—it goes with thinking, for example, that "some man" refers to some man. We must indeed say that, though the predicate is attached to a subject, there is not a predication about anything if the subject in question is an empty general term; and to be sure this goes against our natural understanding of "predication". And we must of course not let ourselves be deceived by the thought: if a predication which is not about anything is about nothing, then it is about the null class, the class denoted by "nothing". But if we reflect on the fact that the use of a general term as subject of predication does not require any knowledge of which things that term names, we may cease to think it requisite that we should know even that the term does name something or other.

There appears, then, no decisive reason for denying a truth-value to propositions that contain an empty general term in subject position. But we have thus far no decisive reason on the other side for allowing them truth-value. It might on the contrary be said that our considerations about "the same dragon" show only that predications with "dragon" as subject have sense, not that they have truth-value.

The commonsense way of dealing with this problem would be to resort to charitable construction of the sentences that give rise to the problem, so that they get assigned a truth-value whether there are dragons or not. Notoriously there are no dragons; but it was once uncertain whether there are live duck-billed platypuses, or whether rather the stuffed specimens were artefacts like the sailor's preserved mermaid; the legitimacy of the term "platypus" should be made independent of such matters of fact. The necessary means are not hard to find. Whenever such a problem arises, the problematic term is subordinate to some term that is certainly not empty, e.g. "dragon" or "platypus" to "animal". Let us then, in sentences where "dragon" or "platypus" occurs in seeming subject position, replace it by the phrase "animal that is a dragon (platypus)", and then apply the technique previously explained for eliminating the relative pronoun "that". This removes all difficulties: the subject is now the nonempty term "animal", and the predicable "―― is a dragon" or "―― is a platypus" may be used in sentences without depriving them of truth-value even if it turns out to apply to nothing.

For example, "I have a sword that will kill any dragon" is rewritten in the first place as "I have a sword, and it will kill any animal that is a dragon"; a second use of our technique for paraphrasing away relative clauses yields:

> I have a sword; and any animal, if it is a dragon, that sword will kill.

This will certainly have a truth-value, given that one can be assigned in general for "F(any animal)". Of course most animals have no proper names and thus cannot be listed; but we shall see immediately that this is no great difficulty for our theory.

107.   There are many nonempty readings of "A" for which we cannot list the things called "A": they may have no names in our

language, or they may be infinitely numerous, or the class of As may be open toward the future. Our task is to stipulate truth-conditions, for predications with "A" as subject, which give the results already obtained whenever "A" is replaceable by a finite list, but which do not require "A" to be thus replaceable. It is not difficult to do this for the applicatives "some" and "any":

> "F(some A)" is true iff "F(a)" is true for some interpreta-
> tion of "a" as a name *of* and *for* an A;
>
> "F(any A)" is true iff "F(a)" is true for any interpretation
> of "a" as a name *of* and *for* an A.

(These schematic conditions are of course to be applied to actual concrete examples by replacing the letter "A" with some actual general term both within and outside the quotes.) It is easy to see that these truth-conditions satisfy our requirements.

If we delete from the above truth-conditions for "F(some A)" and "F(any A)" the restriction to proper names *of* and *for* an A, we obtain truth-conditions for "For some $x, F(x)$" and "For any $x, F(x)$" respectively—cf. section 95. We thus have what we have long been seeking: a clear view of the relation between the applicatives "any" and "some" and the corresponding "———thing" pronouns. For if "F( )" is Shakespearean, then "For some x, $F(x)$" and "For any x, $F(x)$" may be read as "F(something or other)" and "F(anything)" respectively.

Some logicians profess themselves unable to understand absolutely unrestricted quantification: they hold that quantification is intelligible only within a restricted Universe of Discourse, where the identity of the individuals is given once for all. But on the one hand, identity is unintelligible apart from a criterion of identity, and on the other hand there may be no one criterion of identity that fits all the individuals we wish to discourse about. Suppose our old friend Lord Newriche had a row at the Heralds' College, so that someone reporting what happened said "Lord Newriche struck Bluemantle" or "A man struck one of the heralds". There is no one criterion of identity for men and for heralds; a herald like Bluemantle has not even spatio-temporal continuity over the years; "the same material object" of course supplies no definite criterion. So there would be no one Universe within which this simple report would be interpretable. I suppose the way out for those who require restricted Universes would be resort to a many-sorted logic in which we have several Universes to play around with. But the use of quite unrestricted quantification, as in Frege and Quine, looks likely to make life easier; and I see no good reason to dismiss it as unintelligible. (I have indeed rejected their account of how it relates to restricted quantification.)

I cannot see how to devise a similar generalized truth-condition for "F(most As)". There appear, indeed, to be essential obstacles to such generalization. Consider the proposition "Most odd numbers are composite". We might regard this as true, because there are ever wider gaps between prime numbers as we go on in the series of odd numbers, 1, 3, 5, 7, . . . ; however, in view of Euclid's proof that prime numbers never peter out altogether in this series, the greater rarity of prime numbers than of composite ones among odd numbers depends on whether we take odd numbers in order of magnitude or not; and no truth-condition for "F(most As)" could well count as a generalization of the one that works for listable As if it had to bring in some order in which the As must be taken. This difficulty would not arise if we took "F(most As)" to be true, when the As are denumerably infinite, iff "$F(\quad)$" is true of 'almost all' As in the mathematical sense of the phrase—i.e. of all As except at most a finite number of As. But if the class of As is open, I can see no plausible generalized interpretation of "F(most As)".

108.   As regards "F(only (an) A)" only the sort of generalized truth-conditions just given for "F(some A)" and "F(any A)" can be given at all; for even where the As can be listed, no truth-condition for "F(only (an) A)" can be given by specifying a truth-function of predications about the several As: e.g., even if only Bill and Joe are assistants, the truth-condition of "Only an assistant had opportunity to steal the ruby" cannot be given by specifying a truth-function of predications about Bill and Joe severally. It is, however, not too difficult to state a generalized truth-condition:

> "F(only Θ)" is true iff no interpretation of "x" as a proper name makes "$F(x)$" true unless "x" names something that is named in or by "Θ".

I have here used an upper-case Greek letter as a schematic representation indifferently of a proper name, or of a list, or of a substantival general term; that is also my reason for writing "named in or by" rather than "named by", for an object is named *in* a list rather than *by* a list. This account agrees with what Aquinas long ago stated to be the role of "only": that it excludes 'every other object' (*suppositum*) from sharing in the predicate[5]—sc. every object that is not named by or in the subject-term. 'The predicate' would of course be "$F(\quad)$", not "$F(\text{only} \underline{\quad\quad})$".

Medieval logicians were greatly interested in exclusive propositions, but their treatment of them was on the whole superficial. This comes out in their having generally accepted the idea that exclusive propositions were exponible as conjunctions— "Socrates alone is wise", say, as "Socrates is wise and nobody besides (other than) Socrates is wise", and "An animal alone can bray" as "Some animal can bray and nothing besides an animal can bray". Aquinas gives this view of the contemporary logicians, in the article just cited. But in any such case the exclusive force that distinguishes this class of propositions belongs entirely to the second conjunct; the alleged exponibility of exclusive propositions thus throws no light on their distinctive character.

It is formally much more convenient to treat the exclusive proposition as having precisely the exclusive force of its supposed second component, and not to read "$F(\text{only } \Theta)$" as implying "$F(\text{some } \Theta)$" (i.e., in the degenerate case where "Θ" is taken to be a single proper name, as implying "$F(\Theta)$"). This is the way I intended my generalized truth-condition for "$F(\text{only } \Theta)$" to be read. "$F(\text{only } \Theta)$" will thus be true when "$F(\quad)$" is true of nothing at all; for "$F(x)$" will then not be true for any interpretation of "x" as a proper name, let alone its being true for some interpretation in which "x" names something not named in or by "Θ". If the force of the exclusive proposition is to exclude everything other than what is named in or by the subject-term from 'sharing in the predicate', that is no reason for reading in an implication that something named by the subject-term does

[5]Ia, q. 31, arts. 3, 4.

'share in the predicate'; and we certainly cannot exclude from our logic predicables that are not true of anything.

Exclusive propositions have some theoretical interest. In putting "only" or "alone" together with "every" and "no", Aquinas took a decisive step. It is easy enough to think that "all men", "most men", "some men", are respectively used to refer to all men, most men, and some men; it is merely crazy to suppose that "no man" refers to no men and "men alone" to men who are alone, and this consideration may help people to see through the illusion. Even the more subtle medieval theory that the applicatives have the role of showing different modes of reference will not fit either "no" or "alone"; "no" might be explained away perhaps, as a misleading linguistic fusion of "any" with a negation got out of what is being predicated of any so-and-so ("No phoenix is mortal" = "Any phoenix is immortal"), but "alone" resists any such explanation. Aquinas's naïve-seeming statement, which I cited before, that these applicatives serve to show 'how the predicate goes with the subject', is a philosophical thesis whose value becomes clear only through studying the various miscarrying attempts to set up an alternative thesis. Another interesting feature of exclusive propositions, which comes out in the generalized truth-condition, is that in a context "F(only ——)" a single proper name or a list of proper names or a substantival general term may equally stand, *salva congruitate*: this lends plausibility to the view, which I have been maintaining, that when we get incongruities with other applicatives from substituting, say, a list or a proper name for a general term, these are only the result of inessential idioms.

A related form of proposition, which we may call the restricted exclusive form, has some interest and importance, particularly for the analysis of other forms of proposition: we may state the generalized truth-condition as follows:

> "Among the As, F(only Θ)" is true iff no interpretation of
> "x" as a name *of* and *for* an A makes "$F(x)$" true unless
> "x" names something that is named in or by "Θ".

Here too the truth-condition will be satisfied if "$F(x)$" does not come out true for any interpretation of "x" as a name *of* and *for* an A; the intended sense of a restricted exclusive proposition is *merely* exclusive. "Among Lerians, only Prokles is good" will thus not imply "Prokles the Lerian is good"; it will on the contrary be compatible (as the epigram of Phokylides, from which I borrowed this example, insinuates) with "All Lerians without exception are bad".

Once we have unrestricted and restricted exclusive propositions, we can use their logical forms to analyze other propositions. For example, "No other mountain is as high as Everest" may be analyzed as:

(6) Among mountains only Everest is as high as Everest

and "No two men have broken the bank at Monte Carlo" as:

(7) (As regards) any man either (he) has not broken, or among men (he) alone has broken, the bank at Monte Carlo.

In section 74 we encountered a difficulty about the use of applicatives; with 'definable' substantival terms: since relative clauses have to be differently paraphrased away in different cases, there is no uniform relation between "$f(*(A$ that is $P))$" and "$f(*A')$" when "A'" is explained as "A that is P". In part this difficulty belongs to the way things are and we ought not to try to overcome it; for example, if the asterisk stands in for the applicative "only", "$f($only an A that is $P)$" will have different truth-conditions from "$f($only an $A')$", namely those of "As regards an(y) A, $f($that $A)$ only if it is P"—cf. section 72. We can however now use the theory of restricted exclusive propositions to give a uniform account of the relation between these forms wherever the applicative is of the *dictum de omni* kind.

For any such applicative, given that some A *is* P, "$f(*A')$", with "A'" thus explained, and "$f(*(A$ that is $P))$" will alike come out true iff:

(8) Every Θ is P, and among the As only (one of) Θ is P, and $f(*\Theta)$

comes out true for some uniform reading of the thetas, as replacing a proper name, or list of proper names, *of* and *for* As; or else as replacement for a substantival term fitting the criterion of identity for the same A, such as the term "A'''" is being supposed to be. So all that we need further is to introduce a quantifier "for some As, say Θ" that could be prefixed to (8) so as to turn the thetas into bound variables. In fact we explain this quantifier as follows:

(9) "For some As, say Θ, $F(\Theta)$" is true iff "$F(\Theta)$" comes out true for some interpretation of "Θ" as a (possibly single-item) list whose items are proper names *of* and *for* As or else as a substantival term fitting the criterion of identity for the same A.

I must emphasize that this truth-condition for the use of the quantifier must not be taken to imply that we already have in our language such a list or substantival term. (Cf. what I said about the quantifier "for some x" in section 95).

Obviously, what I have just expounded is an extremely artificial way of construing sentences of the form "$f(A$ that is $P))$", and as an account of their syntax it would be inadmissible. But our problem was one of semantics, not syntax: it looked as though, "A'" being explained as "A that is P", there were no uniform connection between the truth-conditions of "$f(* A')$" and "$f(*(A$ that is $P))$". This difficulty is now removed; and the style of quantifier employed in removing it, explained in (9), would be useful for further developing the logic of lists.

One of the applicatives to which the above account is suitable is "almost every" or "most". If we are concerned merely with giving a syntactically satisfactory account of the form "Most As that are P are Q" (with getting rid of the relative clause, as our theory requires should be feasible) then our task is easy. "Most" means "more than not": so we may first turn "Most As that are P are Q" into "More As that are P are Q than are not Q", and then turn this into "More As are both P and Q than are P but not Q". Further discussion of the logic of "most" and "more" lies beyond the purpose of this book.

109.   Instead of (6) and (7) we might have considered alternative analyses, bringing in the pronouns "the same" and "other" rather than "only". "No other mountain is as high as Everest" might

have been analyzed thus:

(10) Any mountain either is not as high as Everest or is the same mountain as Everest

which is not a silly way of putting it, for from this together with "Gaurisanker is a mountain as high as Everest" one may infer "Gaurisanker is the same mountain as Everest", a nontrivial conclusion. (An explorer, observing from an unfamiliar viewpoint the mountain locally known as Gaurisanker, might measure the height of Gaurisanker and so be led to this conclusion.) It is no matter that the conclusion would be false; a logical example need not be true. This seems to be forgotten sometimes, so I spell it out.

Similarly, "Just one man has broken the bank at Monte Carlo" might be analyzed as:

(11) Any man either did not break the bank at Monte Carlo or, if any man did break the bank at Monte Carlo, is the same man as he.

I have used "the same" in (8) and (9), but might equally have used "another":

(12) No mountain both is as high as Everest and is another mountain than Everest.

(13) If any man broke the bank at Monte Carlo, then no man both broke the bank at Monte Carlo and is another man than he.

"The same A" and "another A" can obviously be defined in terms of each other: "x is the same A as y" as "x is an A and y is an A and x is not another A than y", and "x is another A than y" as "x is an A and y is an A and x is not the same A as y". The relation between this pair of pronouns and "only" is one that we cannot yet state precisely. It would be easy to state it if we might analyze "is the same A as" into "is an A and is the same as"; but we have rejected this analysis.

How in fact are we to deal with "the same A" and its relation to the general term "A"? We must distinguish two kinds of use of "the same A": subject-use, and predicative use as part of the two-place predicable "is the same A as". Subject-uses of "the same A" go to signify that a number of predicables are supposed to hold all together of some individual for which the common name "A" stands. Continued and repeated use of a name does indeed involve a criterion of identity, but this is not a problem of syntax; in a regimented language there could simply be repetition of a variable "x" bound to a quantifier that was restricted by use of the name "A". E.g. for "Socrates kicked a dog and the (same) dog bit Plato" we might have "For some dog x, Socrates kicked x and x bit Plato". The relevant identity shows (*zeigt sich*, as Wittgenstein says) in the repetition of the variable; no identity *predicable* is needed.

Let us now consider "is the same A as". We quickly see that "a is the same A as b" is not to be explained as meaning "There is some A that a is and that b also is", i.e. as:

(14) There is some A, say z, such that a is z and b is z.

Formula (14) would be true iff some interpretation of "z" as a proper name of an A made "a is z" and "b is z" both true. But these cannot be read as predications of "z" if "z" is read as a proper name; rather, "is z" must be construed as "is the same as z". Is the same *what* as z? Plainly, the same A as z—and we are back where we began.

However, we can offer "is the same A as *something*" to analyze away the predicative use, "is an A", of a substantival general term. For our using the expression "is the same A as" requires "A" to be construed as such a term, and in that case a thing is an A iff it is the same A as something or other; and there is no risk of a vicious circle, just because "is the same A as" does not admit of the analysis "is an A and is the same as", which would leave "is an A" again on our hands. The substantival general term thus no longer even appears to be characterized by an ability to bridge the gulf between names and predicables; if we eliminate "is an A" in this way, the term "A" will occur only either in subject positions or as forming a part of "is the same A as", which is a two-place predicable with various important logical properties (e.g. reflexiveness, symmetry, and transitiveness).

In counting we go by such equivalence relations. For example, "How many cats?" means "How many different, distinct, cats?"; and "x and y are different cats" means "x is a cat and y is a cat and x is not the same cat as y"; and here the one-place predicable "—— is a cat" must itself be explained in terms of "is the same cat as", namely as "—— is the same cat as something (or other)". To borrow a word from Quine, the one-place predicable is a *derelativization* of the two-place predicable, just as "—— is a father" is derived by the same logical procedure from "—— is father of ——".

We are tempted by our vernacular to think that in such cases the two-place predicable is derived by some procedure from the one-place predicable. But if "A" stands in for some term of kinship, like "father", "uncle", or "mother-in-law", there is no describable logical procedure that would get us from "—— is an A" to "—— is A of ——"; the derivation has to go the other way, "—— is an A" being explained as "—— is A of somebody or other". I remember finding in a logic book an exercise in which the student was asked to construct a schema showing the validity of the argument:

> Any mother is a parent; Jane is Mary's mother; *ergo* Jane is Mary's parent.

Replacement of "mother" in the premises by "mother-in-law" or "grandmother" immediately shows *that* this argument is in fact fallacious; to see *why* it is fallacious, we need to think of "mother" and "parent" in the first premise as obtained by derelativization. There is not, logically speaking, a framework "—— is —— of ——" into which a kinship term may be inserted to make a two-place predicable, e.g. "—— is mother of ——".

I am arguing that the same holds good concerning "—— is the same —— as ——". We must not regard substantival general terms as the kind of terms that can be inserted in this framework to make a two-place predicable; rather, if "A" is such a term, "—— is an A" is exponible by "—— is the same A as something or other". The common verbal pattern of these two-place predicables hints at their shared logical properties, but must not be

The Logic of Lists

taken to show that some one logical procedure is performable on substantival general terms to get these predicables.

110. How is "—— is the same A as ——" related to a proper name *for* an A? To attack this problem, I shall first set forth a paradox that I developed from a *sophisma* of William of Sherwood.

The fat cat sat on the mat. There was just one cat on the mat. The cat's name was "Tibbles": "Tibbles" is moreover a name *for* a cat.—This simple story leads us into difficulties if we assume that Tibbles is a normal cat. For a normal cat has at least 1,000 hairs. Like many empirical concepts, the concept (*single*) *hair* is fuzzy at the edges; but it is reasonable to assume that we can identify in Tibbles at least 1,000 of his parts each of which definitely is a single hair. I shall refer to these hairs as h_1, h_2, h_3, ... up to $h_{1,000}$.

Now let c be the largest continuous mass of feline tissue on the mat. Then for any of our 1,000 cat-hairs, say h_n, there is a proper part c_n of c which contains precisely all of c except the hair h_n; and every such part c_n differs in a describable way both from any other such part, say c_m, and from c as a whole. Moreover, fuzzy as the concept *cat* may be, it is clear that not only is c a cat, but also any part c_n is a cat: c_n would clearly be a cat were the hair h_n plucked out, and we cannot reasonably suppose that plucking out a hair *generates* a cat, so c_n must already have been a cat. So, contrary to our story, there was not just one cat called "Tibbles" sitting on the mat; there were at least 1,001 sitting there! Of course this would involve a great deal of overlap and sharing of organs among these 1,001 cats, but logic has nothing to say against that; after all, it happens on a small scale between Siamese twins.

All the same, this result *is* absurd. We simply do not speak of cats, or use names of cats, in this way; nor is our ordinary practice open to logical censure. I am indeed far from thinking that ordinary practice never is open to logical censure; but I do not believe our ordinary use of proper names and count nouns is so radically at fault as this conclusion would imply.

Everything falls into place if we realize that the number of cats on the mat is the number of *different cats* on the mat; and c_{13}, c_{279}, and c are not three different cats, they are one and the same cat. Though none of these 1,001 lumps of feline tissue is the same lump of feline tissue as another, each *is* the same cat as any other: each of them, then, is a cat, but there is only one cat on the mat, and our original story stands.

Thus each one of the names "$c_1, c_2, \ldots c_{1,000}$", or again the name "$c$", is a name of a cat; but none of these 1,001 names is a name *for* a cat, as "Tibbles" is. By virtue of its sense "Tibbles" is a name, not for one and the same *thing* (in fact, to say that would really be to say nothing at all), but for one and the same *cat*. This name for a cat has reference, and it names the one and only cat on the mat; but just on that account "Tibbles" names, as a shared name, both c itself and any of the smaller masses of feline tissue like c_{12} and c_{279}; for all of these are one and the same cat, though not one and the same mass of feline tissue. "Tibbles" is not a name *for* a mass of feline tissue.

So we recover the truth of the simple story we began with. The price to pay is that we must regard "—— is the same cat as ——" as expressing only a certain equivalence relation, not an absolute identity restricted to cats; but this price, I have elsewhere argued, must be paid anyhow, for there is no such absolute identity as logicians have assumed.

Moreover (slow as I have been to see this) we find ourselves committed to the view of the Polish logician Leśniewski about the category of names: that logic can and must avoid assuming a *syntactical* category of *proper* names. There is a syntactical category of names, but whether a name is a proper name or a shared name is a matter not of syntax but of semantics; and in any event we must say that what a name's sense restricts it to is not being a name for one and the same *thing*, but rather, for one and the same A. As we have seen, a proper name for an A may be a shared name of several Bs, given that each of these Bs is the same A as any of the others.

Let us take another look at an earlier example of ours: proper names for heralds. Let us pretend that "Hilary Handel" is a name *of* and *for* a man, and (with acknowledgment to the late Ian

Fleming) that "Sable Basilisk" is a name *of* and *for* a herald. At a given point of time the man Hilary Handel is a herald, in fact he is (the same herald as) the herald Sable Basilisk; conversely, at the same point of time the herald Sable Basilisk is a man, in fact he is (the same man as) the man Hilary Handel. When Hilary Handel is a herald, "Hilary Handel" is a name of a herald; but "the same herald" does not give us the criterion of identity that is built into the sense of "Hilary Handel", so this is not a name *for* a herald. Conversely, "Sable Basilisk" is regularly a name of some man or other, of Hilary Handel, say, at the moment; but because "the same man" does not give us the criterion of identity that is built into the sense of "Sable Basilisk", this is not a name *for* a man. One and the same man, say Hilary Handel, may at different times be (be the same herald as) different heralds: conversely, one and the same herald, say Sable Basilisk, may at different times be (be the same man as) different men. The relation between proper names for heralds and for men, and between the general terms "herald" and "man", is thus quite symmetrical: I could have brought out this symmetry by further elaborating the example in section 91, which did not exploit any logical difference between "man" and "herald". It is of no concern to logic that "man" is a substance term and "herald" is not: this is as little relevant as that God no doubt cares more for men than for heralds.

If we drop the syntactical category distinction between proper and shared names, this rules out a line of thought I followed in earlier editions of this book. I followed Frege in disallowing empty proper names, but I allowed as names empty substantival terms like "dragon". If, as I have argued, a proper name (for an A) can be a shared name (of several Bs, simultaneously or successively), then this line becomes untenable: and so I reject empty names altogether. Where this use of empty common names seems to occur, we need not harshly dismiss discourse as truth-valueless, but may resort to charitable construction as in section 106.

When used as a name, "cat" is a name *of* each cat, impartially and distributively; but it is not a name *for* a cat, except in the cases, discussed in sections 32 and 34, where it stands in grammatical apposition to a demonstrative. (There is a similar case, which I neglected to mention there, when a common noun is being used *pro hac vice* as a proper name of an object of the appropriate kind: in sentences like "Doctor"—or "Nurse"—"will be with you in a minute", "Cook was insolent to Mother today", "Doctor", "Nurse", "Cook", and "Mother" are used as *ad hoc* proper names of a particular doctor, nurse, cook, or mother.) When a name *for* a cat is used twice over, the implication is that we are referring to one and the same cat (apart from accidental homonymy); but there is no such implication when "cat" is used twice over as a name. The connection of "cat" used as a name with "—— is the same cat as ——" is less direct than the connection a name *for* a cat has: it comes out, for example, in the fact that if there were a finite class of cats, all of them bearing proper names, then "cat" used as a name would be replaceable *salva veritate* by a list of names each corresponding to the criterion of identity given in "the same cat".

I have left to the last one troublesome unsolved problem. If a name "a" is a shared name, a predicable "$F(\ )$" may be true of one thing called "a" and false of another: what then is the truth-condition for "$F(a)$"? As we have now seen, this problem arises for what would ordinarily count as proper names, e.g. the proper name "Tibbles" in regard to the predicable "has hair h_{279} as a part". For a regimented language, with a definite and unexpandable vocabulary of primitive predicables, it is not difficult to give recursive truth-conditions such that there is no danger to *consistency* arising over this; but I have thus far found no solution with the *neatness* that ought to characterize logic. So I leave this as a problem for the reader.

Appendix

The letters used in Chapter One may occur both in 'subject' and in 'predicate' position; e.g., the two schemata "Every S is P" and "Every P is S" would admit of the same readings of "S" and "P". This sort of schema is of course quite acceptable to supporters of traditional logic, since they are committed to the notion of a 'term' which can fill the role of subject or predicate equally well without change of sense. But I have argued in Chapter Two that this notion of 'terms' is incoherent. How then does it lie in my mouth even to discuss, let alone to affirm, the validity or invalidity of argument-schemata whose interpretation would require shift of a 'term' between subject and predicate role? Ought I not rather to have dismissed such use of schematic letters as nonsensical? As Frege said, logic cannot utilize nonsense but only characterize nonsense as such.

It is in fact easy to escape from this trap. The categoricals represented by the schemata in Chapter One may be supposed to apply within a restricted Universe of Discourse (see section 107). Let us suppose, as in Lewis Carroll's logical writings, that the Universe is delimited by some general term such as "cat" or "cake", which gives the criterion for identifying members of the Universe and the sense of counting them; let "U" stand in for this general term. Then "Every S is P" may be spelled out as "Every U that is–S is–P"; here "U" is a shared *name*, but "is–S" and "is–P" stand in for *predicables* that apply or fail to apply to any given U. Similarly "Most MNs are A" in section 13 may be spelled out thus: "Almost every U that is–M and is–N is–A", with use of "almost every", as in section 36, in place of "most". (The predicables thus represented of course need not contain an "is".) No problem about an expression's playing now a subject, now a predicate, role even seems to arise any longer; and my refutations of distribution theory go over without my having needed to use, even provisionally, schemata that make sense only if there are 'terms' as traditionally understood.

Bibliography

The works listed here are those referred to in the text of the book by the author's name (followed by a numeral if several works by the same author have been cited).

Aquinas, Thomas. *Summa theologica, Pars prima.*

Burleigh, Walter. *De puritate artis logicae.* Edited by Philotheus Boehner. St. Bonaventure, N.Y.: The Franciscan Institute, 1955.

Copi, Irving. *Introduction to Logic.* 5th ed. New York: Macmillan, 1978.

De Morgan, A. *Formal Logic.* London: Taylor & Walton, 1847.

Frege, G. (1) *The Foundations of Arithmetic.* German text with *en face* translation by J. L. Austin. 2d ed. Oxford: Basil Blackwell, 1953.

———. (2) *Grundgesetze der Arithmetik.* 2 vols. in 1. Hildesheim: Georg Olms, 1962.

———. (3) *Philosophical Writings.* Translated by P. T. Geach and Max Black. 3d ed. Oxford: Basil Blackwell, 1980.

Geach, P. T. *Logic Matters.* Oxford: Basil Blackwell, 1972.

Johnson, W. E. *Logic.* Vol. 2. Cambridge: Cambridge University Press, 1922.

Kretzmann, N. (1) *William of Sherwood's Introduction to Logic.* Minneapolis: University of Minnesota Press, 1967.

———. (2) *William of Sherwood's Treatise on Syncategorematic Words.* Minneapolis: University of Minnesota Press, 1968.

Bibliography

Keynes, Neville. *Formal Logic*. 4th ed. London: Macmillan, 1928.

Luce, A. A. *Logic*. Teach Yourself Books. London: English Universities Press, 1958.

Ockham, William of. *Summa logicae*. Edited by Philotheus Boehner, G. Gal, and S. Brown. St. Bonaventure, N.Y.: The Franciscan Institute, 1974.

O'Donnell, J. Reginald. "The Syncategoremata of William of Sherwood." *Mediaeval Studies*, III (1953).

Quine, W. Van O. *Methods of Logic*. 3d ed. New York: Holt, Rinehart & Winston, 1972.

Russell, Bertrand. *The Principles of Mathematics*. London: Allen & Unwin, 1937.

Strawson, P. F. *Introduction to Logical Theory*. London: Methuen, 1952.

Whitehead, A. N., and Bertrand Russell. *Principia Mathematica*. Vol. 1. Cambridge: Cambridge University Press, 1910.

Wittgenstein, L. *Tractatus Logico-philosophicus*. London: Routledge & Kegan Paul, 1968.

Index

Italicized numerals show the pages where the term considered is introduced or explained.

"a" phrases:
  "a B" refers to a B?, 36, 60f., 66, 119,
    154
  dictum de omni and, 120–122
  as distributed, 36, 44
  lists (disjunctive) and, 82, 92–95, 196f.
  namely-riders and, 91
  predicative use of, 36f., 60–62, 74, 80,
    95, 171, 213f.
  "some" phrases and, 90–92, 94–96,
    99–102, 123–125, 133f., 196f.
  truth-conditions with, 94f., 97
  as undistributed, 36f., 43–45, 124
"A, if it is P" phrases, 140, 143, 147
"A that is P" phrases, 77f., 142–145, 147,
  149–151, 189f., 210f.
abbreviation, 147f., 150
adjectival terms, *63*
Albert of Saxony, 160
"all" phrases, 29, 34, 75–78, 128f.
all, the, *197*
"almost all", 207
"almost every" phrases, 13, *74*, 108f., 220
  see also "most" phrases
"alone", 35, 38f., 208–210
  see also exclusive propositions *and*
    "only"

ambiguity:
  applicatives and, 192, 195f.
  systematic, 145–147, 172
  with two-place predicables, 125–129
ampliation, *80*
analysis of propositions, double, *see* propositions
Anscombe, Miss G. E. M., 32f.
antecedents of pronouns, *see* relative pronouns
"any" phrases:
  dictum de omni and, 114–116
  distributed, 44f., 124
  "every" phrases and, 44, 96–102, 104,
    122–126, 129, 132f., 160
  as referring phrases, 76f.
  reflexive pronouns with, 160–162
  Russell on, 98–104, 124–127
  scope of, 77, 86–88, 103f., 132
  "some" phrases with, 125–127
  truth-conditions for, 89f., 97, 106
applicatival phrases, 13, *73*, 74f.
  restricted, *73f.*, 89
applicatives, *73*
  "A that is P" phrases and, 145, 150f.,
    210f.
  ambiguity removed by?, 192, 195f.

Index

applicatives (*cont.*)
  Aquinas on, 201f., 209
  dictum de omni, 108f., 111–116, 150f., 193–195, 198, 200, 210f.
  Frege on, 83, 85, 200f.
  incongruous, 192, 195, 209
  Ockham on, 81
  predicates modified by, 85f., 112–114, 197, 200
  redundancy of, 112–114, 195
  "-thing" pronouns and, 170f.
"applies to", *50*
  see also "true of"
apposition, grammatical, 65f., 68, 71, 109, 192, 217
Aquinas, St. Thomas, 10, 187
  on applicatives, 201f., 209
  on 'material' and 'formal' use of terms, 201f., 208f.
  on "only", 208f.
  on substantival and adjectival terms, 63
  on *suppositio*, 84
'Aristotelian' logic, 27, 59f., 171
  see also terms, logic of *and* traditional logic
Aristotle:
  on copulas, 60
  distribution in?, 27f.
  on names, 59, 149
  on negative terms, 64
  on subject-predicate analysis, 54
  on tense, 59
  use-mention confusion in, 50
articles, not in Latin, 8f., 81
"*asher*", Hebrew word, 146
assertoric force, 51f., 53, 203
"attached to", *49f.*

bearer of a name, *55*
  absent or nonexistent, 55f., 69, 114, 186–188, 202–205
Bedeutung: see Frege
Begriff: see Frege
Berkeley, G., 96, 133
Boole, G., 36, 46
Buridan, J., *frontispiece*, 9f., 80
  Buridan's Law, *10*, 60, 80, 117, 152f.
Burleigh, Walter, 124, 159f.

canceling-out fallacy, *88*, 95, 113f., 143, 155
  see also 56
Carnap, R., 8, 181
Carroll, Lewis, 142, 219

cat-and-mouse paralogism, 95, 133
cat-on-the-mat paralogism, 215f.
categories, 15, *178f.*, 185
  of names, 15, 183f., 216f.
  of predicables, 196
  of schematic letters, 179, 185, 210f.
charitable construals, 187, 205
chemical analogy, 84, 130, 164
Church, A., 84
classes:
  designations of, 29, 35, 47, 62, 99, 139
  logic of, 28f., 34–36, 62
  relations of, 35f., 61f., 98f.
  unlistable, 79, 89, 202, 205–207
  see also null class *and* set theory
"class-names", 29
combinations of objects, 83f., 89, 95, 198
common nouns:
  acts of naming with, 53, 59, 65, 69
  demonstratives and, 53f., 65f.
  proper names and, 52f., 59, 68–71, 112–114
  reference of, 69f.
  "same (the)" with, 59, 64, 114
  subject use of, 65, 69f., 201, 213, 217f.
  see also general terms *and* substantival terms
complex terms:
  see "A that is P" phrases; descriptions, definite; *and* "thing that"
confused *suppositio*, 90:
  confused and distributive, 90
  merely confused, 90–96, 120f.
  see also "a" phrases
conjunctive *suppositio*, 97, 160
  see also "every" phrases
connectives:
  with names, *see* lists
  with predicables, 86, 130, 198
    with two-place predicables, 156f., 167
  with pronouns, 140f., 143, 145–147, 150, 210
  with propositions, 14, 51, 58, 86, 103f.
constants, logical, 157f.
contexts of phrases, 75
  intentional, 180–182, 188
  as predicables, 105–107
  see also canceling-out fallacy *and* scope
conversion of categoricals, 36, 47f.
copula(s):
  Aristotle on, 60
  class relations and, 61
  Frege on, 60, 63

Index

Hobbes on, 60
of identity, 67, 74f., 95
  see also "is an A" predicables
tense of, 62, 80, 175
count nouns, 14
counting, 63f., 177, 214–216
criterion of identity, 13, 63f., 68, 70f.,
  173, 177, 181, 199n., 203f., 216f.

dead, predicates true of the, 55f.
definitions, 147–150
demonstrative pronouns, 53f., 65f., 217
De Morgan, A., 117
denoting, 28–30, 57, 83f.
  denoting concepts, 83
derelativization, *214*
Descartes, R., 107
descriptions, definite:
  medieval logicians ignore, 9, 131
  notation for, 139
  predicative use of, 74f., 131, 150
  proper names and, 68, 148, 150
  as referring phrases, 77f.
  unimportance of, 140f.
determinate *suppositio*, *90*, 94–96, 120,
  126
  see also "some" phrases
diagrams for reflexive pronouns, 165f.
dictum de omni, 13f., *115*
  apparent exceptions, 118–123, 161f.
  applicatives governed by, 108, 111–116,
    150f., 193–195, 200
  applicatives not governed by:
    see "a", "every", "few", "just one",
     and "no" phrases, *see also* "only"
  fallacious proof of, 111f.
  reflexive pronouns and, 161f.
  as thematic rule, 109f., 115
distributed terms, *28*, 36, 44, 90
  "all" phrases as, 34f., 47
  "any" phrases as, 44, 47f., 124
  "every" phrases as, 29, 38f., 44, 124
  negated terms as, 36–40
  "some" phrases as?, 44f.
  see also distribution, doctrine of, *and*
    distributive *suppositio*
distribution, doctrine of, 12f.
  for predicate terms, 36–40
  for subject terms, 29–36
  see also illicit process *and* 'undistributed
    middle'
distributive *suppositio*, *90*
  see also "any" phrases

"each" phrases *vice* "any" phrases, 120–
  122
elucidations of names, 147–152
empty general terms, *see* general terms
empty names, *see* names
empty predicables, *see* predicables
"every" phrases:
  "any" phrases and, *see* "any" phrases
  class designations and, 28f., 61f.
  dictum de omni and, 108f., 122f., 195
  distributed, 29f., 36f., 44, 124
  "every A" refers to every A?, 9, 30, 45,
    48, 85, 112, 159
  Frege on, 62, 85f., 200
  lists (conjunctive) and, 97, 99f., 107,
    200
  negation with, 85f.
  as referring expressions, 81–83
  reflexive pronouns with, 9, 159f.
  Russell on, 82f., 99f., 102
  scope of, 86, 107, 129, 131f., 134f.
  truth-conditions with, 97, 106f., 200
  two-place predicables and, 123f.
  undistributed?, 45
exceptive propositions, 131f.
exclusive propositions:
  restricted, 14f., *209–211*
  unrestricted, 14f., 93, *207–209*
    suppositio in, 93, 196f.
  see also "alone" *and* "only"
existence, 10, 185–187, 189

failure of reference, 15, 30f., 80, 153,
  186f., 202–205, 217
"few" phrases, 118f., 108
Frege, G.:
  on applicatival phrases, 83, 85, 200f.
  on assertion, 51
  on *Bedeutung*, 83f.
  on *Begriffe* (concepts), 63, 83f., 200f.
  on copulas, 60, 62, 67
  on countability, 63f., 176f.
  on definitions, 148f.
  on existence, 10, 185, 189
  on identity (equality), 64, 67, 149, 176
  on indirect discourse, 187
  on level of concepts, 85f., 185, 189
  on names, 52, 64, 148f., 201f.
    on empty names, 15, 186, 217
  on nonsense, 219
  on one-one correlation, 14, 176f.
  on pronouns 139
  on quantification, 166, 174, 207

Index

Frege, G.: (cont.)
 on sense and truth-conditions, 182
 on variables, 139

Geach, G. H., 12
Geach, P. T. 39n.
general terms:
 class designations and, 29, 35f., 47, 98f.
 empty, 202–205, 217
 as names, 52f., 59–61, 63–67, 69–71,
  200f., 216–220
 reference of, 69f., 80f., 184, 200f.
 singular reference of, 65f., 68, 217f.
 see also common nouns *and* substantival terms
 grammar to be ignored, 54, 74, 85, 140f.,
  146, 150, 192, 195

Hamilton, W.:
 on intension, 181
 on "most", 40, 117
 on quantification, 27, 46f.
 on "some", 46
historicism, 7, 9
Hobbes, T., 60

identity:
 see copula(s), criterion of identity; Frege,
  G.; *and* "same (the)"
"iff", 89n.
illicit process, 12, *38*, 39–41, 43f.
indefinite indicators, *139*
indefinite pronouns, 136, 169
indirect speech, 179f., 182, 186–188
"intention(al)" etc., spelling of, 180
intentional objects, 181f.
intentional predicables, 180–182, 188f.
interpretations of letters, 179f., 182–185,
 206–211
Irish English, 164f.
"is an A" predicables, 61f., 143, 148, 150,
 171, 213f.

Johnson, W. E., 73
"just one" phrases, 73, 76, 118f., 150–153

Keynes, J. N.:
 on class names, 28, 37
 on denoting and referring, 29–31
 on distribution, 12f.
 on illicit process, 39, 48n.
 on "most" phrases, 41, 117n.
 on particular negatives, 37, 39
 on quantified predicates, 46

on "some but not all", 34, 46
on undistributed middle, 41, 116f.
on undistributed terms, 28f., 34
kinship terms, 214
Kneale, W. C., 44n.

Latin syntax, 8f., 63, 80f., 141, 146
laziness, pronouns of, 151f., 155f., 158f.,
 168
Leśniewski, S., 15, 216
lists, 14
 "and" joining, 82, 97, 99, 106, 122,
  124, 132, 196–198
 applicatives with, 191–200
 Frege's neglect of, 201
 nonrepetitive, 106, 199
 one-item, 75, 78, 107, 192, 195f.
 "only" with, 93, 196f., 207–210
 "or" joining, 82, 92–95, 99, 101, 103,
  106, 124, 196–198
 order of names in, 192f., 207
 reference of, 191f.
  see also combinations of objects
 referring phrases and, 75–79
 as subjects, 195–197, 201
 truth-conditions with, 194f., 198–200,
  207–210
Locke, J., 68f.
Łukasiewicz, J., 28

mass terms, 14, 64
mathematicians and logic, 7, 9
'meanings', 81f.
medieval logic, 8–10, 16
 puzzles (sophismata) from, 9, 43–45,
  61, 124f., 131f., 143f., 155, 215
 technical terms of:
  a pluribus determinatis ad unum determinatum, 126
  ampliatio, 80
  casus, 127f.
  demonstratio ad sensum, 66
  improbatio, 128
  intensio and *intentio, 181*
  probatio, 128
  propositio, 51
  recordatio rei antelatae, 151
  relativa, 140
  restrictio, 74, 77–79
  salva congruitate, 178
  signum, 81
  sophisma, 128
  stare pro, 84
  see also dictum de omni and suppositio

Index

Meinong, A., 30
mental language, 81f.
Moody, E. A., 10
"more", 211
"most" phrases:
  complex terms in, 78, 151, 211
  dictum de omni and, 116, 118, 120
  'illicit process' and, 40
  lists with, 75–77, 106, 191, 198–200
  "most As" refers to most As?, 117
  as referring phrases, 75–77
  "some" phrases and, 40, 43
  syntax of, 74, 191
  truth-conditions with, 106, 127–129,
    198–200, 207, 211
  two in one proposition, 127–129
  'ultratotal distribution' with, 117
  'undistributed middle' with, 42f., 116f.
  see also "almost all"; "almost every"
    phrases; *and* "more"

name *for* an A, 13, *70f.*, 174, 184, 215–
  218
name *of* and *for* an A, *70*, 75, 89, 97, 106,
  109, 113–115, 162, 194, 206, 209,
  211, 215–218
namely-riders, *91*
names:
  Aristotle on, 59, 149
  bearers of, 55
    possible absence of, 55f., 67, 69, 204
  criteria of identity and, 59, 63, 216–218
  empty, 15, 186–188, 202–205, 217
  Frege on, 52, 149, 200
  negatable?, 58f., 64f.
  predicables and, 57–59, 148, 171–173,
    205, 213, 217f.
  shared, 70f., 113f., 149, 174, 184,
    200–202, 213, 216–218
  simplicity of, 148f.
  tenselessness of, 55, 172f.
  Wittgenstein on, 52, 149
  see also proper names
naming, acts of, *52f.*
  demonstratives and, 53f., 65f.
  general terms in, 52f., 63, 65f., 69,
    203f.
  negation of, 59, 64f.
  propositions and, 52–54, 65, 69
  "the same" in, 69, 203f.
negative terms, 64
"no" phrases, 34f., 76, 83, 118, 193, 209
nominal essence, 68

Noonan, H., 13
null class, 34f., 202f., 204

occurrences of expressions (genuine or
  spurious), 85, 120–123, 130, 161f.,
  165f., 179, 201f.
Ockham, William of:
  on applicatives, 81
  on "becoming", 61
  on confused *suppositio*, 92, 94
  on mental language, 81f.
  on modes of referring, 80f.
  "stare pro", *"supponere pro"*, in, 84
  two-name theory in, 61, 80
"one", word for, 8f., 64, 176
one-one correlation, 14, 176f.
"only":
  Aquinas on, 201, 209
  complex terms with, 145, 147, 210
  general terms with, 196, 200, 208
  lists with, 93, 196f.
  predicables formed with, 197, 200,
    209–211
  proper names with, 93, 195–197
  truth-conditions with, 207–210
  see also "alone" *and* exclusive propo-
    sitions
order:
  of filling up places, 129, 131f., 161
  of logical procedures, 129–132, 164f.
  of names in lists, 192f., 205
  of numbers, 205
  of quantifiers, 134f., 138f.
ordinary language philosophers, 7, 9f.,
  119, 128
Oxford philosophers, 10, 146, 189

paralogisms:
  Berkeley's, 96, 133f.
  cat-and-mouse, 95
  cat-on-the-mat, 215f.
  cat-with-three-tails, 34f.
  donkey, 142
  neo-Stoic, 55
  philosophers', 104
  politicians' and salesmen's, 104
particular negatives, 37–40
Peirce, C. S., 132
Polish syntax, 53, 61, 75
portmanteau expressions, 118f., 140f.,
  143, 145, 150
predicables, *50*, *52*
  connectives with, 86, 130, 157f., 167,
    198

227

Index

predicables (*cont.*)
 contexts and, 105–107
 Frege on, 85, 185, 189, 200f.
 level of, 85, 185, 189
 negation of, 57f., 64, 84f., 157
 "only" as forming, 197, 200, 209–211
 Shakespearean, *188*, 189, 191, 200, 206
 tense in, 59, 61f.
 two- and many-place, 123, 126f., 129, 134f., 138f., 156–158, 162–168, 213f., 218
 ungenuine occurrence of, *see* occurrences of expressions
 see also applicatives *and* derelativization
predicate, *50, 52*
 distribution of, 36–38, 40
 extraction of, 54–57
 quantification of, 45–47
 see also predicables *and* subject (terms)
"predicated of", *49f.*
Principia Mathematica, 12, 157f.
Principles of Mathematics, 79
Prior, A. N., 9, 16
pronouns: *see* demonstrative, indefinite, reciprocal, reflexive, *and* "-thing" pronouns; *see also* "asher", "such that", *and* laziness, pronouns of
proper names:
 as abbreviations?, 148–150
 acts of naming with, 53f., 59, 66
 category of, 15, 179, 216
 criterion of identity with, *see* criterion of identity
 descriptions and, 68, 74f., 148–150
 distributed?, 30, 36, 113
 empty, 15, 55, 186–188, 203f., 217
 'genuine', 53f.
 identity statements with, 67, 74, 148–150, 213, 215f.
 impredicability of, 37, 67, 186, 213
 in indirect speech, 180, 186–188
 Locke on, 68
 Quine on, 54, 174, 185
 Russell on, 53, 68
 use or mention of?, 49f., 59, 67, 187f.
 as words in languages, 53
prepositions, *51*
 double analysis of, 54f., 85f., 95, 121f., 124, 128f., 161
 portmanteau, 118
 simple acts of naming and, 53f., 65f., 69
 see also singular propositions *and* truth-conditions
Propositions, *51*, 82

quantifiers, quantifications, 27
 'capture' of variables by, 168
 order of, 134f., 138f.
 of predicates, 45–47
 Quine on, 168, 174–177, 180–182, 184f.
 restricted and unrestricted, 134, 174–176, 178–180, 182–184
 scope of, 137f.
 substitutional, 79, 179, 182–184, 211
 see also variables, bound
quasi subjects, *84*, 121f., 129, 201
Quine, W. Van O., 7, 9, 16
 on abstract entities, 184
 on 'capture' of variables, 168
 "denotes" in, 84
 on derelativization, 214
 on existence ("to be"), 185f.
 on indirect speech, 180f.
 on intentional objects, 181
 on "is" (copula), 175
 on proper names, 174, 186
 on quantification, 174, 177, 181
 on values of variables, 184f.

Realism, 83, 89, 95
reciprocal pronouns, 158
reference, modes of, *79*
 Anscombe on, 32f.
 Carnap on, 181
 confused, 90–96, 120f., 126, 159f., 196, 198
 conjunctive, 97, 104, 160
 determinate, *90*, 91, 94, 96, 120f., 126, 160, 196
 distributive, *90*, 126, 159f.
 indirect, 181, 187
 Ockham on, 80f., 92–95
 "only" and, 93, 196f.
 for reflexive pronouns, 159–162
 Russell on, 80–83, 88f., 98, 102–104
reference, personal, 31f., 119, 153
referring phrase, 13, *75–79*
 see also "a", "any", "every", "most", *and* "some" phrases; descriptions, definite; *and* scope
reflexive pronouns:
 Albert of Saxony on, 160
 Burleigh on, 159f.
 diagrams for, 165f.
 many-place predicables with, 163f.
 "only" with, 159, 164f.
 proper names with, 56f., 159, 164f.
 referring phrases with, 9, 159–162
 symbolism for, 167f.

Index

"that very" phrases and, 162
truth-conditions with, 159f.
relative clauses, 143–147, 150f., 210f.
  connectives buried in, 140f., 145–147, 150, 210
  defining and qualifying, 141f.
relative pronouns, *140*
  grammatically relative, 140f., 143–145, 147–150
  reference picked up by?, *9, 119,* 152–159, 168
  variables and, 136–139, 157, 165–168
  see also laziness, pronouns of
restricted applicatival phrases, *73f.,* 89
restricted exclusive propositions, 14f., 209–211
restricted quantification, 134, 174–176, 180, 182, 189f., 206f.
  see also universe of discourse
restricted terms, 74, 77–79, 150f., 210f.
rules, logical:
  in doctrine of distribution, 12, 38–44
  of elimination and introduction, *110f.*
  medieval, 126
  Russell's, 98f., 127f.
  schematic and thematic, 109f.
  see also dictum de omni
Russell, B.:
  on "a" and "some" phrases, 9, 90, 92, 94f.
  on "any" and "every" phrases, 98
  on "any" phrases with "some" phrases, 99
  on combinations of objects, 82f., 88f.
  on "denotes", 83f.
  on existence, 189
  on "is" (copula), 95
  on 'meanings', 81–83
  "no" phrases in, 83
  on proper names, 53, 68
  on Propositions, 82
  Realism in, 82, 88, 95
  on referring phrases, 79:
    fourfold scheme, 97f.
  on scope, 87
  set-theoretical examples in, 98–102
  on "such that", 145f.
Ryle, G., 91

salva congruitate substitution (syntax-preserving):
  of lists and single names, 107, 192, 195f., 209
  of referring phrases for proper names, 74, 84f.

of "same" phrases for proper names, 69, 114, 174, 203f., 213
  for schematic letters, 70, 178–180, 182, 207–211
  for substantival terms, 191, 200, 209
salva veritate substitution (truth-preserving):
  of antecedent for pronoun, 9, 57, 119, 155f., 159, 164f., 168
  of connective for "such that", 146
  of connective plus pronoun for pronoun, 140f., 143–145, 150
  of definite description and proper name, 68, 148–150
  of lists and referring phrases, 75–78, 92–95, 97, 122–124
  of lists for substantival terms, 191, 200
  of proper name for proper name?, 180, 188
  of simple for complex terms, 147–151, 211
  of "the same A" for proper name, 114
  of unrestricted for restricted quantification, 134, 174–176, 180, 182, 189f.
"same, the":
  in acts of naming, 59, 63, 213f.
  Frege on, 64, 148, 176f.
  and "other", 211f.
  phrases formed with, 63f., 215–218:
    predicative use of, 67, 148, 176f., 180, 182, 188, 212–215
    subject use of, 69, 114f., 118f., 174–176, 178, 183f., 199n., 204, 212f.
  see also criterion of identity
schematic letters, 70, 178–180, 182, 207–211
schematic rules, 109f.
Schroeder, E., 34, 62
scope, 75, 77, 86–88, 103f., 133, 137f.
set theory, used by Russell, 98–102
Shakespearean predicables, *see* predicables
Sherwood, William of, 131f., 215
singular propositions:
  in doctrine of distribution, 30, 36f., 113
  see also truth-conditions
"some" phrases:
  "a" phrases and, *see* "a" phrases
  "any" phrases with, *see* "any" phrases
  distributed?, 44f.
  namely-riders for, 90f.
  reflexive pronouns and, 160
  "some A" refers to some A?, 30–34, 48, 71, 79f., 112, 117, 204

Index

"some" phrases: (cont.)
  truth-conditions with, 89, 97, 106, 160, 200, 206
  undistributed, 29, 34, 38, 45–48, 124
"some but not all", 34, 46
sophisma(ta), 10, 44f., 127–129, 143–145, 215
sophistae, 10
"*stare pro*", 84
statements, 51, 126, 203
Stoic logic, 9, 55, 110
Strawson, P. F., 19, 126, 154f., 175
structure, *see* chemical analogy *and* diagrams for reflexive pronouns
subject (terms), 50, 52
  common nouns as, 65–70, 112, 114, 172, 201–205, 209, 211f.
  demonstratives as?, 53, 65f., 68, 217
  distribution of, 29f., 36, 38
  lists as, 195–197, 200f., 209
  logical and grammatical, 53–55
subject-predicate analysis, 54–57, 62, 171
substance terms, 69, 217
substantival terms, *63*
  apposition of, 65f., 68, 71, 192, 217
  category of, 179, 183f., 213–217
  complex, 77f., 89, 142–145, 147–149, 210f.
  definable, 147–151, 210f.
  demonstratives with, 13, 65f., 217
  negation of, 59, 64f.
  predicative use of, 36–38, 45–48, 59–62, 142f., 147f., 150, 171, 213f.
  in referring phrases, *see* referring phrase
  simplicity of, 148f.
  subject-use of, 65–67, 69f., 172, 200f., 204, 213, 217f.
  see also restricted terms *and* "same, the"
substitution, *see salva congruitate* substitution *and salva veritate* substitution
"such that", 145f.
"*supponere pro*", 84
suppositio, *84*
  confusa et distributiva, 90
  confusa tantum, 90
  determinata, 90
  see also reference, modes of
symbolism, logical:
  author's, 75, 167f., 207–211
  quantificational, 134–139, 165f., 168
  Whitehead and Russell's, 157f.

tense, 59, 61f., 80, 175
terms:

  logic of, 59–62, 64, 171, 219f.
  see also complex, distributed, general, kinship, negative, restricted, substance, substantival, *and* undistributed terms
"term of" (in Russell), 98–102
"that very" phrases, *162*
thematic rules, *110*
theta, as a symbol, 207–211
"thing", 170
"-thing" pronouns, 169–173
"thing that", 170–172
"this" phrases, 13
  see also demonstrative pronouns
traditional logic, 27f., 40f., 43, 59–62, 64, 107, 113, 117, 219f.
"tripodortowser", 93
"true of", *49f.*, 188
  "name of" contrasted with, 29, 57, 59f., 84, 172f.
  see also truth-conditions
truth-conditions:
  with "a" phrases, 94f., 97
  ambiguity of, 93, 96, 125–129, 145, 192, 195f.
  with "any" phrases, 89, 97, 106, 160, 206
  with empty terms, 202–205
  with "every" phrases, 97, 106f., 160, 200
  for exceptive propositions, 131f.
  for exclusive propositions, 208–210
  for existential propositions, 189f.
  with lists, 194f., 198–200
  with "most" phrases, 207
  for predicables' being true-of, 86, 130, 188, 198
  recursive, 198–200
  with reflexive pronouns, 159f.
  sense fixed by, 182
  with "some" phrases, 89, 97, 106, 160, 200, 206
two-name theory, 15, *60f.*, 80

ultratotal distribution, 117
'undistributed middle', 12, 41–43, 116f.
undistributed terms, *28*
  "a" phrases as, 36, 44, 124
  "every" phrases as?, 44f.
  nondistributed terms not the same as, 28, 39f., 41, 45
  predicate terms as, 44f.
  "some" phrases as, 29, 34, 38f., 45–48, 124

Index

universe of discourse, 136f., 174, 182, 206f., 219f.
use and mention confusions, 50, 59, 171f.

variables, bound:
'capture' of, 168
categories of, 179, 183f.
constants and, 157
Frege on, 139, 166
'identification' of, 157, 166, 168
in indirect speech, 179f.
pronouns and, 136–139, 165–168

Quine on, 139, 168, 179–182, 185f.
reflexive use of, 165–168
theta as, 210f.
values of, 182–186
see also quantifiers, quantifications

Whitehead, A. N., 157n.
Wittgenstein, L., 52, 71, 149, 166, 178, 197

zero, 35, 81